"Dr. Magnus is a culture-shaping force. Through his hope-filled teaching, he has equipped leaders toward a model of Spirit-led organizational discernment and development that honours the voice of every person within an organization. In doing so, he has begun to shift leadership culture within the church and beyond."

– GRAHAM ENGLISH, Director of Leader and Church Development, Western District of the Alliance Canada.

"Paul Magnus is a rare blend of pastor, brilliant intellectual, teacher, mentor, and friend. His voice and presence in my life in a critical season was a game-changer for opening pathways of life-giving service."

– CATHIE OSTAPCHUK, MALM, Co-founder and Lead Catalyst of Gather.

"For over 50 years, Dr. Paul Magnus has been a gift to the Canadian Church, to Christian Higher Education, to countless ministry and marketplace leaders, and most certainly to the mission of Briercrest. Paul's leadership, teaching, and scholarship have, without doubt, served in the development of good and godly leadership for so many. Read and reflect thoughtfully as this book identifies some of Paul's key insights in growing Christ-like, effective leadership."

– MICHAEL B. PAWELKE, DMIN, President of Briercrest College and Seminary.

"For almost two decades, I have had the privilege and joy of knowing Dr. Paul Magnus—as a professor, mentor, coach, and dear friend. Every conversation with this amazing man adds benefit to my life and leadership as he pours out decades of research, vast knowledge, and practical experience in the field of leadership."

– MARVIN WOJDA, MALM, Elim Church, Saskatoon, SK.

"Dr. Magnus is a passionate teacher and godly example of leadership."

— JOSHUA BOGUNJOKO, International Director, SIM Mission.

"It's difficult to overstate the impact that Dr. Magnus has had on Canadian Christian leaders over the past 50 years. As I live and serve in the shadow of his legacy, I am so grateful for his ongoing encouragement, empowerment and support. In addition to modelling the practices of effective, sustainable, gracious leadership, he is also modelling how to pass the baton effectively."

— JAY MOWCHENKO, Paul E. Magnus Chair of Leadership and Management Studies, Briercrest Seminary.

"Dr. Magnus has lived with consistency in integrity and excellence. Along with his extensive professional credentials, he is a trusted voice that reaches across generations and contexts for relevance, inspiration, and impact."

— ADAM DRISCOLL, The Evangelical Fellowship of Canada, Board Chair.

"Dr. Magnus has the unique ability to not only teach leadership but also to execute outstanding leadership competence, with a spiritual gift of transferring his knowledge, passion, competence, skill, and stewardship of leadership to any interested student."

— WAYNE DURKSEN, MA, Four Eight Financial.

"Paul lives with eyes wide open. He is alert to people and carefully nurtures their confidence and competence. Always willing to learn and grow, he loves to open doors of opportunity and help women and men solve problems and see with new perspectives."

— DWAYNE UGLEM, MaLM, President Emertius of Briercrest College and Seminary, Senior Associate Pastor, Sherwood Park Alliance Church.

HOLISTIC CHRISTIAN LEADERSHIP
In Class with Dr. Magnus

HOLISTIC CHRISTIAN LEADERSHIP

IN CLASS WITH DR. MAGNUS

By Paul E. Magnus & Team
Edited by Ellen Duffield

Copyright 2023 Paul E. Magnus Centre for Leadership Studies

All rights reserved. No part of this book may be reproduced or transmitted in any form or by any means, electronic or mechanical, including photocopying, recording, or by any information retrieval systems, without the written permission of Briercrest Seminary, except where permitted by law.

Paul E. Magnus Centre for Leadership Studies, 510 College Dr., Caronport, SK, S0H 0S0

Every reasonable effort has been made to attribute concepts to their respective authors.

Cover and book design by Emily Duffield, Shadow River Ink.
Cover image: Adobe Stock

Magnus, Paul E.
    Holistic christian leadership : in class with Dr. Magnus
    239p.
    ISBN: 978-1-9992606-5-1 (Hardcover)
    Includes biographical references and index.
1. Leadership – Christian leadership. 2. Leadership – Education leadership.

First Printing, 2023

Typeset in Linux Libertine and League Gothic

Acknowledgement

The author, editor, and publisher of this work wish to acknowledge the traditional owners and custodians of the land on which this work was produced. This area is now known as Treaty 4 territory and is the traditional land of the *Niitsitpiisstahkoii, Michif Piyii*, and *Ochethi Sakowin* peoples.

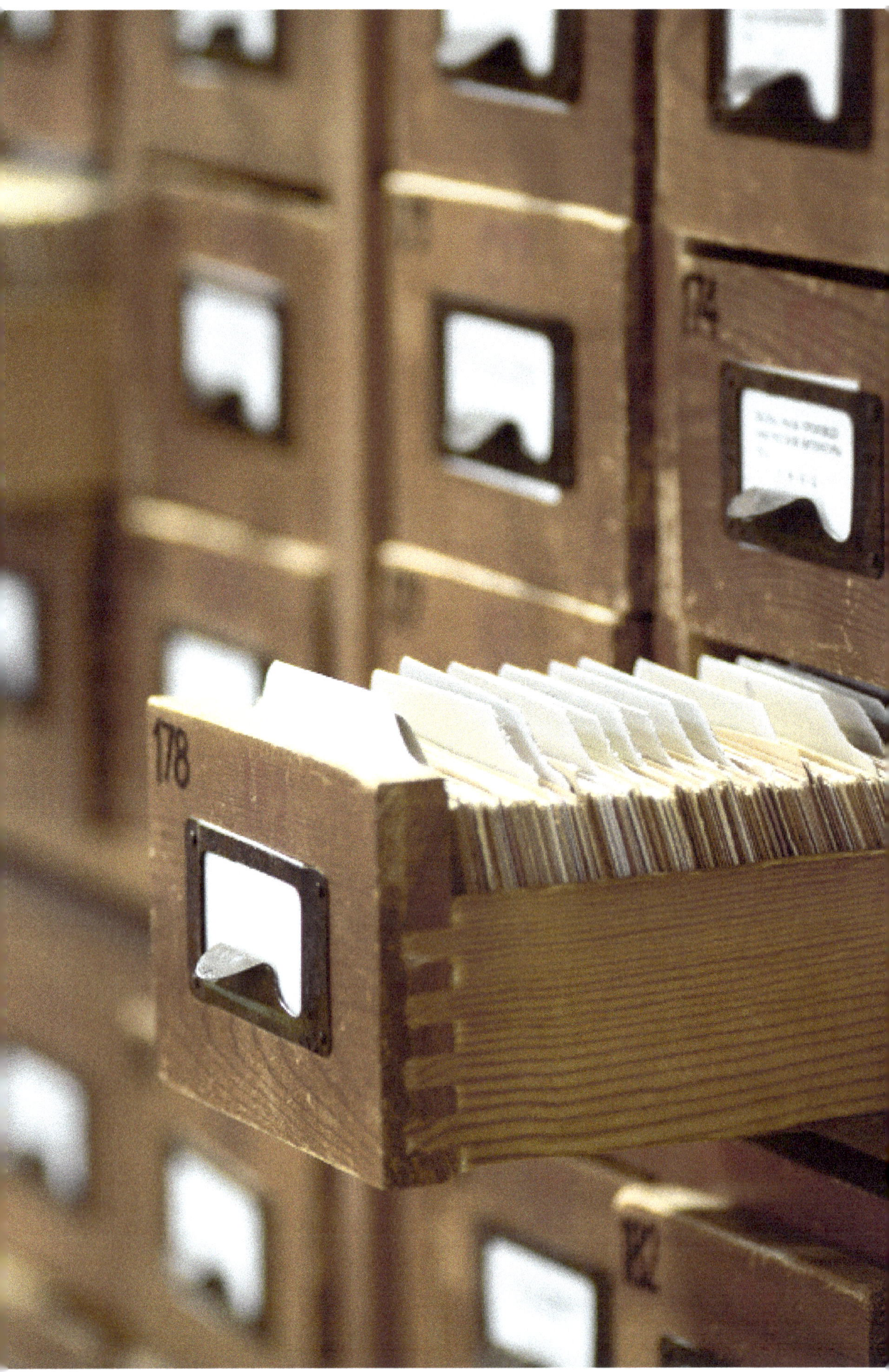
178

CONTENTS

Thanks
Introduction
Prologue

1. The Lenses of Holistic Christian Leadership	1
2. The Heart of Leadership	17
2.1 Soul Care	18
2.2 Mindset Quotient	22
2.3 Emotional Quotient	29
2.4 Trust Quotient	32
2.5 Diversity Quotient	33
2.6 Physical Quotient	34
2.7 Social/Connection Quotient	35
2.8 Ethical Quotient	37
2.9 Vocational/Contextual Quotient	37
2.10 Actualizing Quotient	39
3. The Person of the Leader	43
3.1 The Development of the Leader	44
3.2 The Courage to Lead in Uncharted Times	54
4. The Courage of the Leader	61
5. The Temptations of Leadership	81

6. People	**88**
6.1 Ennoblement	93
6.2 Enlistment	95
6.3 Enablement	99
6.4 Enculturing	103
6.5 Encouragement	104
6.6 Entrustment	106
6.7 Empowerment	108
6.8 Encirclement	110
6.9 Embodiment	112
7. Processes	**118**
7.1 Co-envisioning	124
7.2 Co-mmunication	132
7.3 Co-learning	141
7.4 Co-creating	146
7.5 Co-owning	147
7.6 Co-delivering	149
7.7 Co-measuring	156
7.8 Co-changing	157
8. Purpose	**163**
9. Co-Governing	**178**
10. Succession	**198**
Conclusion	208
Appendix A: Dr. Magnus' Bookshelf	215

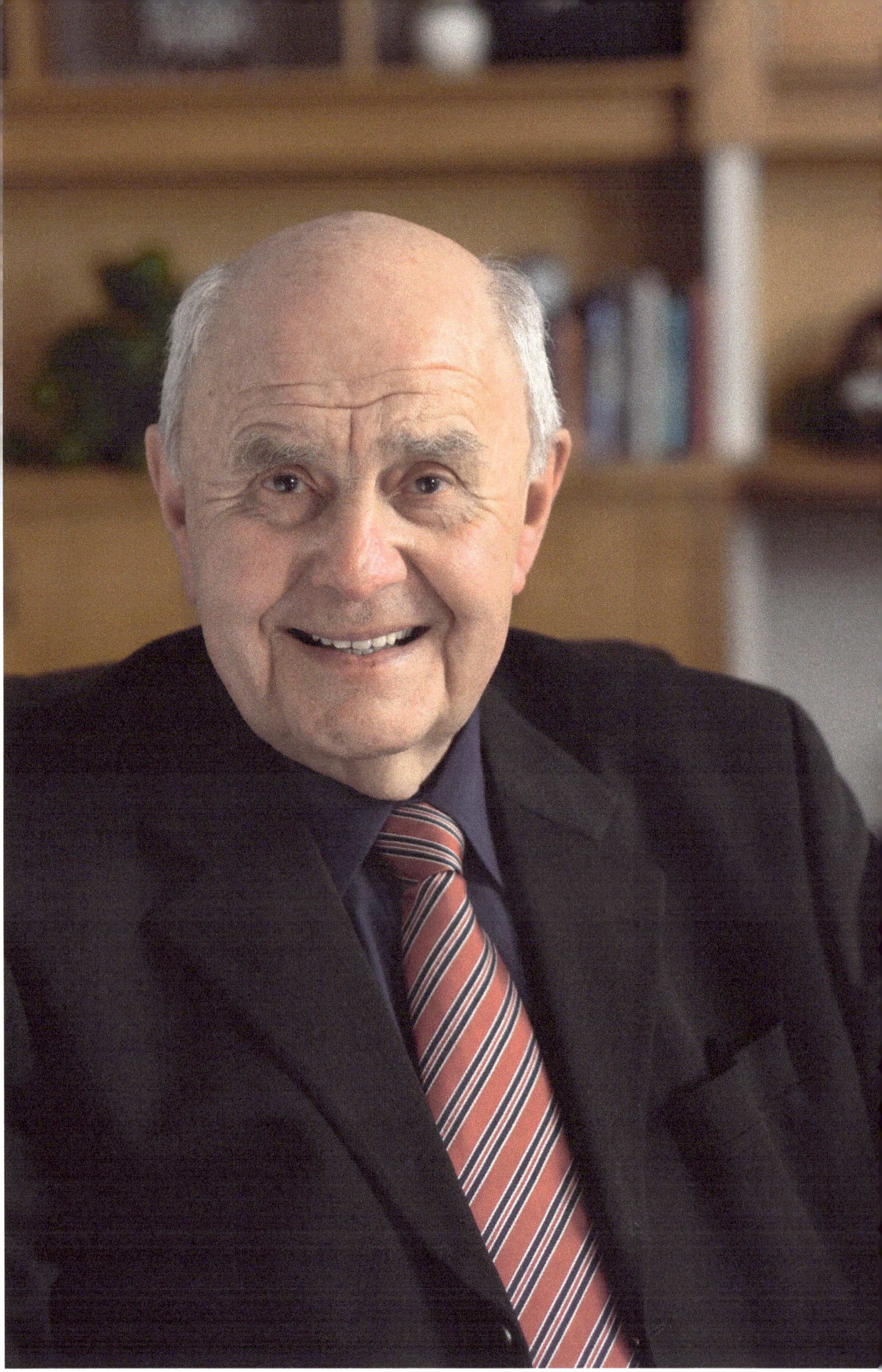

THANKS

WHAT A PRIVILEGE AND HONOUR to practice and teach leadership and management for over 50 years. Looking back, I cannot imagine a life that would have been more meaningful or rewarding. God has been so faithful.

It isn't easy to express the depth of gratitude I feel for the loving support that has been granted to me on this journey. Special thanks go to the Presidents at Briercrest to date. I have been enabled, encouraged, empowered, and enriched by each of them. A special tribute to Henry Budd, who invited me to the team right off the farm so long ago and repeatedly opened leadership-enhancing doors for me. I would also like to mention the exceptional support of Michael Pawelke in the formation of the Leadership Centre and Leadership Studios.

Beyond the Briercrest context, some five-hundred leaders have invited me into leadership and leadership instruction, coaching, and facilitation roles. What is written in this book was significantly influenced by each of you.

To pause my thanks here would be a major mistake. I have had the finest students. While I sought to inspire them to be hungry, humble, and smart learners, they have done for me what I wished for them. These exceptional leaders have taught me so much.

Seeking to capture these foundational thoughts on great and godly leadership would only have happened with your frequent urgings. The student who was most persistent in urging me to write was Adam Driscoll, a leader of profound influence—and also the Board Chair for EFC. We were joined in these early conversations by Barb Elich, a significant leader in the academic world. Friends, the "someday" we spoke of is finally here. I am so grateful to everyone who kept coaching me on this project.

Above all, I wish to single out Ellen Duffield for actively engaging in getting this project planned and launched, orchestrating the ten video recording days, and partnering to capture my thoughts into writing. She has been the co-designer, co-creator, co-developer, and co-author of my rambling thoughts and reflections. My heartfelt thanks to Ellen for this and her creative and skillful contribution to the good work Kimberly McElroy, Tristan Norton, and I began at the Leadership Centre and Studies.

Special thanks also to my wife Jane, whose sacrificial love and encouragement is so exceptional. Words escape me. I also wish to thank our now adult children, their spouses, and our eight grandchildren. Their ongoing support has been so meaningful, even when some of my involvements would lessen the time that I had with them. Unique appreciation goes to our "unofficially adopted" niece, Lori Nicholle Nickel, who was exceptionally faithful in sending inspirational messages every day of the video recordings. These became one of the foundational pieces of this initiative.

And finally, I would like to thank those who have gone before and taught me so much, some who have reached the finish line. I am indebted to you.

Having sought to give honour where honour is due appropriately, I must give the highest credit to God. My guiding life verse is Col 3:17, "Whatever you do in word or deed (Paul), do it all in the name of the Lord Jesus." These words shaped my dream and calling and are the basis for my life mission. They are also the inspiration behind this book.

To our great and gracious God, who has orchestrated my life and, despite my humanity, enabled me with the extended time, energy, health, and strength to put what light I can about great and godly leadership into print and to ensure the profiling of students in the process. I simply want to say a heartfelt thank you.

INTRODUCTION

Although I had taught more classes than I can remember, many of them in this same room, this one felt different. For one thing, S111 has recently been renovated; changed from a classroom to a Centre for Leadership Studies. A barn door now hides the whiteboard behind. Both of these point to my trademark teaching style—covering walls of whiteboards in a single class—and my roots, growing up on the farm not far from the little Saskatchewan town of Luseland. The population was 1200 then and even less now.

The story of my journey from that farm to this space is a story of miracles, mentors, and life-changing moments. As I think of the shy kid I was growing up and the people who took chances on me or took me under their wing, well, gratitude is the only word that comes to mind.

It began with my parents. My mother, an orphan, was the kindest person I have yet to meet. Her view of people and how to treat them profoundly shaped me from an early age. My father was a hardworking man who taught me how to navigate with patience through seemingly impossible challenges. But more about him later, for I owe a debt of gratitude to him and so many others. I was born right in the middle of seven kids, the middle child in so many ways. Little did I know then how deeply this would shape my view of leadership and leading from the middle.

Another reason this class felt different was that it was the students, not the school, who had initiated it, and I was honoured and humbled by their request. When they first contacted me to ask if I would teach a Masterclass in Leadership, I said no. Summarizing a lifetime of leadership theory and practice into a week is no small thing. Then one of them reminded me that I had always said I would rather write on students' hearts than on paper. I realized that this would provide the opportunity for me to continue learning both with and from the students—something I have always cherished.

So here I am, waiting for the first student to arrive.

Graduates of our Masters in Leadership and Management program and others I have coached will be familiar with some voices in the book. There will be business, church, social enterprise, and non-profit leaders in the room, as well as coaches, consultants, and people in transition. However, this resource is prayerfully offered to all Christian leaders hungry for deeper learning and insight.

You are the kind of group I love. Diverse. Hungry to learn. You may have led long enough to come up against your own humanity and been humbled by failure. I pray you have also seen God move in your life and corner of the world.

Someone once accused me of confusing students with friends, and truth be told, in this classroom, we are both. I learn more from you than from any textbook; your stories encourage me to keep going.

You are the people in the trenches of leadership. Some are weary and thinking of quitting. I hope to encourage you if I can because we need you so badly. Others are in a season of fruitfulness, and taking the time to come shows how eager you are to keep learning. Others yet are just starting out, anxious to get going yet wise enough to know the value of resources and peers to call on as needed.

What season are you in? Bring your leadership questions and challenges to "class" with us.

What an important calling leadership is. I realize that it comes with a price. I appreciate your willingness to engage in it anyway. In Romans 12:8, Paul reminds us that if we have the gift of leadership, we are to lead diligently. Not haphazardly or with complacency, but with vigour, teachability, and a sense of responsibility for those entrusted to our care. It has been my life's work to build healthy teams, boards, and organizations; and to enable others to do the same. I offer this book as one more tool in your toolbelt of great and godly resources to serve our truly great and worthy God.

Paul Magnus

PROLOGUE

As I turned off the Trans-Canada highway, the shape of the seminary building brought back a flood of memories. Shaped by the land and the big sky, this school, acknowledged by many as a miracle on the prairie, was an unlikely place to train global leaders. Yet God often uses unlikely spaces, and for decades Dr. Magnus had been at the centre of this.

The classroom was still labelled "S111" but had been completely renovated. Gone were the institutional grey tables and rolling chairs. A fireplace now warmed the room, flanked by bookshelves that stretched from wall to wall. The smell of coffee and homemade baking wafted up as I scanned the room. Farm tables and black Windsor chairs stood ready for students. A bible was open on the stool at the front. And, just inside the door, a plaque acknowledged that we were on Treaty 4 land, the traditional territory of the Niitsitpiisstahkoii, Michif Piyii, and Ochethi Sakowin peoples.

Airplane propellers on one wall recalled the local aviation industry that had later flourished with the needs of WWII and beyond. The same themes of innovation, inspiration, and responsiveness ran through the leadership program.

A green model tractor and sheaths of wheat honoured the agrarian context of the school and Dr. Magnus's childhood on the farm. A picture of him and his wife of over 50 years stood on the mantle beside a cup with his childhood nickname "Pauly Wog"—a glimpse into the bullying he experienced as a child and the compassion he learned from it. His mischievous nature and sense of humour had protected him in countless challenging seasons since.

There are really four main characters in this story: Dr. Magnus and the books, students, and "classrooms" that God used to shape his philosophy and theology of leadership. This combination would impact thousands.

How could I ever fit into a manuscript what this teacher has meant to me and so many others? Here, in the following pages, is my best attempt to share Dr. Magnus with you, as hundreds of students have known and loved him: in the classroom.

Head in with me.
Class is getting started.

Sincerely,
the editor

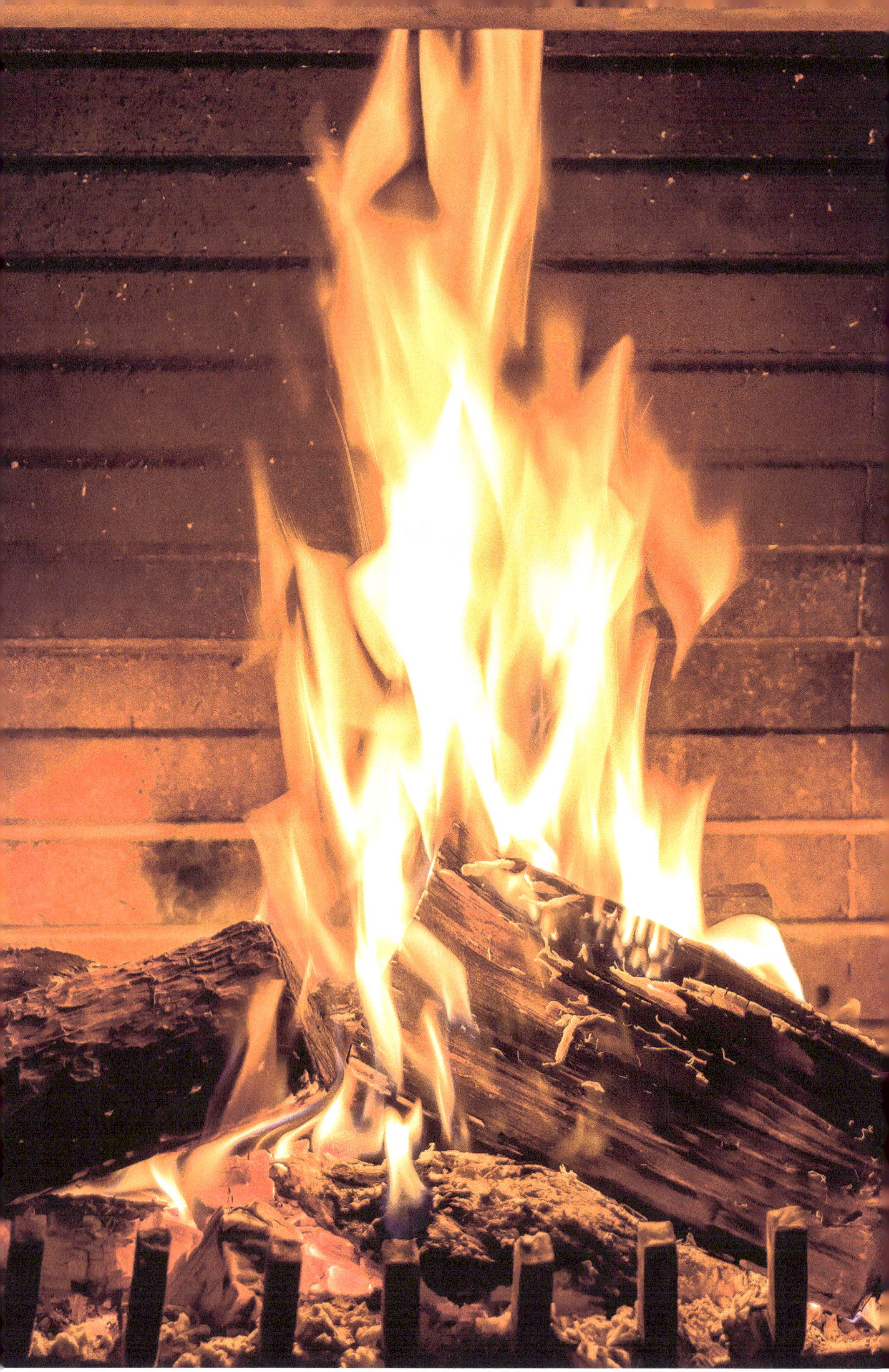

1. THE LENSES OF HOLISTIC CHRISTIAN LEADERSHIP

A COLD WIND WAS HOWLING across the prairie outside, but the fire was on as Dr. Magnus greeted us at the door, his normal suit and tie replaced for this occasion with casual pants and a half-zip sweater; his smile broadening with each new arrival as he welcomed us in.

As we settled around the farmhouse tables, he moved to the rocking chair—a gift from a friend that had sat in the corner of his office for years and from which he had coached and counselled countless leaders over the years. We had travelled from all parts of the country, each with our own leadership successes. And each with significant challenges.

Perhaps you will relate to some or all of mine. I was recently promoted to a more senior corporate leadership role and quickly encountered the complexity of this new responsibility. I felt torn between competing priorities, and there was never enough information or time to make well-informed decisions. I was working hard at communication and trust-building but kept running up against bureaucracy at every turn. Systems that were meant to serve us were holding us captive. I was surrounded by values that did not match my own. And perhaps worst of all, I was quickly becoming someone I did not want to be and wasn't sure how to find my way back. I needed a fresh way of thinking about leadership. A more holistic, holy, and healthy way.

"Shall we begin?" Dr. Magnus asked, opening his well-worn bible and reading from Mark 10:42, "Jesus called them together and said, 'You know that those who are regarded as rulers of the Gentiles lord it over them, and their high officials exercise authority over them. 43 Not so with you. Instead, whoever wants to become great among you must be your servant, 44 and whoever wants to be first must be slave of all. 45 For even the Son of Man did not come to be served, but to serve, and to give his life as a ransom for many.' I am humbled every time I read these verses. Jesus didn't give many directives about leadership, but this one is very clear. And it sets the context for everything that we will be discussing over the next ten days."

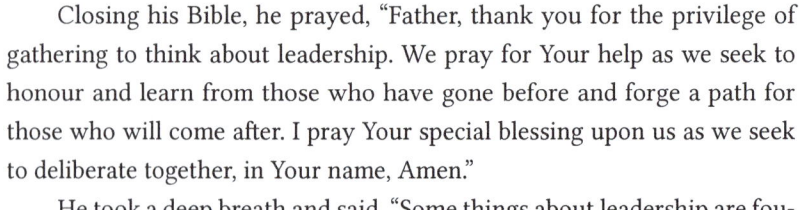

Closing his Bible, he prayed, "Father, thank you for the privilege of gathering to think about leadership. We pray for Your help as we seek to honour and learn from those who have gone before and forge a path for those who will come after. I pray Your special blessing upon us as we seek to deliberate together, in Your name, Amen."

He took a deep breath and said, "Some things about leadership are foundational. Like the passage we just read that applies across generations and contexts and shapes every conversation we have about Christian leadership. I invite you to build from this groundwork up, rather than the other way around. Other things are contextual, and I invite you to contextualize these as we discuss together. I want you to think critically and engage deeply. I want you to disagree and push back.

"Joshua, you are a medical doctor by training who grew up in Nigeria. You have lived and served in many parts of the world and are now leading a global mission organization. How have you been able to adjust and adapt to serve in such different contexts?"

Joshua responded, "I was fortunate to get a good education, part of that with you. And that taught me critical thinking—how to read and interact with diverse views. This helped me to stay open to learning in various contexts. There are many cultural differences, it is true. Yet, as humans, there are also so many things that unite us, and as people of faith, the same biblical principles apply. I read a fair bit. And I have learned to listen carefully to people. Those things, by God's grace, have helped me tremendously."

Dr. Magnus smiled at his former student with pride and warmth, "It has been a joy to watch how God has used you over the years, Joshua, and to see how you have kept learning and growing. We look forward to your contribution to this class."

He looked around at the other students, and his eyes softened again. God had led many of us into leadership in contexts across the country and worldwide.

"I am so proud of each of you," he said with feeling, "so pleased to be in this room together. So thrilled that we will be learning together this week. We will draw from many sources—learning from the leadership modelled and taught by God in scripture; sharing my perspective on the best leadership resources I am aware of; wrestling with concepts, reading research and integrating your real-life examples. When it comes to thinking about these diverse sources, I like to use the language of great and godly. Now, what is the risk of focusing solely on great or godly leadership? I grew up in a Christian environment, and much of my early education was in the theological world; that was the emphasis. Later on, I was often assigned to teach classes like psychology, theology, and leadership. This raised an important question for me. How could I teach in an integrative way rather than polarizing them? Rather than putting them on opposite ends like so..."

He drew a line on the board and labelled it.

Great ——————————————————————— *Godly*

"Early on, I began to reflect on the fact that God's truth permeates all parts of leadership and yet the Bible is not written as a textbook for leaders," he continued. "The word 'great' sometimes frightens us because we immediately think of perfectionism or narcissistic leaders. But the risk of settling for good is that we will stop learning, listening, and discovering."

Several students exchanged knowing glances. You couldn't sit through one class with Dr. Magnus without hearing how important it was to keep listening and learning.

Dr. Magnus continued, "Jim Collins changed the thinking behind leadership in all domains—business, non-profit, and the church—in his book *Good to Great*.[1] In it, he talked about the risk of settling for good. If our goal is great and godly leadership, we need to define these terms. We are not using the word good here in the biblical sense of God's goodness. We are talking about settling for mediocrity. Let's reflect: what's the risk of being good? Collins says it is the enemy of great because we stop before we truly and energetically engage. Before we seek to understand. What are your thoughts on this?"

The discussion that followed was robust and layered. Some argued that pursuing greatness fed their temptation for pride or perfection and had to be managed. Others argued that true greatness differed from popularity, busyness, or perfection.

One asked, "When is good enough, good enough?"

Jacqueline, a corporate consultant dedicated to helping organizations

---

1. Jim Collins, *Good to Great: Why Some Companies Make the Leap... And Others Don't*, Harper Collins, 2001.

build toward greatness, said, "Excellence is an important value. It can also become an unsustainable one if it leads to perfectionism or paralysis-by--analysis. The litmus test for me is whether I can say before God and the people most impacted by my work that I gave it my very best under the circumstances and will stand behind what I have done—to fix it if needed, to enable it to be successful or, if needed, to explain the rationale for the way it was done. To me greatness means doing the right thing, for the right reasons, and doing it right. This is quite different from trying to impress, which is where we start to get into trouble as leaders."

Allowing the conversation to emerge organically, Dr. Magnus perched on a stool at the front. Then, sensing it was time to redirect, he said, "If we focus solely on great leadership—the best that is out there on leadership theory and practice but not necessarily written from a Christian perspective—we miss all that God can teach us through the bible. If we focus only on godly sources, we risk not hearing from those who have spent their lives practicing and researching great leadership. Perhaps shocking to some is the discovery of how close some of these scientific leadership practices come to how Jesus led!"

A student at the back raised her hand. "This reminds me of the sacred-secular conversation from a few years back."

"Yes, exactly. How can we think 'both and'? From my standpoint, one of the most helpful concepts to help us navigate this is polarity management. A polarity is best understood as two perspectives that seem like unconnected opposites but are actually two ends of a pole. Not great or godly, but great and godly leadership. Not head or heart, but head and heart; people and process; autonomy and collaboration; leadership and management; and one of my favourites—organism and organization. In polarity management, the question changes from 'Which is right?' to 'How do we maximize the strengths of both and minimize the weaknesses and risks of both in excess?' And a second, equally important question becomes, 'How do we do this in a team context where people may hold very different views?' But we are getting ahead of ourselves. Okay, what is leadership?"

He rose to his feet and moved to the whiteboard, where he always seemed most at home. With a marker in his right hand, he said, "And a related question, what is the difference between leadership and management? People have argued this for years, elevating one over the other and debating if it is possible for one person to practice both. Marcus Buckingham addresses this beautifully.[2] He says that both are needed, and our focus when 'wearing that hat' must be different. A manager's key focus should be on the individual. Helping direct reports lean into their uniqueness. This is a manager's priority or one thing. A leader's one thing is different. They must focus on the big picture. The manager role pays attention to individual uniqueness to build personal mastery and commitment. The leadership role pays attention to the whole, to build overall momentum and turn organizational fears about the future into hope, faith, and commitment. I find that distinction so helpful. Both are important and needed. Some people are more gifted at one or the other. And you cannot confuse the two.

"When I think of Buckingham's one-thing mindset, I also think of Psalm 27:4. 'One thing I ask of the Lord.' I love the way Eugene Peterson puts it," he said, reaching for his Bible and flipping open to Psalm 27. "'I'm asking God for one thing, only one thing: To live with him in his house my whole life long. I'll contemplate his beauty; I'll study at his feet.' I love that. Live with him. Contemplate his beauty. Study at his feet. That has been my prayer. Whether acting as a leader or manager, our higher purpose is the one thing captured here."

He paused for a moment, deep in thought, before going on, "Definitions of leadership change with the times. At one time, we thought of leaders as those with high technical skill and charisma—the so-called 'Great Man Theory.' Then, as the needs of organizations changed, we began to understand the value of people, so leaders were encouraged to practice benevolence. We could call that the 'Human Relations Theory.' That was through the fifties, sixties, and mid-seventies. That developed into a focus on the use and development of talent and the need for leaders who were strong in Human-Resource Centered Leadership. Then in the nineties, our culture moved towards purpose and meaning, and a focus on Principle-Centered Leadership emerged."

He paused and glanced down at his notes, "Notice how, as each of these leadership movements developed, they layered on the foundation of what had gone before. The last fifteen years or so have focused on the whole person. The whole context. And on collaboration in direction-setting and

---

2. Marcus Buckingham, *The One Thing You Need to Know about Great Managing, Great Leadership and Sustained Individual Success*, Free Press, 2005.

> COMPLEXITY IS THE NATURE OF THINGS. ANY PHILOSOPHY THAT CAN BE PUT IN A NUTSHELL BELONGS IN ONE.
>
> – PHILOSOPHER HILLARY PUTMAN

delivery. Yet even that has changed recently, as we shall see. Now, as we look back through leadership history and if we did a comprehensive review of leadership books today, we would find that there are as many different definitions of leadership as there are spokespersons.

"I am not going to offer a definition. It has been my passion in life to lead wisely and well, and to teach others to do so. I am not sure that a definition helps us with this. Many focus on just one or two aspects of leadership and I think that does us a disservice. We need to think more holistically. What I am going to offer is a series of interconnected lenses that together build an integrative map enabling us to think about and deliver both great and godly leadership."

We flipped open our notebooks as he turned to the whiteboard and labelled the four corners of his model, reading them aloud as he did.

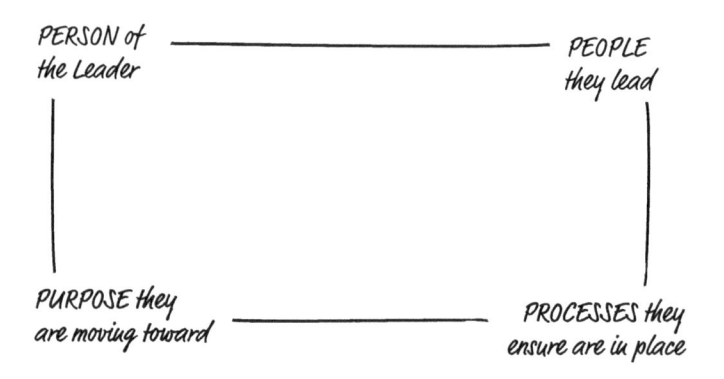

```
PERSON of ———————————— PEOPLE
the Leader                they lead
|                               |
|                               |
|                               |
|                               |
PURPOSE they ———————————— PROCESSES they
are moving toward          ensure are in place
```

"These are the four key lenses or components of a holistic model, in my opinion. However, the connections that link them to each other are equally, if not more, important than the lenses themselves. I have drawn these connections as arrows, as you can see, but of course, the connections between the lenses could be drawn as a web, each one influenced by and influencing the others and linked by the heart in the centre. These connections create momentum, and they can also create tensions. Learning how to maximize both the momentum and the tensions is the work of leadership."

He filled in the model to look like this.

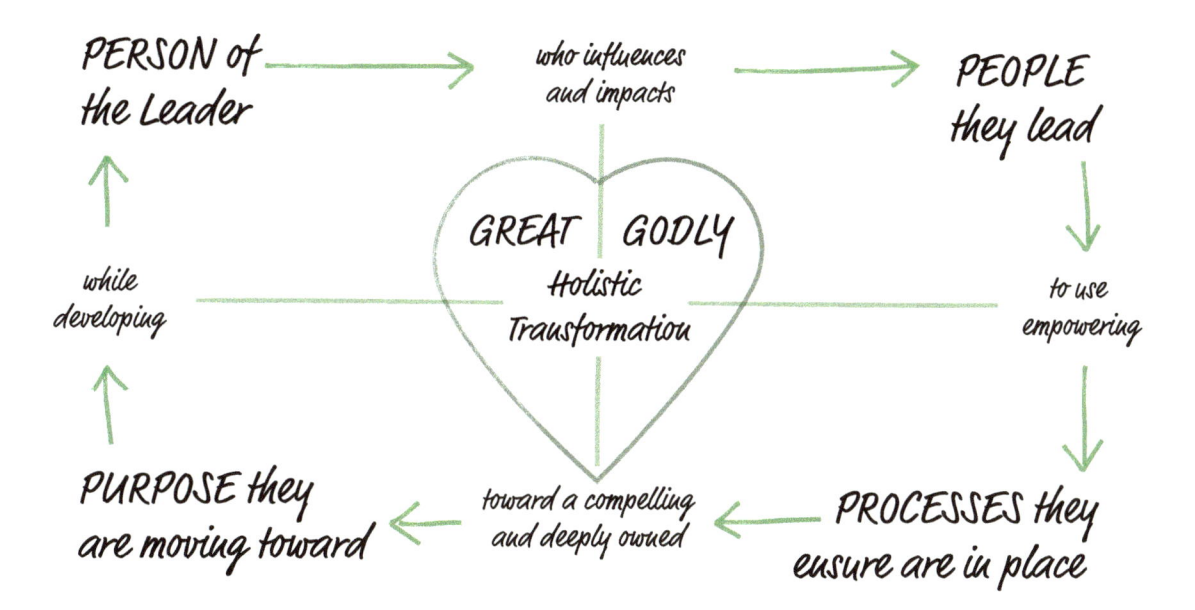

PERSON of the Leader → who influences and impacts → **PEOPLE they lead**

while developing ↑ ↓ to use empowering

GREAT | GODLY Holistic Transformation

PURPOSE they are moving toward ← toward a compelling and deeply owned ← **PROCESSES they ensure are in place**

As I looked at the model, I realized that it spoke to many of my biggest leadership problems: who I was as a person and the gap between that and the leader I wanted to be; how to find and motivate high-potential people; our need to revitalize the systems and processes that made sense when they were adopted but no longer served us well; and purpose, which, if I am honest, I had lost sight of in the tyranny of the urgent. Perhaps that is why our people had too.

With vulnerability, Dr. Magnus added, "This represents my best thinking after a lifetime of reading, teaching, and practicing leadership. It forms a framework or mind map, and it seeks to define a leadership journey that is integrative, progressive, and informed by both great and godly sources.

"You can use it in many ways. As a leader, it is helpful to envision key areas that require intentional focus. As a board member or consultant, it can be helpful to ensure we don't overly focus on one area—for example, the leader or the people, two common scapegoats—without considering how the other pieces may be affecting the whole system. For planning, it can be helpful in ensuring all areas are considered when defining our current situation and envisioning a stronger future. And perhaps most importantly for everyone, it is an ideology that ensures we think holistically and move intentionally towards learning and growth in each area. I use it as a grid to guide my reading, to make sure that I am staying current in each area."

Turning to one of the students, he said, "Adam, when you were a young leader here at the institution, you kept an itemized list of leadership books to read in the back of your journal, if I recall correctly. Do you still do that?"

Adam flipped to the back of his book to show a lengthy list and said, "Not everyone learns through reading, but I have found it to be such a helpful practice."

Dr. Magnus smiled, "Some of you may not know this, but Adam worked in leadership for this organization for a few years. And now, he works at a different academic institution and chairs an influential national board. It's great to have you in class, Adam."

"It's great to be here," Adam answered, then diverted the attention by asking, "You used to read a book a week Dr. Magnus. Do you still do that?"

Smiling sheepishly, he answered, "Yes, I think I can honestly say that there have not been many weeks when I have not read a book or two, mainly about leadership but also about philosophy or theology or psychology. Theology seeks to know God and His ways better. Psychology seeks to understand myself and others better. Leadership seeks to lead more faithfully and functionally. I had a professor in graduate school who encouraged us to develop a life plan. I took that seriously, writing five life goals. One of them was to read a book a week, seeking to spend as much time reading the bible as other sources. I haven't always been able to do that, but most weeks, I have come close. We will look at a few of my favourites together, and you will find a list of others in your notes."

We looked at one another with raised eyebrows and did the mental math. Fifty years times fifty-two weeks. Behind Dr. Magnus was a wall of books. We could point to any one of them and he would tell us not only what the book contained but also how he had used or adapted what he learned in it.

When I was a teenager, my pastor began to invest in me. One of the things he would do was take me to conferences where I met lots of other pastors. At that time, we always had a regulation-size rink in our yard at home, and it wasn't long before our games with friends and cousins grew into the desire to compete with other teams. As a result of the connections I had made at church conferences, my brother and I were able to invite teams from all over to come play. This made for so much fun and gave me lots of opportunities to learn to organize events and gather people around a common cause.

When I was the VP of Education, we were trying to get transfer credit at the University of Saskatchewan for eighty of our courses. There was a receiving committee that was welcoming and ready to review. We presented the syllabi, and the committee agreed that our courses were very comparable to theirs and that there was no reason why students should not be able to transfer them for credit. However, when they took the proposal to their Faculty Senate, one individual influenced a challenge to the committee to deny our request because of our student lifestyle expectations.

I wish to pay tribute to one of my most amazing professors who was on the committee and who also was a strong advocate of the proposal at the Senate level. He had been so supportive on my journey at the university, and I have a fond and deep appreciation for the benefit he brought to my life and all I learned from him, even in processing this. Words fail me to express gratitude to this man.

For the next eighteen years, I met with Deans, Presidents, and teams, but we were only able to get a few courses approved. Eventually, I began to work through government connections to get additional courses and even programs approved. I am so grateful to Dr. Dwayne Uglem, someone I worked with longer than anyone else, and his leadership team, who carried this forward and were successful in gaining university recognition for increasing the number of courses and programs.

The influence one person can make. Positively or negatively.

"One definition of leadership I have seen is someone who has followers, but even that is nuanced. Have you seen 'The Dancing Guy' video? It shows a guy who starts dancing at an outdoor concert. At the beginning he is just someone dancing in a field. Then someone comes to join him, and soon others follow suit until the field is full of dancers. Often it is the first follower, not the initiator, who starts a movement. Dr. Uglem took the risk to step out with me. From what I read of the early disciples it seems that Andrew was a first follower. He is the underestimated one, the one who should get extra pages. He took a huge risk in following Jesus and inviting others along. He started a movement.

"Wayne, you have been in institutional and church leadership for years. Many of those years were deeply challenging. I know because we served together for part of that time. What are your insights on the risks of following God and inviting others along?"

Wayne stopped taking notes and spoke up, "It's often awkward to step out. There are always risks involved. Leadership is not for the casually interested. It takes a lot of persistence and commitment to lead a movement. You're going to need some thick skin. If you have a great cause and resolve—then eventually, you'll see results. From the beginning, God said, 'it's not good to be alone.' And I have found that to be as true in leadership as it is in life."

Dr. Magnus perched on his stool and thought for a moment before responding. "If what you're dreaming about will make a big difference, you will need to find a first follower who is ready to step out with you and invite others to join. That creates its own tensions because having others join in will add complexity and diversity of opinions but without it... well, we are no longer talking about leadership.

"One of the reasons that I knew I needed a team was so I could stay connected to reality. One risk of leadership is that we think we know more than a follower. And another is how difficult it can be for people to be honest with you. Let's talk about that for a moment. What are you doing to make it easier to hear the truth from your team?"

"We have all the regular stuff," said Wayne, "employee surveys and focus groups, suggestion boxes and external consultants. But even with all of that, I often feel I am missing key pieces of information that our teams know but don't feel safe sharing."

Dr. Magnus agreed, "Safety. That is such a key piece, isn't it? How do we make it safe for people to tell us the truth? Here is the irony, the more likely we are to think that people feel safe talking to us, the more out of touch we probably are!

"Now, of course, giving us feedback is not the only reason we need others around us. You'll almost always need a team—formal or informal—in order to move an initiative forward in any kind of significant way. And the more creative or innovative you are wanting to be, the more you will need a team. Amy, you are working in a startup, so the context is a bit different. What are your thoughts on this?"

Amy had been quiet since class began. She was younger than many of the other students and just starting out in leadership. Now she admitted, "This discussion is kind of discouraging to me. How do you work through this as a solo initiative or small organization?"

"That is such an important question, Amy, and I agree it is definitely more challenging. When you are on your own or in a small organization, you will need to count on your informal networks. Learning how to tend and serve our network well is one of the most Kingdom-oriented and fruitful priorities we can set. Studies show that many people dread networking or asking for help. Yet we know that the right kind of networking—being curious about people and offering to assist and promote those whose values align with yours—can lead to countless synergies. And we know that most people, even very busy people, are willing to share expertise or contacts or even practical assistance when what we are asking for aligns with their passions and strengths.

"Two key issues remain the same regardless of the size of an organization. You need to get people to 'want to' and then make sure they know 'how to.' When I was first in senior leadership roles, my challenge was to get people to want to join the team. Then I realized that I also had to progressively ensure they were ready to take on more and more responsibility and authority. The tension of empowering and equipping. Of holding-people-accountable and holding-people-able.

"But we are getting ahead of ourselves again. We were talking about what leadership is. Perhaps it is easiest to start with what it isn't. Despite appearances, it isn't about position or title. It isn't about charisma or education or privilege—although we'd be foolish to think these things aren't factors that affect someone's opportunities.

Warren Bennis defined leadership as the capacity to translate vision into reality. Looking ahead, Bill Gates said that leaders will be those who empower others. Peter Northouse described it as making something happen that wouldn't otherwise happen. There is always an action piece to leadership—a results piece. That is another polarity. When it comes to great and godly leadership, it's not relationships or results but relationships and results! A problem is something that can be solved. A polarity is something that must be managed. Mitch, you have spent many years in this field can you give us some insights about polarities?"

"For me, the discussion of "relationship and results" begins with reflecting on my inward journey of discovering how I am showing up in these conversations and how that impacts others." Mitch began, "'We do out of who we be.' So, who is it that God made me to be? And how can I show up as that in this space?

"Polarity thinking includes an ability to hold two or more thoughts, positions, or ideas in juxtaposition. Traditionally, we thought that these two 'ends' must have contrasting effects. This is either/or thinking. Polarity thinking is a material shift that seeks to envision the comfortable and collaborative contribution of each end of the polarity piece. Holding each pole carefully enough to recognize and receive its fruit. Acknowledging that perhaps the influence of each end will contribute to the unique shaping of its opposite or lead to something new being birthed.

"My favorite book by Parker Palmer is *Let Your Life Speak: Listening for the Voice of Vocation*.[3] He speaks of an internal polarity, saying, 'Leaders need not only the technical skills to manage the external world but also the spiritual skills to journey inward toward the source of both shadow and light.'"

"Dr. Magnus, I like your statement: 'A polarity is something that must be managed.' I try to embrace and nurture the inward work that is to be done even as I do the outward work entrusted to me, in relationship with others who are on the same journey of discovery, self-management, and contribution."

"Such great insights Mitch, thank you. Stan, you are an Athletic Director who works with countless coaches and teams. Do you see similar tensions in the sports world? Can you name a few?"

---

3 Parker Palmer, *Let Your Life Speak: Listening for the Voice of Vocation,* Jossey-Bass, 1999, 79.

"A hundred percent. How do you train coaches to focus on character development and winning games? Discipleship and athletic training. Team building and personal mastery. I couldn't agree with you more, but it is hard, and for that reason, not many people are doing it. I am working to map out what living in that tension means, and it is taking me years to learn. I have my own tensions too. How can I develop best practices for us as an organization and be responsive to the uniqueness and needs of the individuals involved? How can I keep parents and athletes happy with sufficient wins under our belt and spend enough of my time focusing on relationships, character, and discipleship?"

"Thank you, Stan. There is so much in what you shared that we could apply in many contexts. At your tables, take a moment to jot down and then share three of the top tensions or polarities that affect your current leadership context. And mark them as homework for further reflection tonight. How are you managing those polarities? Are you managing to move back and forth along that continuum as needed, or have you become stuck at one end of the pole?"

Heads went down as each of us considered our own context. When we moved to table discussions, there were several overlaps. People and process. Technology and tradition. Great and godly. Team and individual. Planning and execution. Big-picture and day-to-day. Centralization and decentralization. Quotas and merit. Alignment and innovation. Staying true to our niche while staying responsive to customer needs. Culture shaping and personal discipleship. Wellness and work ethic.

After providing a generous time for reflection and sharing, Dr. Magnus said, "There is a lot of pain in organizations. Discouragement. Weariness. Disillusionment. Good leadership inspires hope, help, and clarity. It creates space for people to join into something bigger than themselves and to contribute in ways beyond what they could have imagined or done on their own. Let's talk about space for a moment. Leaders are intentional in creating the space to reflect, the space to learn, and the space to act. By space, I mean time, of course, but I also mean much more than time."

Stepping back up to the whiteboard, he continued, "Space requires safety, and safety requires trust. Trust is difficult to build and quickly undermined. There are several contributing factors: following through on commitments, the ability to honour confidences, our character and consistency. And one that has become increasingly important over the years is vulnerability. If you want to build trust, you have to become vulnerable first. This is true in our relationship with God as well. In Genesis 3, when God asks Adam and Eve where they were, it was more than a geographical question.

> Where are you at? How are you showing up? Where are you going?
> What is driving your holy discontent? Who is going with you?
> How are you wanting this course to help you and those entrusted to your care to get there together?

He pointed to the heart in the centre of the model.

Dwayne raised his hand and said, "The picture you are painting is of a self-aware, God-centered, higher purpose-focused, people-developing leader. This is quite rare in my experience."

"Agreed," Dr. Magnus nodded. Then with a twinkle in his eye and pointing back to the model on the board said, "And I would add 'process developing' leader."

Dwayne continued, "Exactly. As we look at our context, we are noticing a shrinking pool of people who want to lead at all, let alone do the hard work of becoming this kind of leader. Leadership has never been more necessary, yet it seems that fewer and fewer people are willing to step into the challenging contexts that most need wise leadership. We see this happening in almost every sphere and sector."

Dr. Magnus nodded his head thoughtfully, "That is exactly why we are gathered in this room, my friend. Our world needs great and godly leadership." Letting that sink in for a moment, he smiled and added, "We are going to need some sustenance before diving deeper into this, so let's take a humanity break. See you back in 10 minutes."

REFLECT

- Dr. Magnus admitted to a practice of reading a book a week to stay open to learning, current and have something to bring to the various places of influence God set before him. What is your practice of learning and growth?

- Many leaders are stronger with either people or tasks. While it is, of course, situational, do you tend to focus on relationships over results? Results over relationships? Or both equally?

- Do you agree it is important to access both great and godly resources? How do you do this in your own unique way and context?

- How are you creating space for personal and organizational reflection?

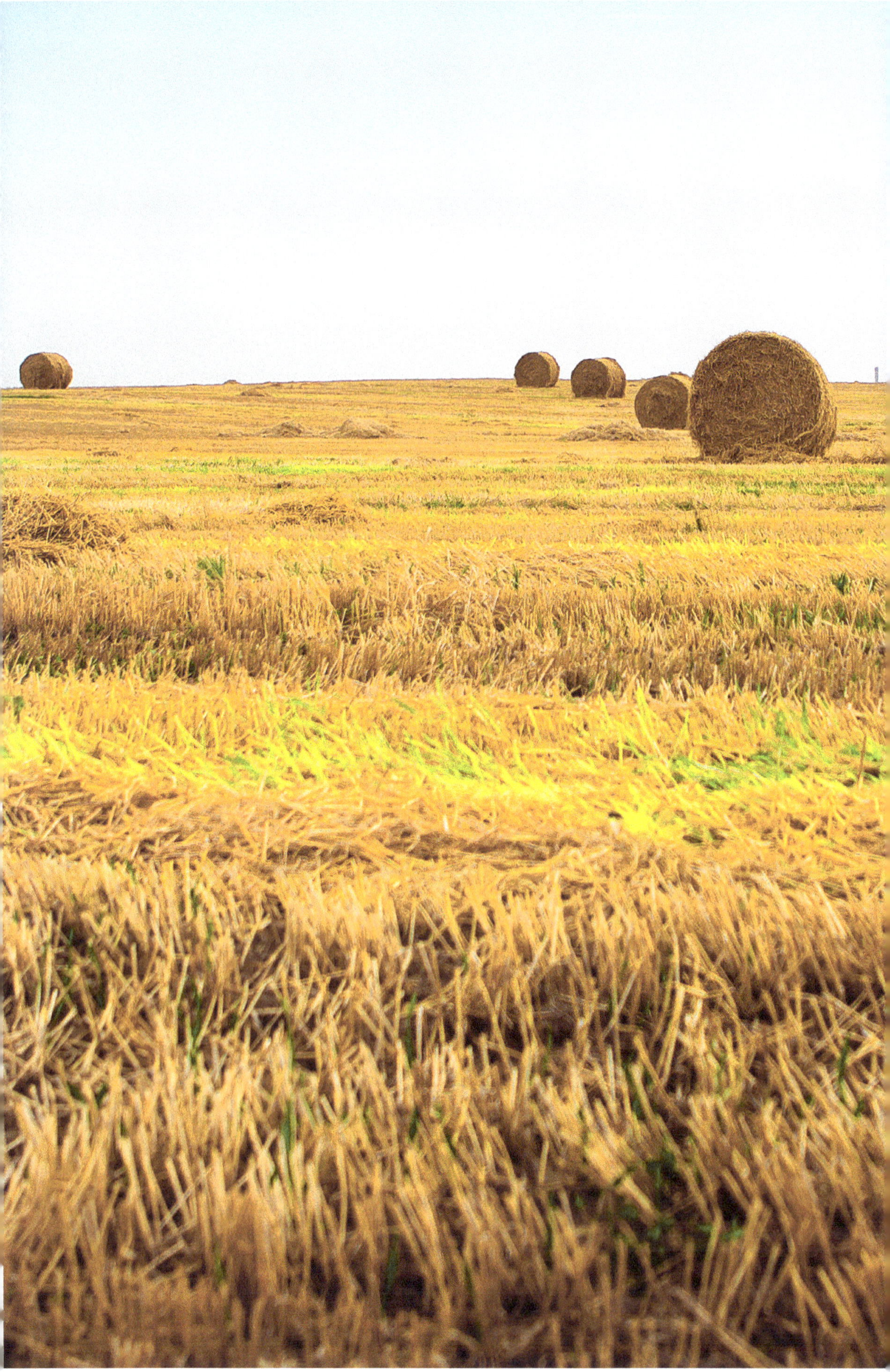

2. THE HEART OF LEADERSHIP

GREAT | GODLY
Holistic
Transformation

"IN THIS SESSION, I would like us to zoom in on the centre of the model—the heart of leadership. What were leaders of the Bible judged by? Their faith and their heart. David was a man after God's own heart. Solomon, even with all his privileges, and the modelling he experienced from the prophets around him, only half-heartedly followed God. Mary, a young and perhaps marginalized woman, had the faith to say, 'Be it onto me.' So, we start here. Turn to a neighbour and share your faith story. Take your time. This is important. How did God pursue you? And, if you were honest, where is your faith at now on a scale of 1-10?"

People began to share. Some smiled as they remembered key moments with God. Some confessed to feelings of emptiness and dryness. Others shared excitedly about insights God had recently revealed. And others yet found it difficult to put into words the journey that they had recently been on. There were lots of nodding heads and hugs, as well as a few tears. Dr. Magnus gave us plenty of time to process and understand how important this was for us at that moment.

I had a hard time knowing what to say. I didn't want to settle for a superficial response, but it was hard to articulate what I had not processed myself. I was doing most of the same spiritual practices as before but without the same sense of expectation and joy. I was concerned about the world but unable to focus on one area outside of work where I thought I could make a positive difference. I wanted my leadership to look different because of what Jesus has done in my life, but could I honestly say that it did? The two words that seemed to describe my soul best were weary and overwhelmed. I needed someone to help me see what was behind that.

Just then, Dr. Magnus said, "Let's look at this holistically. I envision the heart in this model as the cumulation of all your Q's."

Seeing our puzzled looks he went to the board and started a list:

IQ   SQ   MQ   EQ   PQ…

"We are more familiar with IQ and EQ and understand that these are diverse intelligences we can have. I like to expand that list. Imagine that each of these represents a snapshot of our wellbeing and effectiveness in one area. They layer upon each other to either strengthen or undermine our life and leadership. That is why they are drawn at the heart of this model. They affect every part. Every corner and every arrow of this model and of your leadership journey."

2.1 SOUL CARE QUOTIENT

He looked around the room and then started, "I almost never care about someone's IQ, but I care deeply about their soul. When it comes to our Spiritual Intelligence, or Soul Tending Q as I prefer to call it, I really like the way John Ortberg[1] draws a series of concentric circles with the soul as the largest outer circle integrating our will, mind, and body. So many people draw it the other way around, with our soul a small part of us.

I also really like the trellis[2] that Ken Shigematsu draws to demonstrate that God is in and supports every part of our lives. I don't know how to layer

---

[1] John Ortberg, *Soul Keeping: Caring for the Most Important Part of You*, 2014.

[2] Ken Shigematsu, *God in My Everything: How an Ancient Rhythm Helps Busy People Enjoy God*, Zondervan, 2013.

a trellis on top of my model without it looking too complicated but that is how I imagine it. I attribute the idea to him. Here is what mine looks like."

He went to the board and drew:

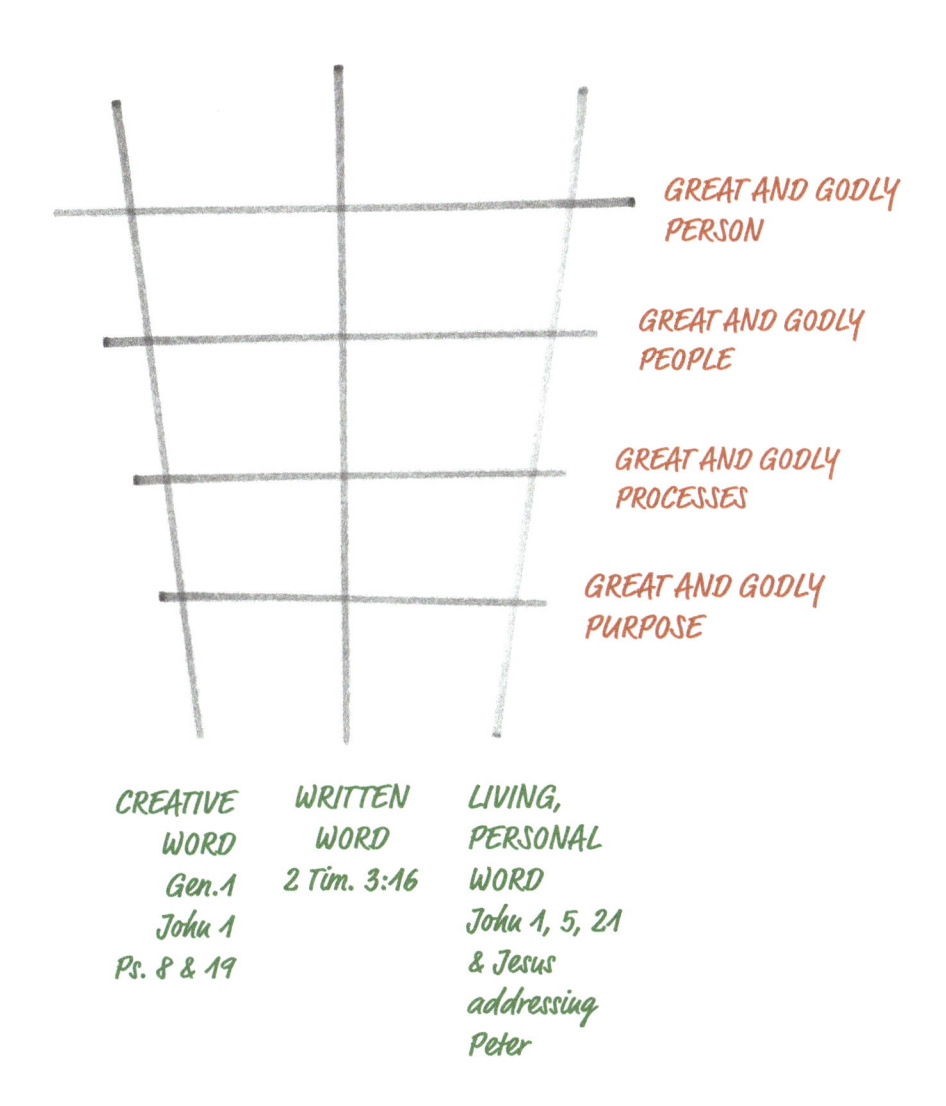

- GREAT AND GODLY PERSON
- GREAT AND GODLY PEOPLE
- GREAT AND GODLY PROCESSES
- GREAT AND GODLY PURPOSE

CREATIVE WORD
Gen. 1
John 1
Ps. 8 & 19

WRITTEN WORD
2 Tim. 3:16

LIVING, PERSONAL WORD
John 1, 5, 21 & Jesus addressing Peter

"Thinking about our soul requires us to think about what it means to be human. When I was a philosophy student, I became interested in Francis Shaeffer's thinking. His books were so thought-provoking. I loved how he offered a holistic view of humanity grounded in theological anthropology. This view led him to a deep appreciation for what he called 'the mannishness of man,' or, you could say, 'the people-ness of people.' This referred to the key attributes the Creator gave us as part of our creation in the image of God."

Dr. Magnus took a step toward us, "These attributes include morality, rationality, creativity, love, and significance. Francis Schaeffer described us as causal agents, able to influence the course of history by the choices we make. He reinforced for me the idea that, restored by Christ, we are called to restorative work. Humans are sinful, yes. Deeply flawed at times. Yet, every human is made in the image of God and, therefore, deserving of our respect and compassion. The alternative is dehumanization! And that we must never allow. Yet, here is what I found so fascinating about Schaeffer's writings: he was not person-centered. He was God-centered, and that was what enabled him to care so much for humanity. God in everything—do you see?"

He looked around the room eagerly, willing us to think critically, deeply, and with faith.

"God is interested in and crucial to each of these leadership lenses. Great and godly leaders, great and godly people, great and godly processes. And, of course, a purpose that is both great and godly. Something worth giving our life to. Regardless of our vocation. Which visual is more helpful for you—concentric circles or the trellis? They are focusing on different aspects but point to the same thing: that our soul is not one small part of us, and God is not just involved in some parts of who we are and what we do. Take a moment and sketch how you would draw this for yourself. Are there any places that you have been making off-limits to God? Perhaps without realizing it? Any places where you have not sought God's perspective, support, and wisdom?"

After a few moments, Dr. Magnus stood and started teaching again. "As a leader, you and God are ultimately responsible for your own spiritual well-being. You must be intentional about spending time with God and finding wise and godly mentors. If you don't tend your soul soon, you will be running on empty.

Carmen, you have been gaining an increasing depth of understanding and experience doing doctoral studies in soul care while also offering graduate-level courses for leaders. Thank you for your willingness to share a case study that grows out of your practice."

Carmen moved to the front of the room and began. "Imagine a woman in her early 50s leading in a long-term care home. Let's call her Sally. Her young adult daughters are both in serious relationships and talking about marriage. Her parents are aging and requiring more care. She had wanted to work four days a week but felt obligated to say yes to five to fill in the gaps. Chronic headaches have plagued her for years, and although she's sought treatment, their cause remains a mystery. With all this going on, Sally did her best to be present at work, but she's already suffered one serious burnout.

"One day, her Executive Director told her that she and her colleagues would also be responsible for developing the structure and staffing of a local hospice. There was to be no pay increase and no additional staff.

"What would you recommend to her to help prevent burnout if she agreed to take on this additional responsibility?"

People shared ideas about building in extra support for herself, chatting with her supervisor, daughters and parents about expectations, and perhaps getting counselling to deal with any of her own unrealistic expectations and limiting mindsets.

After listening to our suggestions, Carmen said, "Too bad she didn't have you to coach her through this. Would you like to hear what happened?"

"Yes," we all said in chorus.

"As a strong perfectionist, the woman paid a lot of attention to every detail. She also worked hard to ensure the right people were hired. Sadly, no one had time to train or guide these new hires. Everyone was exhausted. The Executive Director was task- and project-oriented. When stressed, she could be rude to people. She often called last-minute meetings. This resulted in a rise in organizational anxiety.

"Sally was hanging on by a thread when she came to see me. I asked her the following questions, and these may be helpful for you as well: Where do you have autonomy and agency in this? What is your body trying to tell you? How aware are you of how your body communicates to you? If you were to listen to it, what would you do? If you do not listen to it what might happen? What is God saying to you in the midst of this?

"Sadly, Sally was so depleted that she ended up in a severe burnout and, nearly two years later is still unable to return to work. We are embodied creatures, and we ignore this to our peril."

"Thank you, Carmen, that was so helpful. Before you sit down, would you be willing to pray for all of us?"

After Carmen prayed, Dr. Magnus continued. "We hear this kind of story far too often, good people burning out. You may have been close to this yourself. Perhaps you are now! Or perhaps you sense someone close to you is in over their head.

Either way, I would like us to take some time to craft your own case study by answering the following questions:

What happened or is happening?
What were or are the early indicators of concern?
What should or have you put in place since to tend your soul?
What message might you want other leaders to take from your story?
How would applying this yourself change things moving forward?"

2.2 MINDSET QUOTIENT

After a time of prayer and a break, we took our seats again as Dr. Magnus said, "MQ. We don't often talk about our Mindset Quotient, but we should. Next to our soul care, it is one of the most important areas a leader should tend in themselves and others. Managing the messages that we are allowing to guide our thinking and actions."

He paused, then said, "Come with me…"

We walked over to the part of the bookshelf dedicated to strengthening mindsets, and Dr. Magnus pointed to one book after another that had shaped his thinking about MQ, Mindset.

"Marilee Adams, *Change Your Questions, Change Your Life*.[3] So helpful. The questions we ask shape what we think about, the answers we get and the direction we go. And I am not just talking about organizational questions, as important as they are. I am talking about the questions we ask ourselves when we get up in the morning, when something goes wrong or when someone disappoints us. Our ability to use higher-level thinking often depends on our ability to ask the right question at that moment. As she says, one kind of question moves us toward learning, and the other, more common kind, leads us into the blame-fueled judger pit. That is not a great place to be. And it is a dark and dangerous place to lead from.

---

3 Marilee Adams, *Change Your Questions, Change Your Life: 12 Powerful Tools for Leadership, Coaching and Results,* 4th Ed. Berrett-Koehler Publishers, 2022.

Using our model as a lens through which to think about this, a three-prong question emerges naturally: how can I move more frequently and quickly into learner mode myself? What would need to happen for our people to function more frequently as learners? And how can our processes support this?"

This really resonated with me. Maybe I had been asking the wrong kinds of questions—blame questions that sometimes turned to shame, limiting questions rather than breakthrough prompting ones.

What question have you been asking that, reframed, could lead to a whole different way of thinking?

Continuing Dr. Magnus said, "Another great book. Henry Thompson's *Stress Effect: Why Smart Leaders Make Dumb Decisions and What to Do About it*.[4] Do you see this title? Why some leaders, smart leaders, make dumb decisions. That is why wellness, mindset, and resilience are so important. It's not just about how smart you are. Looking at our model again we see that it's about showing up as your best self. Bringing the right processes into play and the right people into the room to make smart decisions. So helpful.

I was just reading some research from Deloitte about this. Let me find it," he said, shuffling through some papers before reading, "'Organizational leaders in Canada are stressed, strained, and burnt out. And that was before the pandemic. Our most recent study uncovered that 82% of senior leaders were experiencing exhaustion. 50% have also contemplated exiting their roles, resigning, retiring, taking a leave of absence, or moving to part-time work.'

"82% experiencing exhaustion! 50% contemplating quitting! The article goes on, 'What can a board or executive team do to improve well-being, retain senior leaders, and ensure prospering through the inevitable challenges ahead?'

---

4 Henry Thompson, *Stress Effect: Why Smart Leaders Make Dumb Decisions and What to Do About It*, 2010.

"Here are Deloitte's recommendations:

- 'Reduce stigma regarding mental health by demystifying and normalizing dialogue
- Strengthen peer relationships and create community, support, and collaboration
- Enhance organizational mental and well-being support
- Rethink work to enable leaders to work effectively and efficiently'[5]

"The research also focuses on the importance of addressing microaggressions and discrimination in the workplace, something we have not been nearly intentional enough about in Christian organizations especially. And they also stress how climate change impacts human well-being. This is where having a triple bottom line is so important. What we measure is what we focus on. The research demonstrates that companies with robust employee wellness programs outperform those without wellness programs on several important scales.[6]

"So, let's bring this down to personal application. On a scale of 1-10 how stressed are you? How stressed are your people? What practices and processes could you put in place that might alleviate this?"

One of the students excused themselves, saying, "I need to step out for a moment to reflect on this because, to be honest, this is where we are drowning, and some ideas popped into my head as you were speaking that I don't want to lose."

"Go in peace," Dr. Magnus said, adding, "Anyone else need a minute for personal processing?"

A few hands went up. "Okay, let's take a few minutes for reflection."

A while later, Dr. Magnus drew us back together. He paused and perched on a stool, thinking for a moment before saying, "When I was growing up on the farm, one day, I was out on the tractor. There was a big thunderstorm rolling in, and I was afraid. So, I asked my dad what to do, and he said, 'If the storm comes close, take the spare tire and sit on it under the tractor and

---

[5] https://www2.deloitte.com/ca/en/pages/consulting/articles/well-being-and-resilience-in-senior-leaders.html

[6] Lisa MacVicar, Deloitte Canada, 'Well-being: A New Cornerstone for ESG strategy and reporting.' Part One.

keep your head down. That way, you will be dry and safe. After the storm passes, you can get on the tractor again.' After that, I wasn't afraid because I knew what to do. Even when there are storms raging around us, we are less afraid when we know what to do. That is the gift you give to yourself and your team when you communicate with clarity."

"I didn't know you grew up on a farm."

"Yes, rural Saskatchewan. I did the first two years of High School by correspondence so I could stay and help with farming. Perhaps that contributed to the value I place on education and to my understanding of how challenging it can be for people to access it. And perhaps this is where my commitment to help others find a way came from. In 1980, we launched a distance learning curriculum that eventually served over 1,000 students. Three years later, we started a Summer Graduate School. Then a business degree. Then later, at another institution, we co-created a Doctor of Ministry in Leadership.

"I tell you this to show that our values and mindset can move us towards creativity and responsiveness to the needs of those we serve, or they can hold us back. And our mindset is impacted by our life experiences, our training, and the people we surround ourselves with. So, choose wisely."

He stood up from the stool and moved back to the board, "Mindsets. MINDSETS! It's all about mindsets."

Moving along the bookshelf, Dr. Magnus paused and pulled a book to show to us.

"Have you read John Acuff's *Soundtracks?*[7] Another very helpful resource that offers so much light. Acuff uses the analogy of a soundtrack, something that plays on repeat in our head. The kind of soundtrack that leads us to doubt ourselves; and imagine worst case scenarios and that undermines our path forward.

"The apostle Paul the apostle is such a great example to us here. I so love Philippians 1. Paul is incarcerated. He is being held, but not because of any wrong that he has done. He was introducing people to the faith and bringing them to Jesus. While he could have been looking at the downside, he says instead, 'don't worry! I'm here for a good reason! The Roman guards are receiving the gospel and it's moving out through Praetorian guard!' If you were in Paul's shoes, would it be possible that the soundtrack in your

---

[7] John Acuff, *Soundtracks: The Surprising Solution to Overthinking*. Baker Books, 2021.

mind would be negative? Paul continues, 'Because I am here, people are now hearing and telling the good news. Granted, some are doing it out of false motives, but even that is ok.' I just so love Paul's view. The hope that he pours out to others when he could be worrying about the outcome of his trial. Have you ever wrestled during the dark hours of the night with fear, doubt, or uncertainty? Paul had dealt with his soundtrack—his perspective and his posture. He believed that even if his journey was over, that was okay because heaven would be better. Remember, he said, 'For me to live is Christ, but to die is gain.'[8] Choosing what voice to listen to is one of the most important things a leader can do. For Christians choosing God's voice over the voice in our own heads is crucial.

"Back to Acuff for a strategy to help us with that. He offers three questions to ask of the messages overriding our thoughts: 'Is it true? Is it helpful? Is it kind?' So simple. Yet, so helpful! In fact, so helpful that we are going to stop there for a moment. Back to your tables and pull out your notebook. What is the soundtrack that runs through your head?

Where does your mind tend to go when you are anxious or unsure?

"Keep in mind that, as both Acuff and Adams remind us, our minds are more likely to judge than to learn, and our memories cannot always be trusted. Let me ask you this: If you were to apply Acuff's three questions to your soundtrack, what might change?" After a time for reflection, Dr. Magnus gathered us together again. "What did you notice as you did this exercise?"

"That there are almost predictable patterns of where my mind goes."

"That one negative comment or result really can outweigh ten positives."

"Just how powerful our perception of what is happening is, sometimes more powerful than what really occurs."

Dr. Magnus smiled and nodded. "Great insights. Do we need a break? Or should we keep going?"

"Keep going," several voices agreed as we moved to the bookshelf again.

We all took a step sideways as Dr. Magnus moved further along the bookshelf.

"Sarah Summer's book *Leadership Above the Line*[9] came out at just the right time for me. It gave me one more helpful way to understand how

---

8 Phil. 1:21

9 Sarah Summer, *Leadership Above the Line: A Character Based Leadership Tool that leads to Success for You and Your Team*, Tyndale House Publishers, 2006.

different people are wired and how our mindset impacts our wiring. She describes three types of people in organizations: Strategists, who tend to focus on results; Humanists, who, as the name implies, are great with people; and Diplomats, who bring what she calls 'color' to an organization. When we are functioning well in our strength, we bring great value. She calls this leading above the line. However, each of these types has what she calls a 'below the line' presentation when we are not at our best. The Strategist can be impatient. The Humanist can become a people pleaser. The Diplomat may shift their attention to looking good.

When we use our strengths for selfish gain or self-protection rather than service of the greater good, we are functioning 'below the line.' One of her interesting observations is that we tend to view people exclusively by their 'above the line' or 'below the line' traits rather than see them comprehensively. I have done that. I have seen only the strengths or only the weaknesses. Anyone else?"

Which 'type' best describes you? How do you see the strengths and potential weaknesses emerging in your life? Like any model, this is overly simplified, and you may find that none of the categories describes you well or that you respond differently in different situations. This is normal. Just choose one that seems the best fit in most situations.

"Such a good book. It's out of print now, and although I have written a few times suggesting that they bring it back, so far, it hasn't been re-released. Unfortunate. Okay, if you had difficulty determining which is your strength and potential area of concern, it may be that you have not been getting enough honest feedback recently. That is a common problem for leaders, especially if you are a senior leader in your church or organization. Dan, you have done some personal and organizational work in this area. Anything you can share with us that others might find helpful?"

"This talk of 'Mindset Quotient' that you referred to Dr. Magnus resonated with me strongly for several reasons. One is that my theological background kicked into gear. The Bible has passage after passage that describes the importance of our thoughts. If we don't think about what we think about, our thoughts have more power in our lives because we aren't even aware of them.

"In Philippians 4:8, Paul gives us a mental filter to help us sift out thoughts that are unhelpful to our sense of peace and our progress. When we pause to think about what we think about, we can catch ourselves before heading down the 'judger path' and make a turn toward a 'learner mindset.'

"In 2 Corinthians 10:4-6, Paul even tells us that thoughts can become strongholds that imprison us. His solution is to do battle so that instead of them holding us captive, we make them obedient to Christ. There is a very real battle for our minds. What comes into our minds comes out in our lives and leadership and affects the state of our hearts.

"As a pastor, I have often worked with people who are trapped in lies about themselves. 'I could never be loved.' 'I will always be alone.' 'I don't have what it takes to be the husband/wife/Christian/leader/friend/person that I need to be.' 'I will always be stuck in this addiction.' These lies take hold in people's minds, and only the truth of God's Word can truly set them free.

"This affects me personally as well. It is not just theoretical. I have battled negativity and worry in my mind. Even though I see myself as a positive person, I can still find myself at times spiralling down in a thought pattern of negativity or anxiety. Those soundtracks of fear, anxiety, stress, and negative thinking can play again and again in my mind when circumstances don't go the way I have hoped. I cannot agree strongly enough with the importance of leaders considering their mindset quotient. It has helped me live and lead more effectively by training my mind to reframe, focus on what is true and good, and create new soundtracks that remind me of the strength I have in Christ and the hope and future He has for me."

Dr. Magnus gave us a few minutes to reflect on this and record any insights or changes we wanted to put in place before going on.

2.3 EMOTIONAL QUOTIENT

Until the fourth grade, I went to a country school with grades 1-12 all in the same room. In fact, I was so eager to go to school that my mom let me go a year early, and it wasn't until Christmas that the Superintendent got wind of it and told me I was too young. I cried when I found out I had to wait a whole year. So here I am, a little 'grade-oner' in a classroom and out in the schoolyard with all these big high school boys—some of them really rough and tough. Mean.

There were a lot of ducks in the area, so one of the ways they would torment us was by throwing duck eggs at us. One day I ran into the school for self-protection just as the boys let loose. Unfortunately for them and for our long-suffering teacher, Miss Zunti, she stepped into the doorway to see what was going on just in time to be plastered with eggs.

Experiencing their frequent tormenting taught me compassion for the little one, the underdog. I remember what that feels like. It also taught me to expect but not tolerate bullies.

"We could hardly overestimate the importance of emotional wellbeing to leaders. The Bain Institute[10] has done some interesting work around Inspiring Leaders and what they call Centered Leaders. A Centered Leader is inwardly confident, strategically consistent, and focused on their mission. Uncentered Leaders are annoyingly insecure, consistently unpredictable, and focused on their own issues and interests. The hardest leader to follow is an insecure one, especially if they are annoyingly insecure. They are always trying to get you to make them feel better. Jesus, by contrast, was unwaveringly confident in God's love, unreservedly strategic about His Father's business, and always on mission. The language of centeredness may or may not work for you, but I want to give you time to reflect on these concepts."

---

10 Bain Institute, https://www.bain.com/insights/how-leaders-inspire-cracking-the-code/

If you imagined the three criteria listed above as continuums, where are you currently falling on each scale?

Inwardly confident but not cocky ▬▬▬▬▬▬▬ *Annoyingly Insecure*
Strategically consistent ▬▬▬▬▬▬▬ *Consistently unpredictable*
Mission and people focused ▬▬▬▬▬▬▬ *Focused on own interests*

Was it possible that I had swung to the unhealthy end of one of these continuums? Or maybe all of them? The dark side of each felt strangely interconnected, and I could see how I sometimes allowed the pressures of work and the discontent of peers and direct reports to influence my confidence, which undermined our strategic consistency and demonstrated that I had become more concerned with survival—especially my own survival—than our mission. I had confused true humility with insecurity, and our team was paying the price. I made myself a note to learn more about Centered Leadership and began a list of people I needed to apologize to.

Dr. Magnus interrupted my thoughts, saying, "Nowhere is our emotional and social intelligence more tested than when we are in conflict. I love what the Epistle of James has to say. James understood the roots of conflict. Turn to James 4:1. In your groups, discuss what you see in this passage as it relates to conflict you may currently be experiencing. What insights do you see?"

"External quarrels come from internal conflict."

"Yes, thank you. There is so much in that passage, but I want us to reflect on that insight before moving on. When you are in conflict with someone else, ask God to show you what is being triggered for you and why.

"Sherri, you are a leader in the world of healthcare and must experience your share of conflict. How do you navigate conflict in such a high-stress environment?"

Sherri thought for a moment, then said, "These are powerful words indeed —'What causes fights and quarrels among you? Don't they come from your desires that battle within you?' People who know me probably think I am extremely calm in tense situations. I seldom argue or escalate when in conflict. Rather I instinctively look for a collaborative, peaceful process and solution. Yet, while it may appear that I've skillfully navigated conflict, if my heart isn't aligned with my words and actions, resentment and frustration tend to build. Over time, my view of the individual or organization dims, though

I haven't authentically shared my thoughts on the matter. I know that this is unfair to others and to myself. And I realize this is not healthy, helpful, sustainable, or an accurate representation of God's ideal for resolving conflict.

"It does demonstrate the truth of James' insistence that we examine the desires that battle within us. If I'm honest, I have a small three-year-old inside me who is often wailing and shaking her fists at the 'other' while simultaneously seeking shelter in a closet. I resent being told what to do and how to do it, especially if I've shared my ideas and haven't been heard or gotten my way. God has shown me that in these moments, I'm feeling insignificant and overrun by those I perceive as having loud, overbearing voices.

"I realize it also gives insight into what really matters to me. I value engagement and transparency. If I'm triggered, it's often because these values are misaligned with the situation at hand. However, am I also not disingenuous by not fully and honestly engaging in the discussion? And so, I've learned to pray for both Divine revelation and courage when I get that tight feeling in my chest and to trust that God will go before me and stand beside me as I wade into those murky waters of dialogue, listening but also speaking the truth in love."

Dr. Magnus smiled and thanked Sherri for her vulnerability in sharing, "You may have spoken for many of us in the room Sherri. It sounds like you have done the hard work of becoming aware of the kinds of desires that battle within you, what triggers these battles and a more God-centered response to take. There is always a gap between what happens and how we respond to it. We can learn to utilize that gap well. We appreciate you sharing your insights and how you arrived at them. Perhaps others would find similar reflection helpful."

What tends to trigger an unhealthy reactive stance for you during times of conflict? What insights does that give you about what matters to you? About where your insecurities are most likely to surface? What might be a God-honouring way to utilize the gap between 'what happens' and your response to it in times of perceived threat to what matters to you?

2.4 TRUST QUOTIENT

"Let's talk for a moment about trust. Trust is crucial to leadership. People's trust of us and our trust of them is built over time and lost in a moment. Especially when there is moral failure. Trust is inspired by our character, following through on what we promise, our vulnerability and transparency. Listening carefully. Our concern for people. Our personal and professional credibility. All of these build trust. So does truth-telling. When it comes to relationships we tend to focus on grace over truth in Christian settings. This is unwise. When I'm in a relationship and someone is fudging a little—they're not telling the whole truth, even if they're trying to protect me—when I sense that they are, I trust them less.

"A powerful exercise for leaders it to identify what Steven Covey calls 'Trust Gaps' in your credibility and relationships at work. These may be gaps due to what you have said or done or not said or done. Or, they can be gaps between what you perceive and what others perceive.

"The Covey Institute quotes one study where senior managers were asked if they care about their teams. Then middle managers were asked if their senior leaders care about them. There was a 68%-point gap between the answers.[11] Now I ask you, does what the senior leaders think in this case make a difference? It doesn't. If people perceive they are not cared for, then that is the reality they are functioning out of. This is one of the reasons that trust is so much harder to build and maintain than we would think—especially in large organizations.

"In smaller organizations, it may be a bit easier if you spend more time together because that may mean that you give each other the benefit of the doubt and can test your assumptions more. Not always, of course. My point is, the larger the organization, or the larger or more geographically distant your team, the more you will need to be intentional about this."

What trust gaps are you aware of in your team? How might you go about finding others that you are not aware of?

---

11 https://www.6seconds.org/2017/10/31/stephen-mr-covey-three-key-strategies/

2.5 DIVERSITY QUOTIENT

One of the greatest leadership labs I experienced early in my years of service at Briercrest was the opportunity to co-lead an annual youth event. It was the privilege of our team of three to see this event grow over ten years to where there were beyond 4,000 youth in attendance. This was a volunteer role for which we were paid with a new suit each year so the guests and students would know whom to go to if they had a question.

I was the rookie on this team of three extremely different people. One was a very relational and steadying person who loved to have things settled and tightly planned at least two to three weeks before the event. Another was an out-of-the-box creative individual whose best thinking began to flow two weeks before the event. I was trying to find my way to manage this team of opposites from the middle and bring the best from all of us, and so was offered the opportunity to develop systems to satisfy both styles.

This experience, as well as growing up as a middle child in a large family, helped me dream about and experiment with building and influencing diverse leadership teams.

Dr. Magnus continued, saying, "Two of the greatest problems I have observed in organizations are leaders who gather people around them who are all like them, or leaders who gather diverse people around them and then treat them as if they were like themselves and lead them accordingly. Both are huge mistakes.

"Diverse voices lead to diverse perspectives and better decisions. There is a business case that can be made for this, but the bigger issue is that it is just the right thing to do. Companies with strong benches have 22% more women leaders and 36% greater leader background diversity than companies with weak benches. Yet only 21% of the leaders of global companies that were polled said that their company recruits and promotes from diverse candidate pools.[12]

---

12 Global Leadership Forecast, 2023,6, 22-24. Development Dimensions International Inc. (www.ddiworld.com)

"Now, leading a diverse team is harder than one with people who all think as you do. If you don't have the conviction that there is value in that diversity, you will give up too quickly, silence the diverse voices by making it unsafe or only pay attention to the voices that align with your own thoughts. So many teams are doing this. Then they say, 'We tried that, and it doesn't work.' Heartbreaking. Imagine if the early church had done that. Well, I guess in fairness, they did try to do that, but God was having none of it, so he sent Paul to straighten them out.[13] Jesus prayed for unity, not uniformity."[14]

2.6 PHYSICAL QUOTIENT

"Of course, these Q's are all interconnected. By PQ I am referring to not just physical health or fitness but also to our energy. Do you know when your most effective times are? Schedule your most important work—especially strategic decision-making, strategic learning and strategic relationship building—into those times."

"In fact, let's take a few minutes to identify when your most productive times are and compare them to your schedule for next week. Pull out your calendar. Do you see anything it might be wise to change? Are you taking care of your body? Getting enough rest? Exercising? Anything you know you need to build into your schedule so you can be at your physical best and bring your best energy to your family and work?

Dr. Magnus walked to his computer and pulled up his calendar, made some notes and sent an email rescheduling an important meeting. That was the thing about his classes; you always knew they would be challenging, expecting you to engage with each other and the texts in deeper ways than you were used to, and they would require you to apply immediately what you were learning. Yet we loved it, partly because we always knew that Dr. Magnus was genuinely learning alongside us, taking almost as many notes when we talked as we did when he taught and applying everything we discussed to his own life.

---

13 See Acts 15 and Galatians 2:14.

14 See the High Priestly Prayer of Jesus in John 17

Completely unaware that we exchanged glances, acknowledging what we had just witnessed, Dr. Magnus called us back together. "Let's take a break. These next few are so important that I want to follow my own advice and make sure we are at our best to be able to process them together. See you back in fifteen minutes."

Someone put on a fresh pot of coffee as people milled around the room or went outside for a stretch. When we came back, Dr. Magnus was already at the board.

2.7 SOCIAL/CONNECTION QUOTIENT

"I so appreciate the light that Harvard Business Professor Amy Edmondson has brought about Psychological Safety in the workplace.[15] She defines it as 'the shared belief that the team is safe for interpersonal risk-taking.' Places where we can show up as our true selves. Where we can take interpersonal risks. She calls the organizations that achieve this kind of culture Fearless Organizations. These kinds of safe spaces correlate to greater productivity, engagement, learning, and innovation. What are some of the practices you think Psychologically Safe organizations encourage?"

"Speaking up about problems."

"Asking questions."

"Admitting to mistakes."

"Asking for help."

"Learning and growth."

"Handling conflict with care and transparency."

"Seeking the opinions of people who are less likely to speak up."

"I can see you read the book," Dr. Magnus laughed, "but the more important question is, 'what did you do about it?' That is true for all these sources we are talking about. Unless we apply them, they aren't going to help us or our teams. So, turn to your table and discuss how you have intentionally—notice I said intentionally—have put or will put them in practice in more fruitful ways."

---

15 Amy Edmondson, *The Fearless Organization: Creating Psychological Safety in the Workplace for Learning, Innovation and Growth*, Wiley, 2018.

Looking back at our four lenses: How are you as a leader growing in becoming more psychologically safe? How are those around you doing in this area? What processes do you have in place to ensure psychological safety? And, while this one may take some deeper thought, how might your purpose be tied to or even dependent on your ability to create psychological safety?

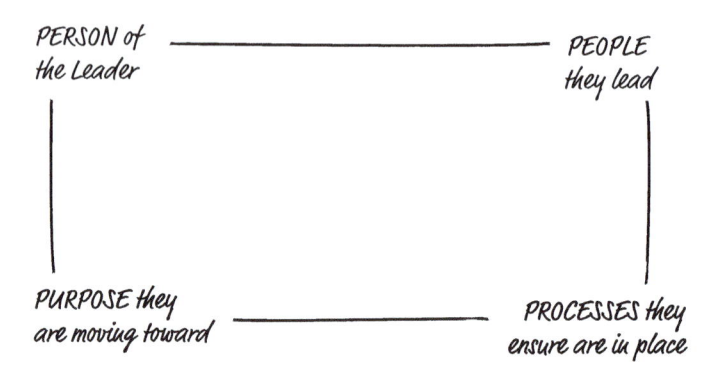

```
PERSON of                              PEOPLE
the Leader  ─────────────────────      they lead
    │                                      │
    │                                      │
    │                                      │
    │                                      │
PURPOSE they                           PROCESSES they
are moving toward ───────────────      ensure are in place
```

Dr. Magnus continued. "Spaces with low safety and low motivation, Edmondson calls Apathy Zones. When standards are low and safety is high, a Comfort Zone is created. These are 'feel-good zone but don't get much done' spaces. The opposite is a high expectations, high standards, and high performance but low safety zone. These are marked by fear and, over time, lead to low performance. When both psychological safety and standards are high, we create a high-performance zone where learning, accountability, and mastery prevail."

Consider the following two questions and apply the insights to your context.
- How are learning and high performance linked?
- How can accountability drive learning and performance in a psychologically safe way?

"Let's change up our groups a bit. Find people who work in similar fields to yourself so you can apply this as specifically as possible… and hold each other accountable to act on what you discuss," he added with a wink.

2.8 ETHICAL QUOTIENT

Gathering us back together, Dr. Magnus continued the conversation around leadership ethics.

"It is amazing how all these Q's overlap. A University of Michigan Study[16] found that leaders who emphasize moral implications to decisions and focus on both the greater good and the collective good are less likely to allow cultures where incivility persists. Of course, it is not enough to perceive yourself to be an ethical leader. This is because we deceive ourselves and because studies show that ethics must be demonstrated through specific behaviours—listening, making fair decisions, and discussing ethics with your employees.[17] When we are intentional about this, levels of respect are more likely to go up around us. The influence one person has! And the responsibility we have as leaders."

What is the next ethical question that your team should be discussing?

2.9 VOCATIONAL/CONTEXTUAL QUOTIENT

Dr. Magnus got our attention, then continued. "This next Q asks both, 'Where can I best serve?' and 'Are the people on our team serving in the right spots?' Assessments and the council of others can be helpful, but in the long run, it is the opportunity to experience different things and, as Marcus Buckingham so beautifully points out, discover not just what our strengths are but what strengthens us when we do it.

---

16 https://www.icos.umich.edu/sites/default/files/lecturereadinglists/Walsh%20et%20al.%20JBP%20-%20Positive%20leader%20norms%20respect%20incivility.pdf

17 Brown, M. E., Treviño, L. K., & Harrison, D. A. (2005). *Ethical leadership: A social learning perspective for construct development and testing. Organizational Behavior and Human Decision Processes*, 97, 117–134.

"You may have experienced a role that just wasn't a good fit for you. Or maybe you have someone on your team who is in the wrong place. Many things can keep us in these roles. Sometimes there is a season for which that is necessary, but over time, this can be both draining and demotivating. Buckingham's research shows that we probably do not have to change vocations. It is the day-to-day details of our job that energize or drain us, and most of us have at least some degree of agency about how we do what we do.

"I found this especially helpful with pastors and people in helping professions who may have gone into their vocation for all the right reasons and be leaving it for all the wrong ones. Buckingham's book *Stand Out* was so important to my understanding of how I am wired and where I can bring my best contribution.

"As I mentioned earlier, I grew up on a farm. It was pretty much expected that I would stay in that line of work. When I started to pursue other educational and vocational work, there were people who questioned me. I would answer, 'I have to obey what I believe God has equipped me for and is calling me to do. This can take courage.' He paused at looked around as heads nodded in agreement.

Looking at me, he asked, "How did you sense your calling into the corporate world?"

No one had ever asked me this before, and I didn't quite know how to answer. "I have always loved business. Even as a kid, I was always selling something or setting up an entrepreneurial enterprise. I was just wired that way, and my parents saw that early on and encouraged it."

Dr. Magnus smiled at me and nodded encouragement, then turned to my neighbour. "Joshua, how about you? How did you discover what God wired you for and called you into?"

Joshua thought for a moment, then shared. "I guess I would describe it as progressive. Towards the end of high school, I sensed God challenging me with the question: 'What about those dying in hospitals?' Although I had never been to a hospital, I began to pursue medical training. At that point, I was not thinking about mission work. However, during medical school, I went to a Christian youth conference where the Lord challenged me again. After reading a missionary biography by Ingrid Trobisch[18] I surrendered to

---

18 Ingrid Trobisch, *On Our Way Rejoicing*.

this calling. Over time God took me from one role to another and each time confirmed that this was the right step."

Dr. Magnus smiled again and turned to another table. "Jacqueline, I know that your journey of discernment has been a bit different. How would you describe it?"

"Like Joshua, I don't view calling as a one-time thing. I view calling as an emerging concept. God made me and called me to live out my life for Him and deploy everything that I have for Him. I believe that whatever emerges as I stay in step with Him is my calling. I want to provide exceptional service to my family, clients, and the world. To experience the richness and freedom this life has to offer while bringing hope, help, and healing to every interaction I have."

Spreading his hands, Dr. Magnus summarized, "Each of us is different, and God speaks to us in different ways. I will say that having a conviction that we are working within our sweet spot is highly motivating. You can see how important it is for us to come to this realization for ourselves and to help others on our team do the same. This is one of the greatest parts of leadership—the opportunity to strategically develop people and help them find places to serve that fit them well."

2.10 ACTUALIZING QUOTIENT

"Moving on to our actualizing quotient, this is our ability to get things done—both what we can accomplish and what we can inspire and support others to accomplish. As leaders, we cannot overestimate how important this is. It's more likely that you have received training in this if you work in the corporate world. For too long, bible colleges have trained pastors to lead small churches. We have not taught them how to scale up when their church grows or when they move to larger churches. We haven't taught them how to lead a team or how to help their Board to adapt to changing circumstances. And you can see the consequences of this. There is nothing that bothers me more than when I see people leaving the church or organization because of poor leadership—often poor leadership from good people. There is so much room for growth in every area, and for many of us, this is one of them."

Jay put up his hand and said, "I was just reading about this." He popped open his computer to a recent survey and read, "Most of the pastors we interviewed and surveyed said their formal theological education did not prepare them adequately for church pastoral ministry. Respondents told us schools were at their best when preparing students for preaching and teaching, and at their worst preparing students for leading change, doing church administration, leading boards, managing church politics, and overseeing building maintenance."[19]

Dr. Magnus thanked Jay and then said, "My point is not to knock bible colleges or universities or to focus on one vocation. My point is that we need to think holistically as leaders and train people holistically.

What skill or attribute would enable you to better serve in your place of vocation? We must keep learning. What is the learning curve for you these days?

"I want to encourage all of us to take what we have talked about here seriously. Leaders around us are extremely anxious and burning out. Some are experiencing moral failure or relational crises. This is important, friends. So important I would like you to turn to a partner, answer the following questions honestly, and pray for each other about this before we break."

---

19 Rick Hiemstra and Lindsay Callaway, Faith Today Publications, 2023. "Significant Church: Understanding the Value of the Small Church in Canada," https://www.evangelical-fellowship.ca/SC, 11.

Step One:
Score yourself on how resilient you are, using a scale of 1-10, with 10 being high and 1 low. Be ready to tell us why you gave this number.

Step Two:
Please also rate yourself on each of the following quotients, again on a score of 1-10 with ten being high and one low.

- SOUL Q.
- MINDSET Q.
- EMOTIONAL Q.
- SOCIAL Q.
- PHYSICAL Q.
- VOCATIONAL Q.
- ACTIONABLE Q.

Step Three:
Plan to follow up and reflectively establish a sentence completion exercise on each.
"Given my score, I will..."

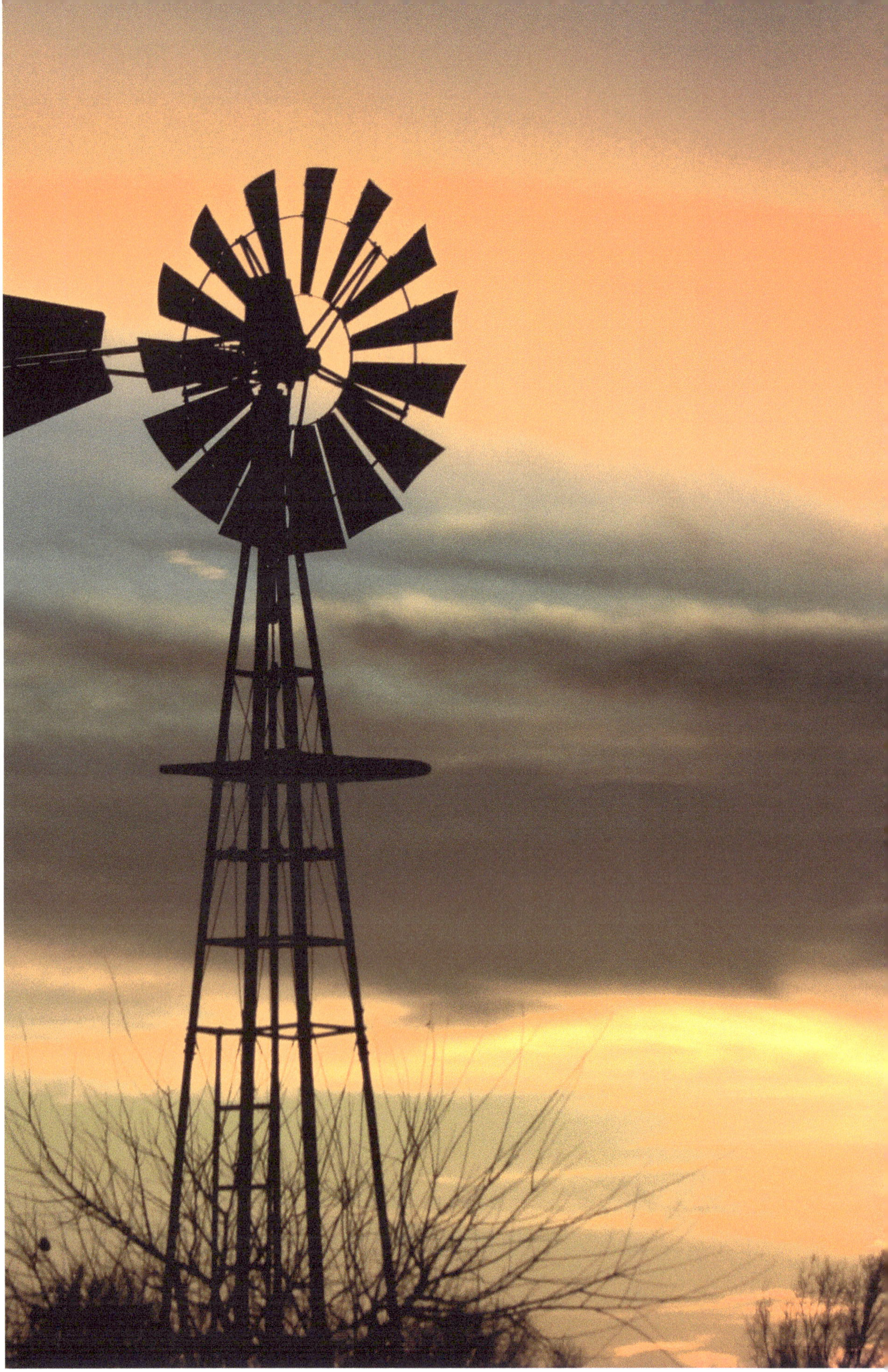

3. THE PERSON OF THE LEADER

"If you want to improve the organization, you have to improve yourself and the organization gets pulled up with you."
- Indira Nooyi

DR. MAGNUS SEEMED TO HAVE RENEWED ENERGY as he began to teach again. "Romans 12 tells us that if we have the gift of leadership, we are to lead diligently. 1 Timothy 4:12 and 2 Timothy 1:6 remind us that our gifts must be fanned into flame. These verses suggest to me that we do all we can to become the best people and leaders we can be. That we do our part. This does not mean that we are not God-dependent. Just the opposite. This does not mean that we don't depend on the Spirit to cause spiritual fruit.[1] Just the opposite.

"Nor does it mean that we pursue leadership the way we see it practiced around us. Just the opposite! 1 Corinthians reminds us that any gift not used in love is worthless. Turn to Mark 10:42. Here we have one of the clearest commands from Jesus about management in the Bible, 'those who are considered rulers of the Gentiles lord it over them...But IT SHALL NOT BE SO WITH YOU!'" Dr. Magnus almost exploded out of his chair. Then taking a deep breath, he continued, "Things are done differently in the Kingdom of God. 'It shall NOT be so with you.' Let's see how this applies to our model."If an organization's mission is to be widely owned, it has to be deeply owned by a few—the key leaders. They must engage with each lens: embodying the purpose, ensuring the organization's processes make traction and sustainability, and enabling the people.

"However, I want to stress that leaders are *human*. How often we forget that. A human being that is both God-centered and fallible. We're often surprised if we fail. Other people are surprised when we make mistakes. Yet there is something wonderful about being human. One of the things Jesus revealed to us was what it looks like to be fully human. He called us to take back the image of God in our humanity. I'm a human being, but I'm a human being who is transformed and also becoming transformed." Dr. Magnus was getting passionate, "So how do we seek to lead diligently while holding in tension the fact that we are human?"

---

1 Galatians 5:22,23

Ellen spoke up, "I have been thinking about true humility recently. Lots of things had been going well for me, and without realizing it, I was becoming a bit complacent. Then I went into a meeting less prepared than I should have and got blindsided. Things went sideways really quickly, and I contributed to the hurt someone received. Ironically, the person I had gone into the meeting to try to advocate for. That brought me back to reality and reminded me of just how easy it is to allow self-sufficiency to carry us and how quickly that can get us and others into trouble."

"Yes, good. Our humble, Holy Spirit-infused presence is so important. The condition of the leader affects all the other parts of leadership. And it's so important because the health and resilience of an organization are closely linked to the condition of the leader."

Dwayne put up his hand and said, "This is a really important topic for me. In my early years of leadership, I spent a lot of time on processes. In the last ten years, I've spent much more time working on myself. I need to, as sadly, I'm way more sophisticated at lying to myself than I want to believe."

Now that was an honest assessment. I looked across the room at Dwayne to see if he was joking and was reassured to realize he was not. The nodding heads of many seasoned leaders in the room showed me that he and I were not alone.

3.1 THE DEVELOPMENT OF THE LEADER

Dr. Magnus confirmed this, saying, "This part of your story is common, Dwayne. Emerging leaders are often more interested in learning how to lead others than themselves. Yet, God's plan starts with our own transformation. Seminal work in this area was done by Robert Clinton in *The Making of a Leader*.[2] Who has read about the stages of development he discovered after studying hundreds of biblical and other leaders?"

Several people put up their hands as others, like me, made a note to read the book.

---

[2] Robert Clinton *The Making of a Leader: Recognizing the Lessons and Stages of Leadership Development,* The Navigators, 2012.

"I thought I had a long reading list before coming to this class," one person at the front whispered in a stage voice, and everyone laughed.

"Welcome to a Magnus class. Prepare to smoke your credit card," Mat, a Communications Director and consultant, gently teased.

Dr. Magnus laughed with us and then drew a large chart that filled most of the wall of whiteboards. "Whether you agree that this applies in all or even most cases, Clinton's mapping of a leader's journey normalizes some of the challenges we may be going through and helps us to think about the priorities for each season of our leadership.

Phase 1 refers to the life-shaping experiences that prepare us to be set apart for God's calling on our lives. One of the key things God wants us to develop as a young leader is integrity. In study after study, the two things that employees expect from their leaders are integrity and empathy."

> *"The supreme quality of leadership is unquestionably integrity."*
> Dwight D. Eisenhower

He continued, "I want to stress that when I use the word ministry, I am not using it in the traditional sense of church or other overtly Christian ministry. I am talking about the work of our hands, wherever that may be, and the way that we do it for God's glory. Clinton's Phase 2 is a season of discipleship and experimentation with vocation. Learning the job. Learning to lead in areas of greater responsibility. Learning to lean on God in those areas of responsibility. In Phase 3, ministry becomes a prime focus. We have greater clarity on our unique abilities and interests. We see God moving in and through us. In Phase 4, we rediscover that our work flows from who we are, and we craft our own philosophy of ministry based on what we understand of God and His call on our lives. In the final chapter of our lives, what Clinton calls Phase 5, the pieces of our lives and ministry converge with greater clarity."

He stepped back from the board and said, "All of this is set within the context of our growing relationship with God and our developing relationships with others—learning to love God and our neighbour. Each stage includes a learning opportunity or tests around, for example, our integrity, or obedience, or ability to receive a word from God."

Dr. Magnus set down the marker and handed out work pages with graphics and questions for us to complete.

Let's apply this to ourselves. How would you chart where you are at in your leadership development journey? Have you observed any of the patterns that Clinton mentions?

———

When I was in my last year at seminary, a professor gave us the assignment to lay out a life plan with five big purposes for life. Then we needed to identify what our objectives were and what realization procedures we would need to actualize these. I still have it.

I committed to learning for life. I wanted to learn from God, and I had three objectives that went with that: to learn from His word, from His person in Jesus, and from the other people, mentors who had moved along the path well. Then I identified what action steps and realization procedures I would need to actualize that commitment. What action would best serve as leading indicators of growth?

When I read Cole's book The Journeys of Significance, *which is based on Clinton's* The Making of a Leader, *I loved how Cole aligned Paul's journey with Clinton's six steps. I tried to do that with my own life, where am I on my own Pauline journey. One-to-three-year time frames worked well when I was younger. Five-year windows worked well through my thirties and forties. Then I shifted to ten years, and now I think in life quarters. You must be real about this. I credit that professor for helping me to see life as a long game and plan for the totality of it. This has profoundly shaped the way I think and plan, both personally and in the organizations and initiatives I have led.*

———

Quite a while later, Dr. Magnus invited us to move into round-table discussions of the insights we had gleaned from the exercise. An animated conversation broke out that lasted until the break.

Once we had settled back in, Dr. Magnus said, "Another framework for thinking about a leader's development comes from seminal research by Jim Collins.[3] He describes five levels of leadership effectiveness. This changed the paradigm of leadership. One of the insights I found so helpful from Collins

---

3 Jim Collins, *Good to Great: Why Some Companies Make the Leap and Others Don't*, Harper Business, 2001.

is that leaders that are still ego-driven seek to inspire people to follow *them*. What he calls Level Five leaders are those committed to a cause larger than themselves and seek to inspire people to serve the *cause*. When you have a charismatic cause, you don't need a charismatic leader. This is a mistake many organizations make, hiring someone charismatic and then watching the whole focus move to that person rather than the cause they serve. The essence of Level Five leadership is service. Or 'ambition channelled outward,' as Collins likes to say. Level Five leaders are personally humble yet deeply committed to the outcomes of the organization. Frances Hesselbein, the highly effective and well-respected CEO of Girl Scouts, used to say, 'to serve is to live,' and that is how Level Five leaders genuinely feel."

> *"Before you are a leader,*
> *success is all about growing yourself.*
> *After you are a leader, success is*
> *all about growing others."*
> Jack Welch

I have worked for very diverse leaders over the course of my tenure, and this has been helpful in unexpected ways. In learning to work with different styles of leaders, we see up close that there is no one way to lead. This has helped me to find my own way and to see leadership traits in people that others, who have not had this exposure, might miss. When we must adapt to other people's approach, it strengthens us. We have to be creative in finding ways to support them in a way that both enables them to move their priorities forward while also, candidly, making room for you to have influence in the areas where you can best bring value. Don't be afraid to surround yourself with different kinds of leaders or underestimate how much you can learn from and about how to work with people who are really different from you.

"Bill Joiner and Stephen Josephs identified five levels of leadership agility."[4] Listing them on the whiteboard, he continued. "90% of leaders are

---

4 Bill Joiner and Stephen Josephs, *Leadership Agility: 5 Levels of Mastery for Anticipating and Initiating Change,* Jossey-Bass, 2006.

**Joiner & Josephs'
FIVE LEVELS OF
LEADERSHIP
AGILITY**

HEROIC
[Pre-expert]
1. Expert
2. Achievers

POST-HEROIC
3. Catalyst
4. Co-Creator
5. Synergist

working in the heroic catagory. They may be skilled at strategic thinking, motivating people, and getting things done, and can be highly effective in moderately complex settings. Agile leadership, however, happens at the post-heroic level.

"Moving to a Catalyst Leadership style requires a change in thinking and behaviour—a move from heroic to post-heroic ways of being. Catalysts are much more likely to facilitate the development of their team and include them in decision-making. But we are still only at stage three.

"Joiner and Joseph describe stage four leaders as Co-creators. As the name suggests, they are more likely to genuinely value collaboration. They are agile, able to use both assertive and accommodating styles as needed. Now listen, only four percent of leaders—according to their research—have mastery in doing this, and increasingly, leaders are expected to facilitate co-creation. Our employees expect that of us, yet few of us are skilled in developing collaborative leadership teams where there is shared responsibility and accountability.

"The final Joiner-Joseph stage is the Synergist or Holistic leader. This type of leader is empathetic and unafraid of diverse perspectives, and they are skilled at using diverse team leadership styles as needed. As such, they are more agile and able to respond to complex, uncertain, and changing circumstances. Synergists may represent the long-term future of effective leadership, yet the research suggests that only one percent of today's managers fit this description. That confirms the importance of what we are talking about here—holistic leadership.

"And it begs a question: How do we create organizational cultures where Synergists are more likely to emerge? And what is the development pathway for those at the first levels? Joseph and Joiner suggest that actually, 'the vital challenge most companies face today is the need to develop Achievers at the upper levels of an organization into Catalysts, and Experts at the lower and middle levels into Achievers.'[5] This is one of the most important, and sadly often overlooked parts of leadership, developing the leaders in our organizations, creating leadership rich cultures."

---

5 Gyzel Pialat, What is Leadership Agility?, https://www.stratx-exl.com/industry-insights/what-is-leadership-agility

Are you able to identify which level you are leading from most days? And equally importantly, if you were to develop a plan for the development of leaders, what would need to be in place so that more and more people are growing toward catalysts and co-creators and synergists? This is a bigger question than we might think but well worth the effort. You will be a better leader, and your team will thank you for your strategic investment in them.

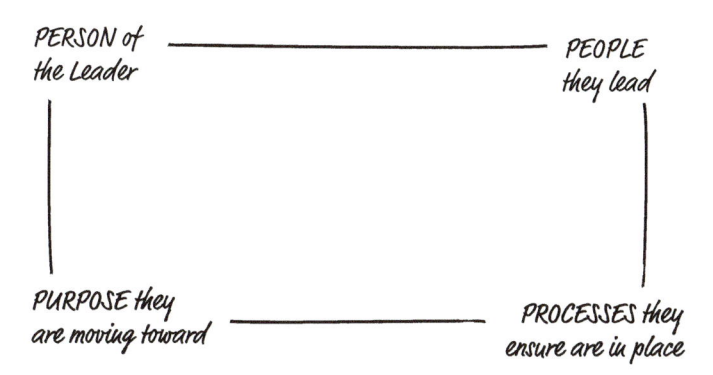

```
PERSON of                              PEOPLE
the Leader  ────────────────────       they lead




PURPOSE they                           PROCESSES they
are moving toward ──────────────       ensure are in place
```

Dr. Magnus continued, "It may not surprise you to know that I think of this through the lens of our model. I like the language of the Engaging Leader. Someone who is fully engaged themselves knows how to engage people. They create engaging processes and enable people to use these processes to move towards an engaging purpose."

Dwayne raised his hand and said, "It's hard to stay in the person part of the model because we've completely bought into 'purpose' and 'fixing the world' being our whole mission. I think of all the chapels that I sat in that called me to 'make a difference in the world.' The emphasis is not on the person, it's on the impact."

Dr. Magnus responded, "This is so true. Perhaps that is part of the reason that I put purpose last in the model. Vision and purpose are incredibly important. They give us a why. However, I agree that they can become an unhealthy focus if it is all about the end and not how we get there. Or all about the purpose but not about the people. Or, if I understand you correctly, all about the purpose without adequate consideration of the preparation of the leader. We used to say, 'hire a leader with vision,' and almost secondarily, we considered teachability or character or their ability to develop people."

Crystal, a respected Executive Leadership Coach, added, "There's also a tension between the person and their action. Between the person and their achievements. We need to execute as leaders, but so much focus is given to that at the expense of other areas."

"This is a perfect segue to talking about self-awareness. Tasha Eurich says that 95% of us are not self-aware.[6] Ninety-five percent! Life provides opportunities for us to take off our blinders—both through everyday situations and earth-shattering events that show us what we couldn't see otherwise. Eurich describes two parts of self-awareness: how we see ourselves and our ability to accurately perceive how others see us. Her research suggests that people who are strong in both have healthier relationships, fewer biases, are more creative, and make better choices. So, if only five percent of us are truly self-aware, this is something we probably need to work on."

Dwayne agreed, "This is so true, yet it's almost impossible to find someone who will give honest feedback. Self-awareness is really tricky because everyone is nervous about telling me how I'm doing."

Dr. Magnus nodded, "It's true. The more influence and authority you have, the harder it is to get honest feedback, and the less likely it is that people will think you want or need it. Even though we do! Therefore, the more advanced we are, the more intentional we must be about seeking it. There is a perceived fear. You can work as hard as you want to make the situation safe, but people will still be cautious."

Jacqueline added, "As a coach and consultant, I have found that we always have to be speaking to the potential of people—not where they are, but where they could be. This means that I need to be more direct than I wish to be at times."

"You are right, Jacqueline. Leaders need more direct feedback. Truth mixed with compassion and grace. In my estimation, self-awareness is still not emphasized enough in some circles. It not only helps us capitalize on our potential but also to realize the gaps we need to accommodate for. It also influences who we hire and who we are coached by, because they are best at seeing and pointing out what we feel challenged to see or be or do. We need people who are very different from us to best help us see more broadly."

---

6 Eurich, Tasha. "What Self-Awareness Really Is (and How to Cultivate it)." *Harvard Business Review,* https://hbr.org/2018/01/what-self-awareness-really-is-and-how-to-cultivate-it

Bonnie spoke up, "Can I just jump in here? In my opinion, there are at least three types of feedback we should be seeking. Appreciation. Advice. Assessment. Just using that language, asking for targeted feedback according to those three areas, can greatly impact the feedback we receive."

Dwayne interjected. "But, we can't talk about this without considering power differentials. No matter how much you try to manage this, others will see you through your role. It is almost inevitable."

Crystal agreed. "There is absolutely a power differential influencing how people think and act. I coach employees to use empathy to look at a situation through the lens of their supervisor. What are the pain points they might be feeling? How might my feedback help them to move beyond their stuck-ness? However, I do agree that the onus is on the leader to make that safe. On the one hand, we know that we are imperfect humans, but we still get defensive when someone points that out to us. Why? Because we may be working hard at it, or we focus on our intentions rather than outcomes. Or we see it only through our own limited lens. When we can set that aside, it makes it more possible for us to think, 'it's possible that our employees see this differently, and they would be giving me a great gift by sharing that insight.' And here is where empathy for them comes in. Now I need to put myself in their shoes and consider how challenging it would be for them to come forward. Now I can ask, how could I minimize that challenge?"

Bonnie spoke up, "This is where I can legitimately give a strong plug for coaching. These conversations can be difficult to navigate on your own, but a coach can help both parties. One of the tools I often use is called Reality Testing. This is done with a series of questions. What is true? What is *really* true? How do I know it is true? How am I showing up in this situation? What do I know about myself that might help or hinder me here? How do I know that is true? What do I really know about this other person? How do I know that is true? How can I be appropriately vulnerable in this situation so we can meet in an honest space?"

Dr. Magnus continued, "That is so helpful, Bonnie and Crystal, thank you. There is so much in there I hope people were taking good notes. Okay, time for some truth-telling."

Dr. Magnus smiled and shifted on the stool. "Almost every person I talk to about leadership is struggling with a relationship with a superior. And they feel there is nothing they can do about it. Some of those people may be working for you! None that I know of, but it's possible."

Take a few minutes to make a plan. How are you going to access the information your team has that could so help you to lead better?

―――

My parents farmed with horses when I was little, so there were always forty or so of them to be cared for. We loved the horses, grooming them, riding them, racing them. We went by horse to school—horse and buggy in the summer and horse and sleigh in the winter. Probably younger than I should have, I was driving four- and six-team horses. One of the teams had a horse that would sit down anytime you stopped, and it was impossible to get him back up. One time I had to walk home to get my dad to help me because I just could not get that horse up again. That was the day my dad taught me how to get a horse going that didn't want to go. I've never forgotten it. Whether it's schoolyard bullies or horses that don't pull their weight on their team, all of these life experiences were teaching me how to control my own emotions and learn to read the room.

Sports also played an important role in this. I played football (until I dislocated my shoulder farming) as well as hockey, soccer, and wrestling. Here is what I learned. The faster the sport, the more emotional intelligence you needed if you didn't want to spend half the game in the penalty box. When things are happening quickly, situations quickly escalate. If you can't manage your own emotions and, equally importantly, help your opponent to manage theirs, it won't go well for either of you. Sports are great for teaching you team play, but it is invaluable in teaching you self-leadership.

―――

"My next question is: how do you get light on areas that are unknown to you and unknown to others? This is something I have thought about for a long time, and in my opinion, the best approach is to broaden your exposure. Do different assessments. Read books that open areas you had not even thought of. Talk to people who are very different from you and expose yourself to very different experiences where your cultural and other blind spots are more likely to become evident. I discovered so much from learning and listening to others by reading widely and travelling as much as possible.

"We have agreed that feedback is important, and so is knowing how to adjust my behaviour considering that feedback. In my experience, many leaders want to do better. They don't know how to. We need help on both," he emphasized, pointing back to the leadership model on the board. "Jesus showed people how as well by inspiring them with the why and what. He modelled and taught. He apprenticed. We have not done well with this, and then we wonder why leaders, even after receiving feedback, are not consistently improving. We need to address both motivation and skillsets."

"Several years ago, I wrote a life mission statement. I keep it near me." He pulled a paper from a file and read, "*I will be a lifelong strategic learner in hot pursuit of wisdom, understanding, and knowledge to equip me to influence and impact persons. I am in significant contact with others who are becoming strategic life learners, stewarding my life and God-given gifts, calling, and resources of leading, communicating, and coaching to bring maximum glory to God.*" He put the paper back in the file and said, "This is not theoretical to me. I have devoted my life to it."

Then he took a long drink of water and said, "The fact is, a leader casts a broad shadow. They have greater influence than they think. And this can be very positive. It can also easily lead to overuse or downright abuse of power, of course, but let's focus on the positive for a moment. Consider how many people's lives you could make better if you intentionally used the platform God has given you even a little bit more strategically or intentionally."

Take a moment to consider the people in your sphere of influence and what you could feasibly do that would genuinely make life better for them.

"And whatever you do, in word or deed, do everything in the name of the Lord Jesus, giving thanks to God the Father through him."

Col. 3:17 ESV

3.2 THE COURAGE TO LEAD IN UNCHARTED TIMES

After the break, class started again, with Dr. Magnus pulling a book from the shelf. "Who has read Brene Brown's *Daring to Lead*?" Looking around the room at the raised hands, he asked what stood out to us from the reading.

"The importance of courage."

"The courage to have tough conversations."

"And the courage to show up wholeheartedly."

"Good," Dr. Magnus encouraged. "Leadership takes courage. In some seasons, more than others, undoubtedly, but this has always been true. When I think of leadership courage, I think of the biblical story of Nehemiah. The book of Nehemiah is a study in courageous leadership. In chapter one of Nehemiah, we see the courage to ask hard questions, to find out what's really going on, and to fast and pray. Chapter two, the courage to speak to the king, to honestly assess the damage, and to call together a team to 'rise up and build.' I love how he defines the current reality for them and identifies personally with the challenge. Do you see how he invites the people's participation and encourages their hearts with stories of what has already been accomplished? It's masterful. He is inviting them to rebuild the wall, but ultimately, he is painting a vision of who they are and what they could be as God's people.

"Notice that some people were already mocking. Anyone relate to this? Just as you get started on what you believe God asks of you, the mockers emerge. See also how Nehemiah deals quickly with them. He knows how dangerous those voices can be. How demotivating they can be to others. Chapter three, the leaders build shoulder to shoulder along the wall, except for those—see verse 5?—who 'would not stoop to serve their Lord.' Ouch. That is not what I want written about my life.

"Chapter four. Outright opposition. The first of three waves. This first wave is external, and that is difficult to deal with. The next is internal opposition, which is much more difficult. If you have been leading for a while, you know what I mean. Opposition from and conflict with your most trusted teammates. In chapter six, the opposition turns personal. There is an attack on his character. His integrity. And that is the hardest wave of all to deal with. What does Nehemiah do? How does he deal with it? He goes to God in prayer rather than respond to them in anger. Then he strengthens his team with what he has reminded himself. Look at Nehemiah 4:14. So helpful. Let me read it so we don't miss anything, 'Do not be afraid of them. Remember the Lord who is great and awesome, and fight for your brothers, your sons, your daughters, your wives, and your homes.' I love that. He reminds them of the mission and the meaning behind it. He reminds them of God's nature and their own history of God's faithfulness. He reminds them of the stakes and who they are doing this for. There is a whole course on leadership resilience here. And probably other ones on change, leading in a crisis, handling conflict, and shaping culture. Nehemiah offers such an important case study for us as Christian leaders.

"Sure enough, God moves, frustrating the plans of their opponents and enabling the work to carry on. Now notice how the people adapted. There were additional challenges now, so they worked with a weapon in one hand and a shovel in the other. They adapted! Nehemiah set the tone and the pace. And a wall of wonder began to arise from the rubble. I use a Wall of Wonder all the time. We will talk about this more when we talk about Appreciative Inquiry and Appreciative Leadership. The people built on the foundation that had been laid and the wall went up."

Dr. Magnus paused for a sip of coffee from his travel mug and smiled broadly.

"Now, chapter five is a part of Nehemiah's story we often forget. He stops the oppression of the poor. He is not so focused on building the wall that he forgets about people. Remember? Result *and* relationships. People *and* task. Stewardship of the mission *and* care for people. Prayer *and* action. Wall building *and* character building.

"Look at verse seven, 'I took counsel with myself.' I love it. Just like David who led himself first,[7] or the NT woman who kept telling herself to go to Jesus until she had the courage to do it,[8] Nehemiah investigates his own heart and acts again with courage. This time he speaks to his own nobles and officials.

"Look at what he says about his own behaviour in 5:15, 'The former governors laid heavy burdens on the people...but I did not do so.' Remember

---

7 1 Samuel 30:6

8 Matthew 9:21

what we read in Mark 10:42?[9] Why did Nehemiah not do what other governors had done? 'Because of the fear of God.' Nehemiah understood that God had entrusted him not only with a task but with a people. A people. Doesn't this remind you of the situation with the widows in Acts 6? The disciples encountered a similar challenge. Look it up later to see how they handled that. They, like Nehemiah, understood what godly leadership entails. Justice. Compassion. Generosity. Service. Courage. Not entitlement or the ability to look the other way at things that are happening under our noses. Not a laser focus on results that forgets the bigger picture. Okay, there is so much here that we could spend all week on it and more but let me make a few summarizing points before I give you some time to apply this to your own context.

- OPPOSITION IS INEVITABLE. EXPECT IT.
- PRAYER IS INDISPENSABLE. PRACTICE IT.
- CHARACTER IS NON-NEGOTIABLE. DEVELOP IT.
- GOD IS SOVEREIGN AND CAN BE TRUSTED. COUNT ON IT.
- COURAGE IS NEEDED. GO TO GOD TO COUNSEL YOURSELF FOR IT.

"Okay, on your own with a notebook. What stands out to you from the story of Nehemiah? What parts do you relate to in your current leadership situation? What insights can you glean from this book that may help you? Is there one of these points that you need to apply at this point in your journey?"

Sometime later, we gathered back together.

"Courage." Dr. Magnus mused. "Before we move on, I want us to take one last look at Nehemiah. Turn to chapter thirteen. The wall was built in fifty-two days. The people celebrate. The scriptures are read. Houses are built. People took up residence. Then, over time, complacency settled in. See that? The Law wasn't kept. The people forgot God. The children were not able to speak the language that would enable them to understand God's word. Spiritual negligence led to a cultural decline, as it inevitably does.

---

9 Mark 10:42-45 Jesus called them together and said, "You know that those who are regarded as rulers of the Gentiles lord it over them, and their high officials exercise authority over them. Not so with you. Instead, whoever wants to become great among you must be your servant, and whoever wants to be first must be slave of all. For even the Son of Man did not come to be served, but to serve, and to give his life as a ransom for many."

"What does Nehemiah do? He could have said, 'Surely, I've done enough. It's someone else's turn,' but he doesn't. He follows the pattern he has learned. Finds out what is happening. Speaks up about what is happening. Points the way to something better.

"There are two important lessons I want to stress here.

"The work is never really done. Beware complacency in yourself and others. We must be intentional to preserve what is sacred—to ensure we don't slip back.

"Patterns that we think we have dealt with often re-emerge—just in different ways. We can learn from what God has taught us in past experiences and apply that, but we can't expect the challenge or the solution to be identical. It rarely is. This is why it is so important that part of our practiced response to both challenge and opportunity is that, like Nehemiah, we go first to the Lord for counsel and courage.

"Thoughts? Comments? Ellen, you have been leading in camps, organizations, and churches for many years. Have you experienced some of what Nehemiah does?"

Ellen spoke up, "Oh, absolutely. The waves of opposition. The disillusionment and discouragement that can come with it. Nehemiah's story is such a helpful roadmap for purposeful leadership. His style reminds me of Bass and Burn's Transformational Leadership."

"Say more..."

"Well, at the risk of oversimplifying, my understanding is that Transformational Leadership includes raising the level of ethics and the level of motivation in a group. William Wilberforce used a similar approach. He knew that he had to help people see how evil slavery was and deepen their resolve that another way was both crucial and possible. And he knew that it would take time to build the critical momentum to move the needle. Yet, here we are again now with higher levels of slavery than during the Transatlantic Slave Trade. Without persistence, we cycle back to old ways so quickly. We need Transformational Leaders to stand in that gap, like Nehemiah. Pointing to a higher way and helping the people believe that it is possible. Nudging them towards it gently at times and dragging them towards it kicking and screaming at others."

Adam interjected, "Sometimes it feels like that, doesn't it? Dragging people kicking and screaming. Surely that isn't leadership, though, its authoritarianism. And even if it is well-intentioned, that is still a benevolent authoritarianism. How do we reconcile that?"

After a lengthy conversation in the room, Dr. Magnus said, "So it sounds like we agree that showing courage is not the same thing as being authoritarian, although we also agreed that there may be rare times when an authoritarian approach is warranted—but only with several caveats and safeguards in place.

"I want to clarify that there is a big difference between raising ethics and being a moralist. Nouwen calls someone whose identity is firmly rooted in God's love for them a mystic. Here is one of my favourite quotes from his little book *In The Name of Jesus*: 'Christian leaders cannot simply be persons who have well-informed opinions about the burning issues of our time. Their leadership must be rooted in the permanent, intimate relationship with the incarnate Word, Jesus, and they need to find there the source for their words, advice, and guidance.'[10] He goes on, 'Dealing with burning issues without being rooted in a deep personal relationship with God easily leads to divisiveness because, before we know it, our sense of self is caught up in our opinion about a given subject. But when we are securely rooted in personal intimacy with the source of life, it will be possible to remain flexible without being relativistic, convinced without being rigid, willing to confront without being offensive, gentle, and forgiving without being soft, and true witnesses without being manipulative. For Christian leadership to be truly fruitful in the future, a movement from the moral to the mystical is required.'[11] I am interested in hearing your thoughts on this, but let's give the internal processors a chance to process on their own first. Take five minutes to record some thoughts. Use this as a critical thinking exercise, pushing yourself beyond platitudes and Sunday School answers. Then when the time is up, we will have a chance to learn from each other."

Some people began to scribble quickly. Others closed their eyes to think or flipped open their bible. There was silence except for the rustling of papers.

Could this be part of my challenge? Was the outer disorder I was allowing around me rooted in my own inner divisiveness?

---

10 Henri Nouwen, *In the Name of Jesus: Reflections on Leadership*, Crossroad, 1992, 45.

11 Henri Nouwen, *In the Name of Jesus: Reflections on Leadership*, Crossroad, 1992.46-47.

After an extended time of reflection and discussion Dr. Magnus moved to the front of the room, signaling that we were to come back together. "John 5:39-44 is so powerful, and I love the way Eugene Peterson puts it in *The Message*:

"'You have your heads in your Bibles constantly because you think you'll find eternal life there. But you miss the forest for the trees. These Scriptures are all about me! And here I am, standing right before you, and you aren't willing to receive from me the life you say you want. I'm not interested in crowd approval. And do you know why? Because I know you and your crowds. I know that love, especially God's love, is not on your working agenda. I came with the authority of my Father, and you either dismiss me or avoid me. If another came, acting self-important, you would welcome him with open arms. How do you expect to get anywhere with God when you spend all your time jockeying for position with each other, ranking your rivals and ignoring God?[12]'"

Dr. Magnus closed the Bible and said, "Such a powerful interpretation of this text. God came in the flesh, and some people couldn't see him because of their religiosity, self-aggrandizement, and self-righteousness. That last line! 'How do you expect to get anywhere with God when you spend all your time jockeying for position with each other, ranking your rivals and ignoring God?' If the possibility that we could become like them in our desire to live righteous lives doesn't scare us to our knees, I don't know what would!

"Notice also that Jesus says, 'I'm not interested in crowd approval.' Why not? He seeks God's approval. This is so convicting. And it creates another tension for us, doesn't it? How to live non-judgmentally while calling people to live according to godly values. This takes wisdom and courage. And like most leadership, it begins with our own lives. Choosing the narrower path. Doing what is right even when there is a cost. We sometimes describe that as moral courage, which is one of the many types of courage we could talk about. But first, let's take a break. I want us to be fully alert when we dive into this topic together."

---

12 John 5:39-44, *The Message*

STRATEGIC MANAGEMENT
CONCEPTS AND CASES
FOUNDATIONS of STRATEGY
SHAPING YOUR ORGANIZATION'S FUTURE
MIGLIORE
ORGANIZATIONAL BEHAVIOUR
ULTIMATE

4. THE COURAGE OF THE LEADER

Diagram: radiating lines from center word "COURAGE" labeled: EMPATHETIC, MORAL, SOCIAL, INTELLECTUAL, EMOTIONAL, DISCIPLINED, PHYSICAL, TEACHABILITY, PERSERVERANCE

AFTER THE BREAK, Dr. Magnus went to the board and, while drawing a series of radiating lines, said, "When we are talking about courage, we could include things like Moral Courage, Physical Courage, Intellectual Courage, and Emotional Courage. And while you might argue that this is a subset of the emotional, I would see Perseverance as an important and underestimated form of courage that leaders need.

Adam put up his hand and said, "Can I push back on that? I think I understand what you mean by it and agree, but I have also seen perseverance, taken to an extreme, become such a destructive force in leadership."

"Sounds like there is a story behind that."

"Yes, a painful one, actually. When our organization was going through a period of uncertainty, the board hired someone that presented as strong and confident. I think we were fearful and wanted someone who seemed to know what to do and have the courage to do it. Things started out well, but when it became clear that they were pushing hard in the wrong direction, they refused to consider alternatives, and they shut down conversation and sought to motivate everyone with pep talks about discipline and grit. It was like their determination precluded them from looking at the facts. Everything became something to overcome rather than something to inform."

"This is such a good case study. What happened in the end?"

"They eventually left, with some encouragement from the board, but by then, so much damage had been done."

"I was going to talk about what I call Teachability Courage in a minute but let me bump it up the list and add it now. The courage to seek out alternatives that oppose your own. I am not talking about agreeing with everything or zigging and zagging our team back and forth with every shifting wind. I am talking about genuine curiosity and openness to learn that enables us to make decisions more thoughtfully and know if and when we need to change our strategies. I am so glad you brought this up. Any of these, taken to an extreme, can be so detrimental.

"Intellectual courage is the courage to challenge mindsets and assumptions, even if it means admitting to having been wrong in the past. Or perhaps wrong now.

"Disciplined courage is the courage to stay the course when things get tough. To overcome obstacles and distractions, and failures. To focus on the right things and move consistently toward them.

"Moral courage, as we said, is the courage to do the right thing, even if there is a cost."

Jay blurted out, "I know you want us to process this later, but I must ask, does anyone else find moral courage failures the hardest to come back from? Not necessarily something big that takes you out of the running but the little things that you knew you could have done differently and should have done differently."

Many heads nodded.

"What do you do with that?" he continued.

"This is an important question. Take some time at your tables to discuss."

Dr. Magnus joined a table group, and we were soon all deep in conversation. One brave person at my table described a series of poor judgements early in their career and how long it took to rebuild trust. Another shared about the hard time they have filtering what comes out of their mouth and how often that has gotten them into trouble. I admitted that, although God had protected me so far, I was terrified of infidelity, having seen so many of my peers, often the ones I least expected, fall.

Personalize it: what moral courage failures are you most prone to? What do you have in place to help protect you from slipping?

Dr. Manus gathered us back saying, "Empathetic courage is a bit different from the other kinds. It is the courage required to set yourself aside long enough to enter someone else's world. To see things from a different perspective. To acknowledge and address your biases. I like this one. Why does true empathy take courage?"

"It requires self-awareness and listening skills."

"It may lead to insights that are uncomfortable."

"Or mean we need to stay present while someone else reveals pain or emotions that we don't know how to help them with."

"Or we may jump in to want to fix instead of having the discipline to stay present and let them process for themselves."

Dr. Magnus smiled again, "Such helpful answers, thank you. Sounds like some of you may have learned this from personal experience. I know I have had to learn the hard way. Okay, switching gears here a bit. Oh, let me pause, I can see some of you are still writing and reflecting. Let me give you a moment. This is important."

There was silence in the room again as people processed. Then sensing we were ready to go on Dr. Magnus began again, "Of course, we could also talk about Physical Courage, the ability to act in the face of physical harm. We tend to think of firefighters, police officers, military, and medical personnel here but it can apply to anyone. Or we could nuance this a bit and talk about Social Courage—the willingness to do the right thing for the sake of the group.

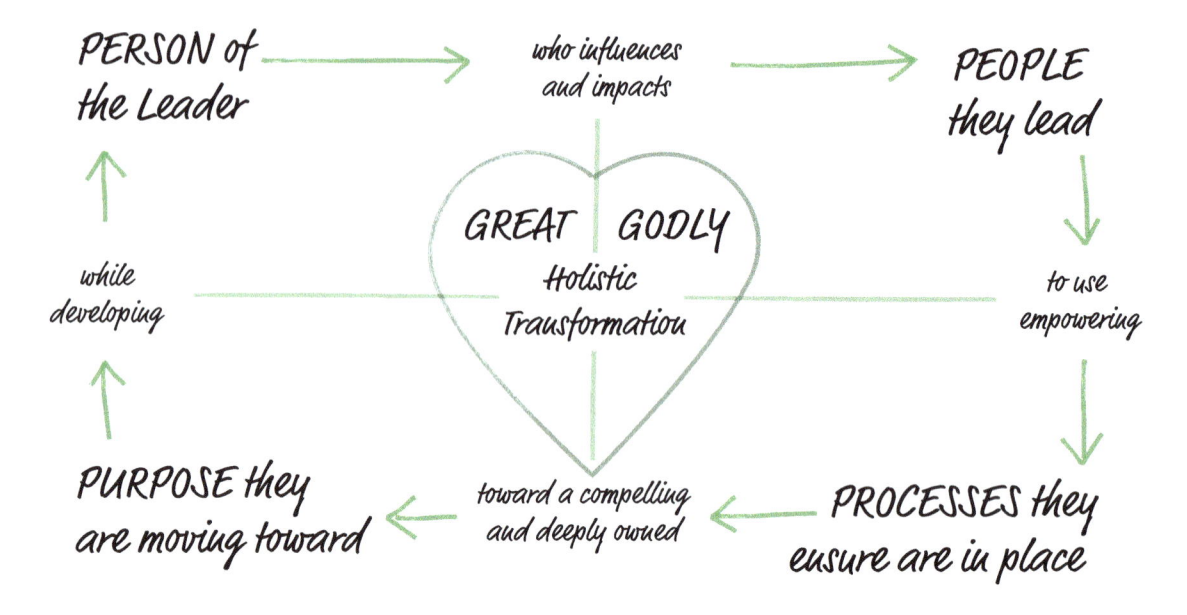

PERSON of the Leader → who influences and impacts → PEOPLE they lead

↑ while developing

GREAT GODLY
Holistic Transformation

to use empowering ↓

↑ PURPOSE they are moving toward ← toward a compelling and deeply owned ← PROCESSES they ensure are in place

"Looking at the model we have been using to help us think about holistic leadership, we can see that courage is needed in each area. The courage to tell people the truth, the courage to look at entrenched processes and make changes, the courage to reevaluate our purpose and if it is no longer relevant, change it but if it is still relevant continue to pursue it under more difficult circumstances.

"Is there one of these you would like to pay more attention to? Make a note in your book and come back to that later to reflect on more deeply."

———

My parents had come to Canada as immigrants, as young single adults from different parts of Germany, between WWI and WWII. They met and were married in a small farming community in Saskatchewan. My grandparents on my dad's side had lost everything, as the money from the sale of their major farm in Germany/Poland was never released to come to Canada and hence they had to start over. My mother was an orphan and had nothing. As a consequence, our family was very tight on funds, and we all helped significantly on the farm. School was secondary in importance, even more for my older siblings than myself. We were needed on the farm, especially at seed time and harvest time. I normally did not find school too challenging but at harvest time did miss more days of school than I intended or felt good about. This left me feeling conflicted because I knew I was needed.

When I was in grade nine, I had an experience that marked me for life, and I initially allowed myself to feel wounded, ashamed, and like a failure. Only later was I able to reimagine it as a gain, when I could see how it helped me understand and benefit others.

Having been away from school to help with harvesting for a couple of weeks and then coming back, a teacher called me an absolute idiot for not knowing how to do the algebra questions he set for us. He did this aloud in front of the entire class of thirty or so students with whom I had been in class for five years. What made this even worse was that, although I attended the public school, he was a Christian teacher who attended our church and knew our situation. At the time, I took the comment seriously and failed to process it in light of the circumstances. I felt such shame and a sense that I was not enough, and it affected me so deeply as a grade nine boy that the rest of the school year and church attendance were agony for me. I decided to end my schooling and help with farming before the year ended and hence did not finish the grade at the time.

After two years of farming, my hunger to learn was felt deeply enough that I did both grade nine and ten by correspondence in one year and then attended Caronport High School for grade eleven and twelve.

It was not until a professor—in my doctoral studies program at another school—taught me a mindset and mind process strategy to reject unfair shaming that I began to heal from this comment. I learned then that although I could not manage what someone else did or wrongly conferred on me, I could and should manage how I reprocessed and responded. I do not need to accept such a conferral on me or my value as a person.

This lesson was invaluable to me, when—in my doctoral studies—a new Dean attempted to shame me into doing what felt unfair and unreasonable. He called me into his office the second day of my final summer and told me that my dissertation—which had been written, graded, approved, and signed by the prior Dean and team—was not acceptable. Keep in mind that this was the first day of my last couple of classes. I simply said, "Sir, I will consult with a few people and return to talk to you in two days. If that is still your conclusion it is that I likely that I will not want the name of an institution that would approve this seemingly unethical step on my resume." His response was not pleasant. I sought counsel and approval from my supervisor at Briercrest and a very good friend who was also the Dean of a new PhD in educational leadership at Trinity Evangelical Divinity School, in Deerfield Illinois. Two days later I returned to tell the Dean that I would complete the remaining summer classes I had come to take but would not start again on another dissertation or seek graduation from their institution if this was their process without recourse. I was able to have that crucial conversation without feeling high emotion and have never looked back.

While this appeared to be very unethical to numerous people and a shame, it served as a gain in many ways.

1. *Being in educational leadership myself, it meant I became known as an advocate for students or anyone without a sense of voice. Numerous students would tell me my door was the last recourse for them. The experience left its mark for good for me and others.*
2. *I did go on to Trinity Evangelical Divinity School to do their doctoral program and at the graduation with my doctorate, was awarded the research scholar of the year, and I credit God with reassuring me through that.*
3. *I did learn that the only real failures in life are failure to learn from a "perceived" failure! No one has ever since conferred "failure" that I accepted or taken from them again, though a number of people attempted such, I had learned to take charge of what is in my control.*
4. *I also learned that God does indeed keep His promise in Romans 8:28, when He assures us that, "all things work together for good for those who are called according to His purpose."*
5. *I frequently say to myself when I begin to think I have or am failing, "thank you for the opportunity to learn" what I would otherwise likely never have learned.*

I selected this story because I carried the fear of being shamed and fear of rejection with me as a failure longer than any other failure until I learned how to gain victory over this by managing my mindset. This has likely been my most significant navigation toward learning from every experience of life, rather than letting an experience or fear of loss or failure overwhelm me.

Failure, and our response to it, takes a different kind of courage.

"There is another kind of courage that I would like us to think about. I call it Crisis Courage. The courage to not run away from a crisis. In one sense nothing can prepare us for crisis but in another sense, as followers of Jesus we have to believe that the Holy Spirit will use our whole life to prepare us.

"Not all of us will experience extreme crises. However, to be human is to experience hardship. To be a leader is to lead during challenging times.

"Here is another homework assignment for you. Read James 1. Then create a timeline of your life to date that includes the trials and challenges you have experienced and what you learned from them. I am not talking about insights like 'don't trust people,' I am talking about insights like 'God can be trusted even when others let you down.' Turn to a fresh page in your notebook and draw a line across the page. Now label that 'My Character and Courage Development Path.' When we look at our lives through this lens it helps us to see how God has been using even the hardest of situations to enable us to lean on and learn from Him."

He gave us a moment, then said, "Now what if we apply courage to an organization? Kilman, O'Hara, and Strauss[1] describe Courageous Organizations not as ones with superhero staff or a higher-than-normal percentage of risk-takers, but as places where two things are true: There is a high level of fear about performing acts of courage and there is also a higher-than-average opportunity to observe acts of courage. Isn't that interesting?

"It turns out that acts of courage are contagious. We saw that in the story of Nehemiah, didn't we? Courageous organizations are not organizations where there is no fear. They are organizations where fear is balanced by acts of courage—big and small. See that, just observing acts of courage over time, from our leaders and peers, builds our corporate courage. Ellen, you talked about transformational leadership earlier. Here is a great example of how raising the level of ethics—knowing what the right thing is—and motivation—doing the right thing—is so important. One of the ways we do this is by modelling in ourselves and celebrating in others acts of overcoming fear. I'd like to give you a few minutes to reflect on that. How intentional are you about creating a courageous culture and highlighting the courageous actions of your team? And how willing are you to be vulnerable about the fears you are facing and the ways you are moving forward in spite of them?"

When he could sense that most people were done processing, Dr. Magnus

---

[1] Kilman, O'Hara and Strauss, quoted by Ian Day and Dr John Blackley, in "The Meaning of Courage," https://challengingcoaching.co.uk/the-meaning-of-courage/

stood up again and asked, "Graham, you led a large congregation through a season of great change and uncertainty. What are some of the most important things you learned during that time? And what role did crisis courage and everyday courage play?"

Graham responded, "I was pastoring a mid-sized church when we had a massive fire that destroyed one of our two main buildings. As a result, the church had to relocate to a school in a different community about twenty minutes from where we were meeting. It doesn't sound like a big move, but we went from an established church to 'startup mode' overnight. Our church went into quite a crisis. At first, we were in shock and simply responding to the impact of the fire. We had to find a new facility, relocate our offices, and completely rethink how we did ministry. A crisis like this raises all kinds of existential questions. Who are we? Why are we here? What is important to us?

"Using an Appreciative Inquiry approach, we engaged our congregation in a series of conversations that ended up being important for the overall health of the church. We had to discover who we were again and what strengths remained true for us. We started to craft a dream about what we sensed God was calling us to. We decided on four main priorities that we would focus on over the next few years. This was helpful in that it reminded us that the fire hadn't changed us substantially. While it had changed us significantly, there were many strengths that remained among us and our vision for helping people come to know Jesus and experience God's abundant life had not changed either.

"I think the greatest lesson I learned as a leader through that process is that I don't have to bear the whole weight of leadership on my own shoulders. I have a community of people with whom I can engage. The greatest source of encouragement and help for me were those who would lean in to help in the process of leading the church forward. Quite simply, I would have been crushed under the weight if I had to go it alone. As well, leading through the process is way more engaging, fun, and liberating because others co-own the vision with you.

"Finally, using Appreciative Inquiry introduces the group to adaption and experimentation. Rather than significant changes, we made small changes and kept trying new things. For the first time in my leadership, I felt free to try new things, and failure felt normalized.

"On courage… When the fire hit, I felt like I was a first responder at the scene of an accident. I had to jump into action and make important but quick decisions with our leaders. There weren't a lot of processes to work through because we just had to react. This required 'crisis' courage and it was necessary or else the group would have been stuck. Someone had to stand up and say, 'We are continuing to trust God and move forward.' But I wasn't alone. My board was a great source of encouragement in these early days. I also had a group of younger leaders, who were from a construction background, offer their help. They had a strong sense of call to rebuild, and this group of young people became the core of the building committee. Many people in the church supported, prayed, and encouraged us. As a leader, I had a strong sense that God would refine us and that we would eventually emerge from this as stronger and more fruitful.

"The church decided to purchase new land and build a new facility. This was a significant leap for us. We had met in the same location for 75 years. Our people stepped forward courageously and made the commitment to take on this challenge. The building looks great now, but it took lots of perseverance and hard work from a lot of people, over a sustained period of time to get this done. People setting up in a school, people praying, people giving, people sacrificing time, talent, and treasure. All of these small acts dedicated toward a rebuild and a revision were where I saw everyday acts of courage. Personally, for me, it was trusting in God as we navigated through the loss of many things, while still remaining hopeful about the future. Daily courage was not found in one big act but in day-to-day faithfulness even when things got really hard. As a leader, I worked hard on daily disciplined acts to sustain my health such as prayer, meditation on Scripture, exercise, and Sabbath. As well, my family was a significant source of encouragement. Life doesn't stop during a crisis, and I think it takes daily courage to stop, trust that God has it and enjoy the good gifts of life.

"I feel it's important to state as well that the COVID-19 pandemic hit while we were in the final few months of our build. Also, I would end up transitioning out of the role of Lead Pastor and into a denominational role to serve our wider church body. As a result, I never got to move into the new building. However, when the building was completed, I did a walk-through. As I stood on the platform and looked out over the new auditorium a wave of sadness swept over me because I would never experience the benefit of a new building after pastoring in the church for twenty years, the last four of them through the crisis. In that moment of sadness, the Lord reminded me that everything that I had worked through was not for my benefit but for the church and community. Pondering this actually brought a great sense of satisfaction that I had done what God has asked me to do."

"That is so helpful. Thank you, Graham. I love how you started with the questions: Who are we? Why are we here? What is important to us? These are the fundamental conversations every team must have, and as you have so thoughtfully articulated, especially during seasons of change or crisis or uncertainty. They build clarity and courage. Every team must ask these same questions within their sphere of influence and ensure they align system-wide. We will talk more about Appreciative Inquiry later but now let's focus on these questions."

Personalize it: When is the last time your team asked itself who they are, why they are here and what is important to them? If you asked those questions today, would there be team alignment? This could be a great exercise to do together.

"Leaders today are in uncharted waters. That is part of the reason so many are stepping back. We lack courage to wade into such uncharted water."

His voice grew louder and more passionate as he added, "I understand. We don't know how to lead during such complex and uncertain times—and the stakes are high—but this is exactly when wise leaders are most needed! Leaders of character and stamina who can create agile systems and lead adaptive teams. This is where Todd Bolsinger's work is so helpful," he said picking up *Canoeing the Mountains*.[2] "The title says it all, and his description of the kind of leader needed in this world is succinct but helpful. Notice the polarities in his descriptions."

He wrote on the board.

TECHNICAL COMPETENCE
ADAPTIVE CAPACITY
RELATIONAL CONGRUENCE

"Technical and relational. Mastery and adaptability. Such a good book.

---

2 Todd Bolsinger, *Canoeing the Mountains: Christian leadership in Uncharted Territory*, PRAXIS, 2018.

Well worth the read to see how these three interact and overlap. Here are your homework reflection questions. What parts of your journey feel uncharted? Where might you need to develop technical competence? Adaptive capacity? Relational congruence?

"Let me give an example. A few years ago, I had the idea of a virtual teaching room. In the end it turned out to be a godsend as so many of the college and all the seminary classes moved online during the pandemic, but at the time it took almost every form of relational congruence I had to get this idea taken seriously. Our high value of community and incarnational presence were important to us but, in this case, they created challenges that were difficult to see past. Additionally, we needed another level of technical competence and adaptive ability to make it happen, including the willingness to try something we had never done before, make some mistakes along the way, and carve a new path for online learning. It was really back to the drawing board in many ways for us as we had to manage the tension of adult learning and professor preference in teaching. If a teacher isn't comfortable, you won't get the best from them, and if a student isn't being well served, we have missed the mark. But sometimes these things are at odds. We had to think those kinds of things through to find win/wins. Bollsinger calls this 'calmly confronting the unknown.' And what does that require of the leader?" he asked holding out his hands to show he expected us to answer.

"Staying humble enough to listen, learn, and change ourselves first," we recited together.

"I have taught you well," he laughed. "Writer Marie Forleo says that growing up her mother would say that something may not be fixable, but everything is figure-out-able.[3] My dad taught my siblings and I the same thing. He was a patient man. His father, a millionaire in Germany, had lost everything when he came to Canada and had to start from scratch. Together, they built a life and built up a profitable farm under very challenging circumstances. He expected us to do the same, to find a way. To figure things out. I know that I would not have lasted as long as I have in many of the roles I have been given if not for the lessons learned from him. If Plan A doesn't work try B, then C, then D and E until you find a way. Angie, I would love to hear your thoughts on leading in today's world."

"We are at an interesting point in history." Angie acknowledged.

---

3 Marie Forleo, *Everything is Figureoutable,* Portfolio, 2020.

"Leading through a global pandemic, societal polarization, widening economic disparity, and rapidly rising cost of living. Our teams are stressed, and we can't fully address the impact that these external factors are having on them and their families. This for me is the hardest part of leading today. As a mission we focused on a Matthew 25 calling to serve the poor in one of the most expensive cities in Canada. I am constantly seeking God's wisdom and looking for ways to support our staff as they seek to support the community, both from a financial and mental health perspective."

Mini-case study: Ministry XYZ has experienced significant challenges because of a financial downturn and the reduced involvement of volunteers. The road ahead looks uncertain, and funders are asking hard questions. How can you keep yourself and your team from becoming reactive or paralyzed from fear?

Personalize it: How have you responded to changes in your field recently?

When I first came to work for the institution every faculty was expected to also volunteer as a sports coach. School didn't start until October, because so many of our students were needed to help bring in the harvest and, in the winter, everyone curled. That was the culture. It revolved around academics, sports, and farming. You have to learn how to adapt to the priorities of your context. In this context, if you wanted to talk to certain people the best place to do that was on the ice with a rock in one hand and a broom in the other. There was one Dean who refused to have conversations anywhere else! Every organization has its idiosyncrasies and eccentricities. I could have thought these ones odd, or I could take up curling. I took up curling.

"Wherever you sit in an organization you *have* to figure out a way to facilitate the learning of those with whom you have relational congruence."

He paused and then, pointing to the model on the board, said, "You have to help the people around you to think holistically. Okay, enough of me talking. Break into groups and discuss how this applies in your context.

How intentional are you at studying the complexity of your current system and engaging the whole system in deep strategic learning? I would like for you to plot that out somehow. If you need time to think on your own feel free to move over here to do that. If you are ready to talk lean in around your table and go to it."

"Before we start can you clarify what you mean by Strategic Learning?"

"Oh, good question. I will let you discuss that as well in your groups but let me get us started. The simplest way to think about this is to create opportunities for learning in each area of our model."

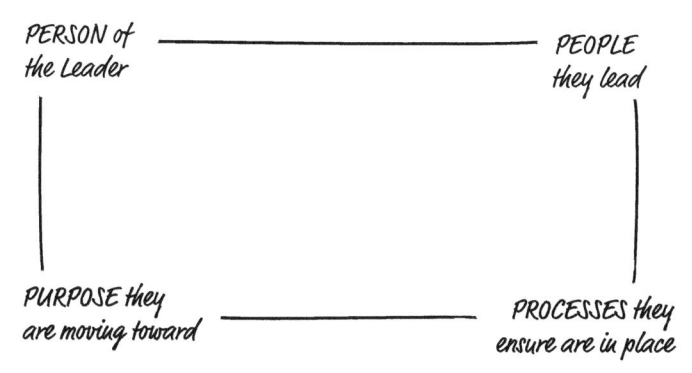

```
PERSON of                          PEOPLE
the Leader                         they lead



PURPOSE they                       PROCESSES they
are moving toward                  ensure are in place
```

"More broadly, I am using this phrase to refer to the will and skill to exegete our context. This includes seeking to deeply understand our current reality so that we can unearth and overcome barriers. We can empower and enable people. We can activate the strategies, processes and systems that will allow for forward movement. And, finally, we can ensure feedback loops are in place to measure effectiveness and alignment with purpose."

We scrambled to take notes as he spoke.

"This may include experimenting so you can learn from failure and success alike. Here is another polarity. How can we create short-term pilots and experiments while at the same time playing what Dorie Clarke calls 'The Long Game?'[4] Incidentally, she says that when we take the long view it builds our courage and enables us to focus on what is most important. I love how she talks about thinking in waves, riding one wave while looking ahead to the next. The challenge is staying long-term focused without losing

---

4 Dorie Clark, *The Long Game: How to be a Long Term Thinker in a Short Term World*, Harvard Business Review Press, 2021.

sight of the present. Riding the waves helps us to do both. I think it can also help us to watch the trends and patterns that are emerging as well as pay attention to the Positive Deviants that may be harder to find. Can someone remind me what Positive Deviants are?"

Dr. Magnus looked around the room, waiting for someone to indicate willingness. "Yes, Amy?"

Amy started, "Positive Deviants are people in communities that are doing something differently from others—with great results. Farmers who have found a way to maximize their crops in their context, when their neighbours are using more mainline practices with less success. Parents whose children are healthier despite experiencing similar deprivations to their peers. Leaders who are leading differently, counterintuitively even, yet with great impact. Organizations that have found an unusual but highly effective path. It is asset based, problem solving and community driven.[5] It is a way to ask, 'what is in our hands?' and then use what we have in unexpected ways, exceptionally well."

"Well explained," encouraged Dr. Magnus as others chimed in with examples they had seen.

Then Dr. Magnus said, "One of the things I am hearing from your stories is how, as Christian leaders, riding the waves means looking in multiple directions—back at where we have come from, down at where we are now, to the sides to watch out for what might side swipe us, and forward to the next wave or waves. Not to mention above the waves, so to speak. To keep our eyes firmly fixed on God's nature and ways."

"That is such a good metaphor for me," Eric said, "I often feel buffeted, like I am just struggling to the top of one wave when another hits. Reimagining that as riding the waves may be a more helpful metaphor."

"That is a great insight. Do you have any more clarity on what difference

---

5 https://positivedeviance.org

it would make for you?"

"Not yet, but it has given me more hope. I am going to talk to the team when I get back. I think I may take our team out on the water somehow, maybe sailing. Then I may reach out to you for some coaching when we have some ideas to bounce off you."

"I'll look forward to it. Riding the waves is not easy. We may go overboard from time to time. We may become discouraged. Leadership takes courage and persistence."

There was a moment of silence before one brave soul admitted, "I've kind of forgotten what you asked us to talk about in our groups?"

"And how you defined Strategic Learning?" added another.

"Let me give some bullet points to get you started," Dr. Magnus went to the board and wrote as he spoke,

"Strategic Learning Includes:

- ADDRESSING BOTH MOTIVATION AND COMPETENCIES.
- CAREFUL EXEGESIS OF THE ECOSYSTEM.
- UNCOVERING BARRIERS AND OPPORTUNITIES.
- OPENNESS TO DIVERSE WAYS OF THINKING AND FINDING NEW DATA IN NEW WAYS.
- CHANGING MINDSETS.
- EXPERIMENTING AND LEARNING FROM FEEDBACK LOOPS.
- THINKING LONG TERM AND SHORT TERM, LOOKING AT THE MICRO AND THE MACRO."

Then his voice increased in passion as he added,

- "BEING INTEGRATIVE AND HOLISTIC IN OUR THINKING."

Turning he asked, "Did I forget anything?"

"I think that is enough to get us started," someone quipped.

"No biggy," someone else joked and we all laughed.

"In other words, lead?" someone else asked.

"In other words, lead a courageous and collaborative learning system," Dr. Magnus countered. "And as hard as that sounds when we talk about it here, it is even harder to do when we get back into our context. Which is why after you have shared in your small groups, I would like you to pray for each other's leadership, and ministries or organizations. And lest you underestimate how important these next several moments are let me remind you of the research that shows that 97% of leaders identify strategic thinking as crucial to their success yet 96% say they do not have time to do so.[6] Okay, in your groups discuss how this applies in your context. Then on your own make some notes about how intentional you are about studying the complexity of your current system and engaging it in strategic learning? And, as I said earlier, it may be helpful to plot that out somehow."

How would you plot your organization's ideal strategic learning plan?

Gathering us all back together Dr. Magnus suggested we pull our chairs in a circle. Then he asked, "What has taken courage for you this past year?"

People sighed and shifted in their chairs and then began to answer.

"If I say *life* will that seem like I am sidestepping the challenge of answering more specifically?"

"I was thinking along the same lines because it is the overlap of diverse and constantly changing challenges in our organization with some painful personal challenges."

"This may seem like an odd answer but for me I would describe it as the courage not to allow my own discouragement. Or at least not to allow it to get to a point of cynicism or apathy or negativity. I was—let me correct that—I am, deeply concerned about how my response to things may impact key relationships and outcomes."

"Thank you for saying that. I can relate to that too." We sat in silence for a moment, honouring such honest sharing.

"For me it's the courage to wade into polarizing conversations."

"Or to make some tough calls."

"Or to admit to failure."

"The courage to delegate some things I wanted to hold on to."

"These are all important insights," Dr. Magnus said, "Thank you. We

---

6 Dorie Clarke, If Strategy is So Important, Why Don't we Make Time for it? June 2018. https://hbr.org/2018/06/if-strategy-is-so-important-why-dont-we-make-time-for-it

need places where we can talk about these kinds of things. Turn to a partner and give as much context as you are comfortable sharing then pray for one another. We need God's help for wisdom and courage."

The day was drawing to a close when Dr. Magnus announced two guests. "I have asked Jeremy and Judith to share real-world examples of leading when the path is unclear and unpredictable. In these seasons, stakes may be high, and emotions elevated, making it even more difficult. Judith, can you start us off by sharing your example?"

Judith readily agreed, "Like many organizations we have come through a few challenging years. During this season of polarization, I've found it crucial to listen carefully, suspend assumptions, and, when needed, be willing to have the courageous conversation. Many topics during and post-Covid became quite polarizing, and I became concerned about how many leaders shut down just when people needed guidance to navigate this wisely. So, I intentionally chose a posture of courage and honesty in conversations.

"Let me give one example. I had someone challenge me around my stance on vaccination *and* women as pastoral leaders. Two very different and very polarizing topics. He was quite forthright and the way he engaged around these kinds of topics was normally very divisive. So, I set the stage for a healthy conversation by saying, 'I look forward to engaging in this conversation if you are okay with hearing my perspective as well and committing to a healthy process even if we disagree. Two markers of this conversation will be that we both choose the posture of listening and learning, and that we honour the other person even if we have a difference of opinion. And lastly, can we commit that we will still be friends—even if we are in disagreement?' The outcome of the conversation was beautiful—we both heard one another, and we both learned something."

Dr. Magnus thanked her and invited Jeremy to share next.

He began, "Interestingly enough Judith, my story has some elements similar to yours. In our denomination, provision has been made for churches to study and discern for themselves if they believe the Scriptures put restrictions on the roles of women as it relates to church governance—for example eldership. Historically, this has tended to be a divisive issue, and though we were uncertain of the outcome, our Elders wanted to ensure we led through this conversation and vote with the utmost humility, honour, and transparency. There were four words we used to describe the process.

"Clarity: Five months before the vote, our Elders laid out a clear process for how we were going to engage this conversation. In an eight-page document, we articulated the motion we were voting on, the 'why, what, who, when, and how' of the process, primary scriptural views, Elders' recommendation, guiding values, and steps towards heart preparation.

"Story: Knowing that story humanizes people, I began by sharing my own journey, including family of origin dynamics for both my wife and me. I did this in part to highlight that we all have a backstory that shapes our thinking and interpretation. We provided opportunity for every person to share their story and perspective with someone from our leadership team.

"Resources: Our hope was that people would have the humility to understand the scriptural convictions of both 'sides' of the matter before voting, and so provided the congregation with the best resources we could find supporting both positions.

"Listening: At the end of the process, but before the vote, we did a follow-up survey to assess our congregational readiness to vote on this matter. The final question in the survey was: 'Having prayerfully studied and considered this matter, are you ready to vote?' This gave us the humble confidence that we understood where our congregation was truly at to ensure we could vote on this matter and remain unified and healthy regardless of the outcome. All of the above was saturated with prayer, and by God's grace, we were able to navigate these sometimes-turbulent waters with peace and calm. I am intentionally not going to tell you the outcome as the focus here is on the process, but I am happy to chat with you later about that piece."

Dr. Magnus commented on the case studies before adding, "I so appreciate that each of you spoke of both posture and process. Whether for a one-on-one conversation about a topic that has the potential to be polarizing or a group process that lasts several months. The way we show up during seasons of uncertainty is so important. A wise leader is intentional in the design of collaborative listening and learning processes. We know that even then, things do not always go perfectly. This is where courage comes in and takes us back to that topic: the courage to not tap out when it gets hard; the courage to have the conversations that are needed but to have them with grace, having done our own inner work first; the courage to lead, to look at the facts, even when they are brutal; the courage to make changes when they are needed. Take another look at the model we are centering our conversation around. Do you see how courage is needed by the person and the people? And for the purpose and the processes?"

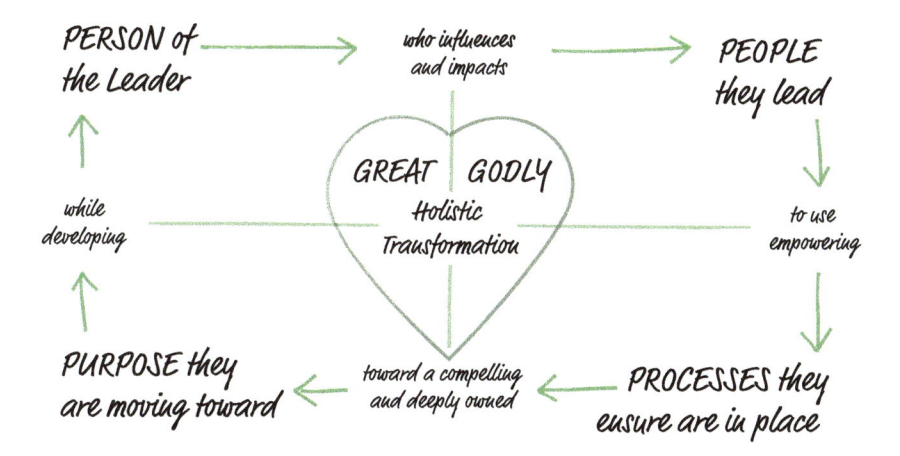

PERSON of the Leader → who influences and impacts → **PEOPLE they lead**

GREAT GODLY Holistic Transformation

while developing ↑ ↑ ↓ ↓ to use empowering

PURPOSE they are moving toward ← toward a compelling and deeply owned ← **PROCESSES they ensure are in place**

"I want us to keep coming back to this to ensure we are thinking holistically. Here is your homework." He went to the board and wrote four questions:

- What do you as a leader need to say or do that is going to take courage? Where do you, or your team, need courage to lead bravely?
- What is required of the people in your organization that is going to require their courage?
- What changes, enforcements or expansions of processes are needed that will take courage? And how will these changes enable us to be more courageous as an organization?
- How does, or how might, your purpose draw you and others out of your comfort zone and into courageous spaces?

"Courage is closely linked to resilience—being able to hold the course when things are rocky, getting back up when knocked down. I first taught a course on leadership resilience years ago, but it is even more important now. Resilience includes the strategies of wellbeing we talked about with our list of Q's, but it also means being as aware as possible of the things that could trip us up in the first place. And that involves taking a deep dive into the temptations of leadership.

"Okay, get a good sleep. You are going to need your best energy tomorrow."

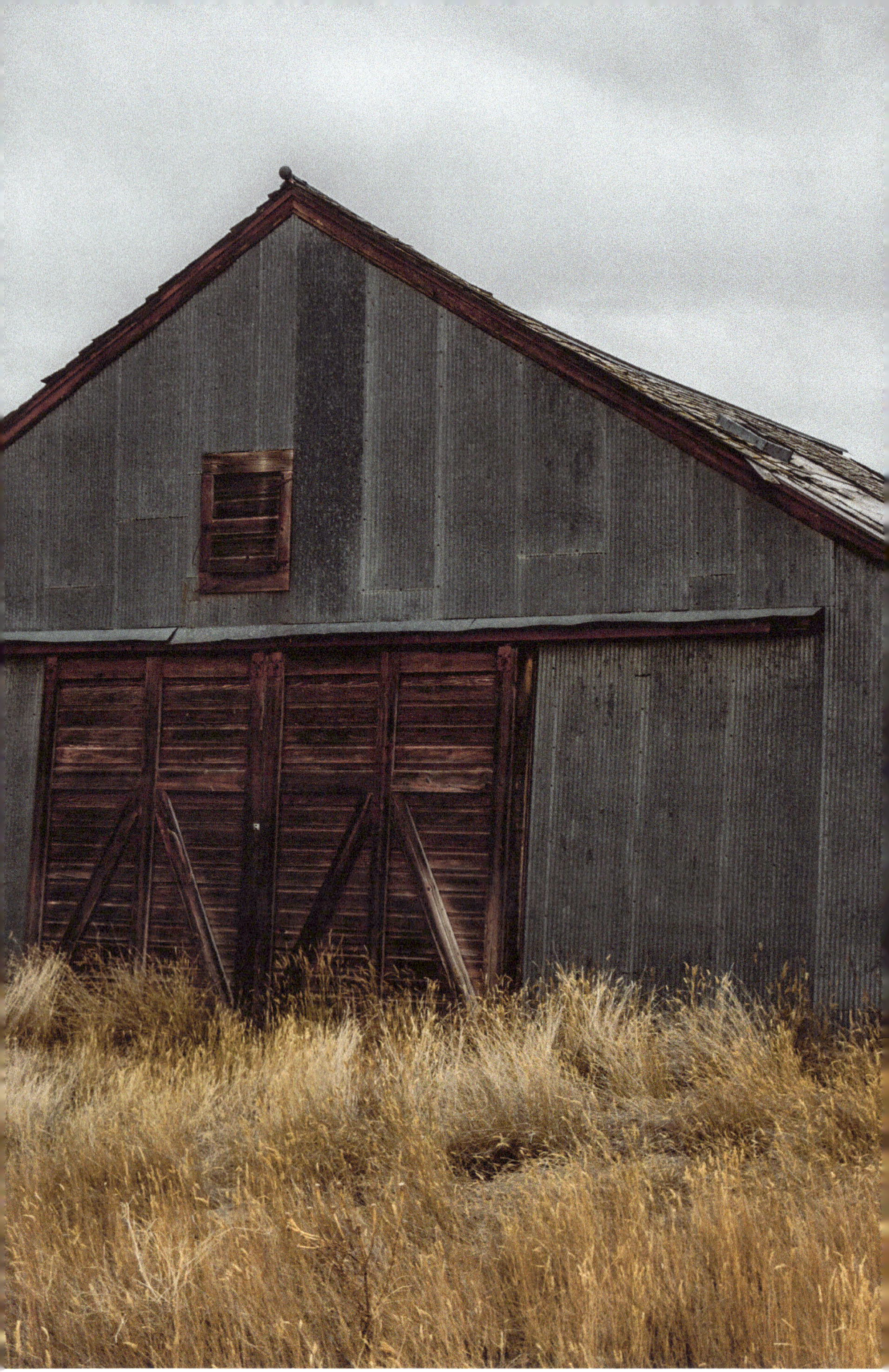

5. THE TEMPTATIONS OF LEADERSHIP

I WAS ALMOST AFRAID TO COME TO CLASS that day, knowing our topic would be temptations of leadership. It had been easy to judge when I was new to my industry, but now that I held a position of influence, things didn't seem as simple as they once had.

After reading us selected Old Testament stories of Saul and David's failures, Dr. Magnus turned the conversation to us. "We have talked about self-deception in leadership, and I would like to return to the topic of leadership temptations and derailers. No one goes into leadership thinking, 'I am going to make as big of a train wreck out of my life as possible,' yet somehow many of us end up on the slippery slope that heads in that direction.

"As we keep emphasizing, the great thing about leadership is that, when called and equipped, it enables us to have a positive influence. The bad thing about leadership is that it means we can quickly, and without meaning to at times, have very negative influence. Power can be easily misused, even without us realizing the path we are on. Leaders cast a larger shadow than they know. What they say has more impact than they know. That just goes with the territory. It means that we need to be especially careful about our words and actions. Add to that the additional pressures you may carry, the lack of honest feedback you may be getting, the sense of entitlement that creeps in when you think about how hard you work, the access to favors and gifts you might have from people seeking to sway your opinion, the publicity of the mistakes you make, and the growing belief that you need to hold on to your position for the good of others… not to mention the target that is painted on your back. No one should go into leadership without counting the cost."

"Are you trying to talk us out of it?" someone joked.

Dr. Magnus chuckled, "Sounds like it, doesn't it? No, of course not, but I am trying to scare you enough that you take this seriously. Henri Nouwen wrote a succinct but profound little book called *In the Name of Jesus: Reflections on Leadership*.[1] Have you read it? So helpful. Can anyone recall the three temptations of leaders he pulls from the story of Jesus in the wilderness?"

Stan flipped open his Bible to Matthew 4 and read the notes he had scribbled beside verses 4-9. "The temptation to be relevant. The temptation to be popular—to be liked. The temptation to be powerful—to be strong, invincible even, to be a hero."

"Yes, good. And what is the antidote, at its core?"

"Remembering our identity is rooted in God's love."

"Yes, good! What does this remind you of? Centered leadership as modelled by Jesus. Jesus understood His calling in light of His Father's deep love for him. Not the other way around. He didn't need to prove anything. We still think we need to," he raised his eyebrows and looked around the room, letting the silence do the heavy lifting.

"*And* we think we need to have the right answers. Remember we talked about that when we discussed Nouwen's differentiation between a moralist and a mystic?"

Dr. Magnus looked at us again. Then he went on, "Patrick Lencioni picks up on similar themes in his book, *The Five Temptations of a CEO*.[2] He talks about our:

- Enjoyment of status
- Need to be liked
- Need for certainty
- Preference for harmony
- Need for invulnerability

---

[1] Henri Nouwen, *In the Name of Jesus: Reflections on Leadership*, Crossroad, Crossroad, 1992.

[2] Patrick Lencioni, *The Five Temptations of a CEO: A Leadership Fable,* Jossey-Bass, 2008.

"This isn't the only list we could consider. David Dotlich and Peter Cairo[3] list eleven potential leadership derailers as:

- Excessive eagerness to please
- Perfectionism
- Passive resistance
- Aloofness
- Mischievousness
- Habitual mistrust
- Excessive caution
- Volatility
- Arrogance
- Melodramatic behaviour
- Eccentricity

"I would be remiss not to mention moral temptation here. The examples of clergy and leader abuse that have come to the surface recently are both appalling and upsetting. Friends, this must stop. Financial temptation, sexual temptation, addictions of any kind, these always start small and seem manageable, justifiable, and inconsequential. Beware their allure. Read the book of Proverbs. Establish healthy rhythms. Seek accountability and get help where needed. God has a way of bringing a thing to the light if we are not willing to. I say this not to frighten us but to encourage us. Friends be wise," he pleaded. "Okay, enough said."

Which of these temptations could be an Achilles Heel for you? And what have you, or will you, put in place to enable you to mitigate it as wisely as possible?

By this time there was sufficient trust in the room for people to be vulnerable, so the conversations ran deep. Accountability companionships were agreed to on the spot as people exchanged contact information and prayed for one another.

---

3 David L. Dotlichi & Peter C. Cairo, *Why CEO's Fail: The 11 Behaviors that Can Derail Your Climb to the Top and How to Manage Them*, Jossey-Bass, 2003.

He smiled and added, "We tend to think of temptations on a personal level, but we could also consider organizational or leadership team temptations. As a team, we can practice hubris. As a team, we can value harmony over healthy dissent. And as a team, we can under or overestimate risk. There are so many high-impact low-potential risks out there that it would be impossible for us to consider them all. However, it is important to identify the risks that matter. This is sometimes called risk ID, the discipline of identifying risks that could seriously undermine your mission. Predictable risks include things like natural disasters, financial downturns, epidemics, and leadership moral failure. Some leaders fixate on potential risks and are paralyzed. Others neglect the possibility, often to their peril. What risk management processes do you have in place to identify potential organizational derailers, and set in place plans to reduce their likelihood and severity?"

"Okay, I have left this final temptation to last. Burnout. Turn to 1 Kings 19:1-19 and discuss it at your table. Elijah was weary, afraid, and alone. Not the best conditions for him to remain centered, or to remember God's promises. Notice how he turns to self-pity. Self-absorption. Yet God does not condemn him. Instead, God gives him the one thing he most needs in that moment. Discuss at your tables. What does God give Elijah?"

Sometime later, Dr. Magnus called us back together, asking, "Okay, what did you decide? What did God give to Elijah?"

Josie answered, "An encounter with his God."

"Yes, exactly. When we are weary and most likely to run away from God, the very thing we need is to reconnect with Him. Don't you love the question that God asks? Twice! 'What are you doing here?' I don't think that is just a geographical question. That is a call to rethink our mindset, for some of us, maybe our pace or posture. Look at verse 14. Can't you almost hear God sigh as Elijah repeats his same 'poor me' lament? What does God do? Reminds him he is not alone. Reminds him of God's power. Reminds him that this is God's work, and these are God's people, not his. And here is a piece that is close to my own heart. God gives Elijah the gift of a renewed calling and the promise of a successor. We will come back to that when we talk about succession later, but for now, I wanted to point out that God is showing Elijah that he understands his weariness and is going to provide help. So helpful.

"Judith, from your perspective as a church planter and leader of other church planters, what is important for leaders to do to protect themselves from burnout in this complex and uncharted season?"

Judith thought for a moment and then answered, "Our team has a horizontal landscape regarding leadership. Two assessments have been very helpful. Each of our team members has done the APEST Assessment[4]—the Apostle, Prophet, Evangelist, Shepherd, and Teacher designations from Ephesians 4. This gives us clarity regarding how we function in ministry. We affirm each other's gifting and encourage each team member to take on various initiatives as the lead depending on the situation of what we are doing. If we need an event planned in detail, we have our Teacher take the lead. If we need to be taken care of, we call on our Shepherd. If we have an innovative launch, we ask the Apostle and so on.

"Functioning with this shared leadership model helps to protect us from burnout. The other tool we have found helpful is the Enneagram Assessment. This has helped our staff understand how each person on our team interprets the world and manages their emotions, allowing us to understand ourselves and the other team members in greater depth. The greatest benefit is the Emotional Awareness, grace towards one another. It has definitely strengthened how we function together. All our programs are run by a team. We can lean on each other for ideas, shared responsibility as well as the opportunity to lean on one another if a team member needs that extra emotional support. We noticed during Covid that team members at different times needed one another as it was quite an emotionally draining time. Some are experiencing post-Covid stress and the team structure is very helpful.

"We have weekly team check-ins to pray for each other and we share a meal at least once a month. These help us to build trust and community. And I am very intentional about making sure that I meet each of our leaders every other week for a coaching check-in to see if they need extra resourcing or support. During those time we dream about where the Lord is leading them and their ministry. The time together is authentic and inspiring, and we've built trust together over a long period of time.

"The last thing I would say relates to mindset. Our focus is on Holistic Health. Our organizational culture is all about Healthy Team, Healthy Organization, Healthy Leader, and Healthy Family. We are quite clear about

---

4 APEST Personal Vocational Assessment, available online.

what we value and what our expectations are as a part of our organization. We encourage a balance at work and also in their homes with family. Having that focus makes making most decisions a lot easier. Sustainability, giftedness, holistic well-being and community are all filters that help us hear what God is saying."

Dr. Magnus thanked Judith for these insights and then said, "I especially appreciate you mentioning the importance of building and understanding your team and being intentional about community. This is the longer, slower approach but, in the long run, so much more powerful, sustainable, and rewarding.

"Wayne once asked me what leadership feels like, and I answered, 'It feels like waiting.' Waiting for people. Waiting for information. Waiting on God's timing. In my experience, one of the most important traits that I have had to develop is patience. And there have been many times I have had to coach myself. I think we will leave it there for now, as that is a perfect transition point for when we come back to talk about communication.

"For now, I want to stress that a leader who is tending themselves and growing in both their great and godly leadership is infinitely more ready to intentionally, irresistibly, and impactfully tend and lead others. This is what Jesus did and calls us to."

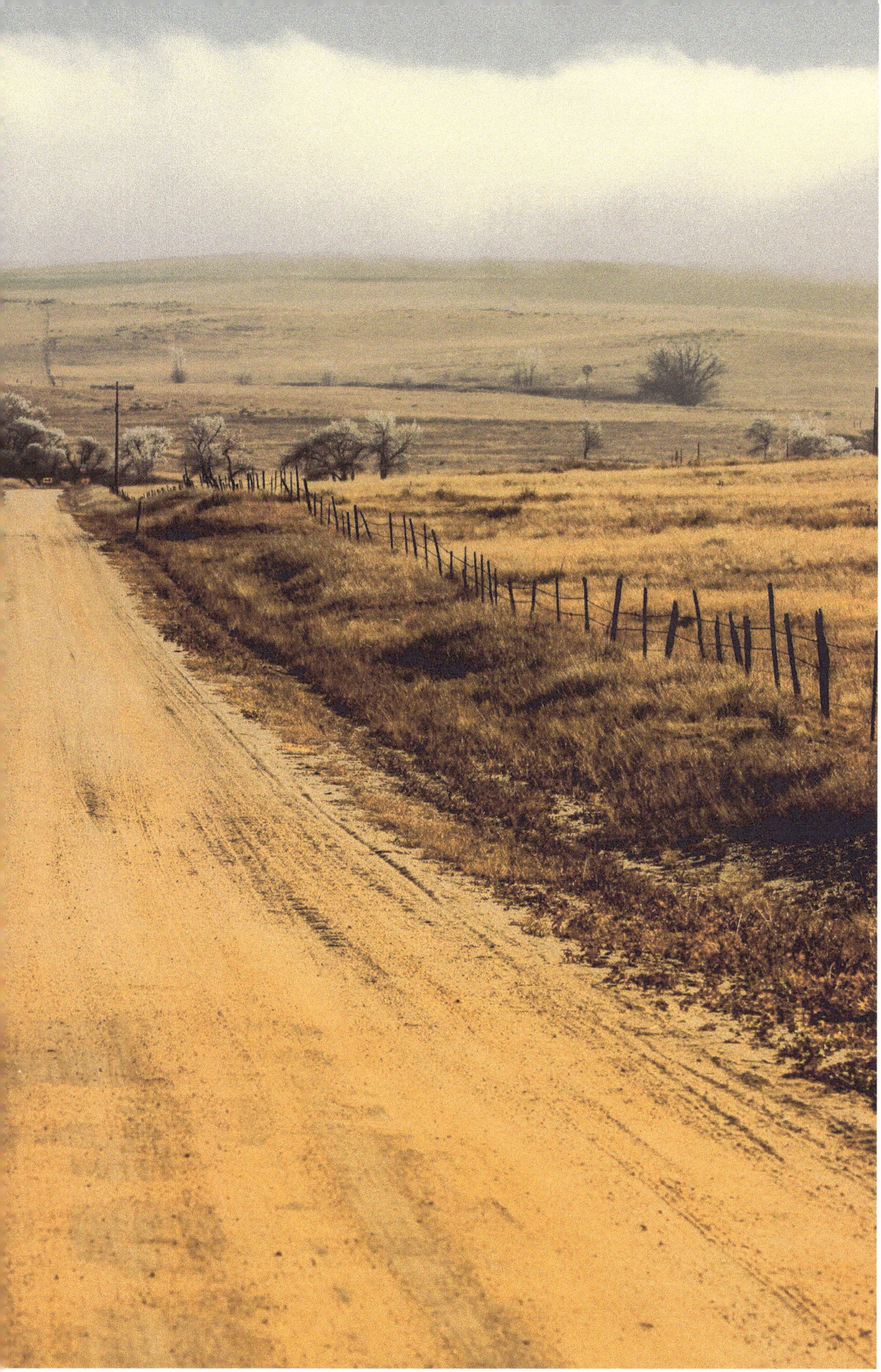

6. PEOPLE

"A boss has the title. A leader has the people."
Simon Sinek

Dr. Magnus met us in the hall and assigned us places at either end of a long rope. Without further instruction, he counted down, "Three, two, one, pull!"

"What?"

"Pull harder."

Soon we were sweating and laughing as the rope pulled in one direction, then the other then finally dragged half of us halfway down the hall before we fell in a heap, exhausted.

"Okay, back to our room," Dr. Magnus commanded as we staggered to our feet.

We sank into our seats as he said, "There are tensions within our model. Polarities. Tensions between the person and the people, between people and processes, between processes and purpose, and between purpose and the person of the leader. And our model represents the tensions that cut across from person to process and people to purpose as well. All are influenced by our personal and corporate core. The heart is in the middle. What do you think some of the tensions between the person of the leader and the people might be?"

"The will of the leader and the will of the people?"

"The power differentials that exist."

"Levels of engagement."

"Different perceptions of reality."

What tensions do you see at work in your organization?
Giving neutral names to each pole enables us to have a healthier conversation. For example, 'individual work' and 'teamwork' are much better names than 'loners' and 'people who can't work on their own.'
What neutral names could you use to label your polarity?

Each pole has positive and negative traits. We could draw them like this.

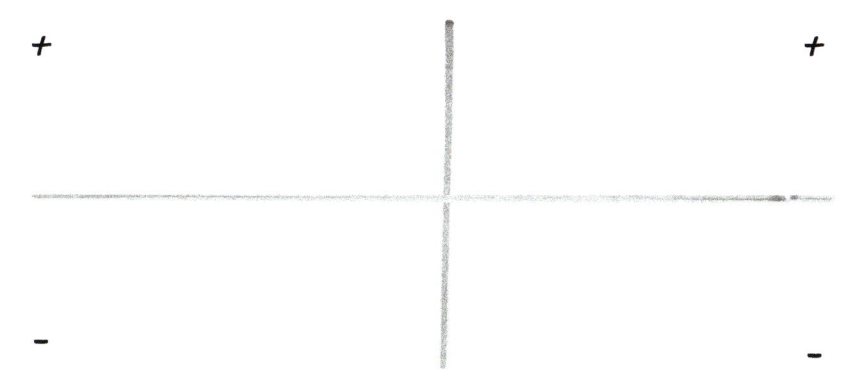

```
+                           |                            +
                            |
                            |
────────────────────────────┼────────────────────────────
                            |
                            |
-                           |                            -
```

Populate the four quadrants of your polarity map. This not only helps us to see when and where to focus on one pole but also enables us to find the higher purpose that links the two ends.

Dr. Magnus began, Bible in hand. "To learn how to navigate this, we turn again to scripture. I believe that John 14-17 gives us one of the clearest pictures of how God functions within the Trinity. It is so rich. The mutuality. The unity. The honouring of the other.

"I personally believe that this may also be one of the clearest pictures of what Jesus wants for and from His Body. Self-emptying love. Relentless respect. The genuine pursuit of unity. There should be no competition among leaders.

"There will be challenges, of course; look at John 15:18. Leadership is a calling to servanthood, not glory. Look at verse twenty of the same chapter. Thank goodness that a few verses later, Jesus promises a Helper.

"Remember the context. Jesus is preparing the disciples for his departure. Actually, let's back up to John 16:25. This is so rich. Two verses each, starting with Sam, please."

As we took turns reading aloud, Dr. Magnus stopped us from time to time to add a comment, but more often, he sat, head down and nodding at parts that meant the most to him, almost overwhelmed by the impact of the words. Then he summarized, "The Father loves us. In the world, there will be tribulation, but Jesus has both left us His peace and has overcome the world. And he prays for this one thing. One thing. That we be sanctified in the truth and be one, even as He and the Father are one. Outstanding."

> *IF THE WORLD HATES YOU, KNOW THAT IT HAS HATED ME BEFORE IT HATED YOU.*
>
> JOHN 15:8 ESV

DR. PAUL MAGNUS

A silence fell over the room as he read the whole passage aloud again, then repeated, "That they may be one, perfectly one, with Jesus where He is. That the love with which the Father loved him may be in us and Jesus in us." He looked up and then said, "Jesus was irresistible. Jesus is irresistible. His outrageous love and compassion for people translated after His resurrection into a church that cared for the hungry, the poor, the widows and the sick while the broader society looked on in amazement. His disregard for social norms informed a church that opened its doors, albeit begrudgingly by some, to all. Read Galatians 3:28!"

Walking to the whiteboard, he wrote "irresistible" and underlined it as he said, "I dream of leaders of irresistible influence, building cultures of irresistible influence. That is why I come to work. And the Trinity models for me, for us, what irresistible influence looks like."

He opened an old dictionary and read, "Webster defines irresistible as 'impossible to resist.' Hmmm… that isn't too helpful, is it." He chuckled. "But listen to this. Influence is defined as 'the act or power of producing an effect, in tangible or intangible ways, without apparent exertion of force or direct exercise of command.' Now that is interesting!"

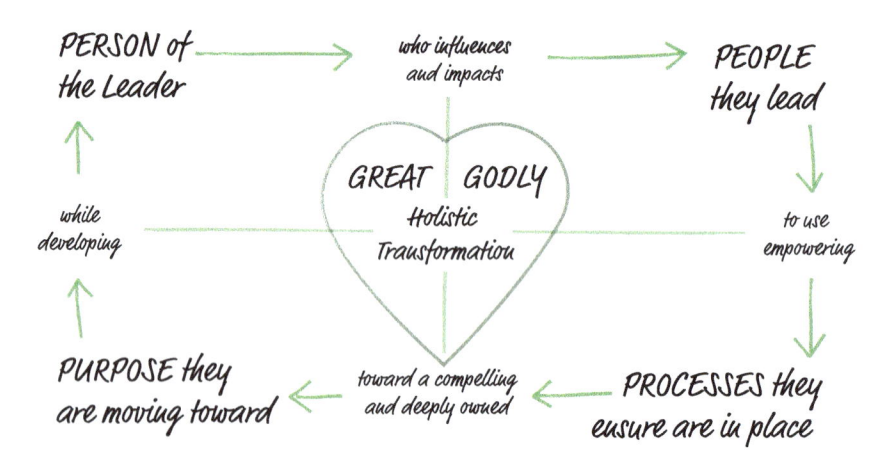

PERSON of the Leader → who influences and impacts → PEOPLE they lead

while developing ↑ ↓ to use empowering

GREAT GODLY Holistic Transformation

PURPOSE they are moving toward ← toward a compelling and deeply owned ← PROCESSES they ensure are in place

Pointing to the model as he spoke, Dr. Magnus said, "We started by talking about the core. The heart and how it impacts every other lens in this framework. Then we talked about the person of the leader and how important it is to practice self-leadership: growing in our spirituality, emotional regulation, physical well-being, social skills and so on. Effective leaders tend and steward themselves before they seek to tend or steward others.

"Now we want to shift to think about people. The team. Whether or not we realize it, leaders have significant influence. The question is: how intentionally and irresistibly are you using that influence?"

"What would intentional and irresistible look like when it comes to leadership influence and impact? Notice also that I use the words 'influence' and 'impact.' What do you think the difference between these might be?"

Dr. Magnus moved to the front of the room to get our attention, "What makes someone's influence irresistible?"

"I am reminded of the passage that tells us not to muzzle the ox. For me, someone who gives the right mix of inspiration and freedom has irresistible influence."

Dr. Magnus nodded and said, "That's an important insight. The role of leadership is always to manage the polarity of order and freedom."

We talked about how this will be different for different people, so that took us back to the conversation about the one thing managers must do is know the individuals on their team well enough to know how to best support and challenge them.

"Another great polarity," Dr. Magnus agreed, "balancing the big picture of the organization with the individual wellbeing and development of the person."

"Someone is irresistible to me, at least in the way we are defining here, when they have earned my trust and respect."

"And when they treat me like a human, a partner rather than a peon."

After a rich time of discussion, Dr. Magnus spoke again. "John 14-17, one of the most beautiful passages in the Bible, in my opinion, not only gives us such rich insight into the way the Trinity co-lead but also gives us a sense of how Jesus intentionally discipled and developed people. He knows that He is about to leave them, but instead of asking that they take care of Him, He cares for them. In the early chapters of John, we see the first followers coming to Jesus. He asks, 'What is it that you are seeking?' In John 21, we see Him on His knees beside a fire cooking them fish and restoring Peter to the fold. And in between these passages, a constant stream of learning opportunities and growing ministry opportunities ensure that they were humanly ready for the task He has for them. Then, knowing that they would need more than human capacity, He makes two astounding promises.

He will be their Advocate and Companion.

He will send a Helper, a Comforter, a Teacher who will guide and lead them.

"Astounding. This passage has caused me to completely rethink leadership and how to influence people. Vanessa Bohn's research[1] shows that we tend to overestimate the negative impact we have on people and underestimate the positive. People listen to and respect us more than we think. Her book offers science-based strategies for observing the effect we have on others, reconsidering our fear of rejection and maximizing our influence."

What would you do differently this coming week if you truly believed that you have more positive influence than you think?

"Jan, having grown up in Europe and being part of a global mission for so many years must have shaped your thinking about leadership significantly. What do you see when it comes to developing and influencing people?"

Jan thought for a moment and then answered, "Over the past 30 years, I have seen an eruption of leadership development endeavours. Most of these are around what I would call the Messiah model; boards appointing a leader to take the organization to the next level of success. While I agree that organizations are in a better place with leaders equipped with skills, there is one aspect of leadership that needs more attention and emphasis: the character of the leader. I still see too much of a 'lording over' use of power rather than influencing power that sets people up to succeed and flourish. Sadly, I see this tendency across many cultures and think it is something we must be much more intentional about."

"That is helpful, Jan. Thank you. For me, it is helpful to have a set of guiding principles. I call this list my '6 E's.'" He went to the board and wrote:

ENNOBLEMENT
ENLISTMENT
ENABLEMENT
ENCULTURING
EMPOWERMENT
ENCIRCLEMENT

---

[1] Vanessa Bohns, *You Already Have More Influence Than You Think: How We Underestimate Our Power of Persuasion and Why It Matters*, 2021.

6.1 ENNOBLEMENT

"Hopefully, by now you know how seriously I take the responsibility of leading people made in the image of God. In my years of leadership, I have seen how quickly we can forget this and how devastating the effects can be. There are several ways we could think about this, and today I have chosen the Arbinger Institute's research on Leadership and Self-Deception.[2] In our world and in ourselves, we observe this tendency to forget that the human in front of us has both God-given dignity and similar personal and professional challenges to ourselves. Arbinger calls this a form of self-deception that leads to self-betrayal. Anytime our goals outweigh our humanity, or we act in a way that is contrary to what we know we should do for others, we have betrayed our own humanity and dehumanized another. This causes a dissonance within us, so we begin to reframe the way we see the world in order to enable us to justify our behaviour." Dr. Magnus paused, letting the silence carry the weight of these insights.

Then he continued, "This greatly decreases our ability to influence, because we now have a distorted view of reality. This is, of course, much more devastating for people of Christian faith as it means that we have not taken seriously that people are made in the image of God and are precious to Him. Let's flip to Ezekiel 34:1–24. This is a passage written to leaders."

He read it slowly and somberly, letting the impact of the words hang in the air. Then he repeated, "'The weak you have not strengthened, the sick you have not healed. The injured you have not bound up. The strayed you have not brought back. The lost you have not sought. And with force and harshness you have ruled them.' Ouch. Jesus picked up this same theme when he said, 'The rulers of this world lord it over them but it shall not be so with you.'[3] Friends, be careful. We can so easily judge others and deceive ourselves. Look at the number of Christian leaders who have experienced major moral failures. Consider how easy it is to forget how sacred people are. We are called to steward those who are precious to God.

---

2 The Arbinger Institute, *Leadership and Self Deception: Getting Out of the Box*, Berrett-Koehler Publishers, 2018.

3 Mark 10:42

"Be careful. Be wise. Establish rhythms of right living and compassionate leadership. Ensure you have adequate accountability. The Bible teaches us that 'the heart is deceitful above all things.' Pull out your Bible and mark Jeremiah 17:9,10. God alone can reveal the deceitfulness that so easily settles in. This is, again, too important to breeze over. So, we are going to take a break here and give you time to pray for one another."

Dr. Magnus paused and looked at each of us in turn. "Brothers and sisters, this is incredibly important. Please pray with intentionality and authenticity. And make it your practice to pray for yourself and each other about this.

"There are two key parts of this. The first one is remembering that people are made in the image and likeness of God. If that doesn't change how we look at people, I don't know what would! And secondly, helping people to become more fully aware of who they truly are. As human beings, even if you are in a setting where you can't talk about Genesis 1, you can still raise awareness about the dignity of humanity."

Putting down the marker, Dr. Magnus settled in his rocking chair. "Before we leave this topic, I'd like to talk for a moment about consistency. Something we don't often discuss when it comes to leadership. You know my wife and I have been married for over fifty years. We are in a covenantal relationship. That is very different from a contractual one. And that covenantal relationship is both confessional—by which I mean bound up in our understanding of the scriptures—and convictional—it is something we live out. There is something in there for us as leaders too. I am not comparing our leadership role to a marriage, but I am saying that we are in a covenantal relationship with God and that there is something to be said for thinking of our relationships with the people in our organization as more than transactional. In the family of God, our relationship is familial, not contractual. Okay, but back to applying this through the lens of our model."

Are we practicing personal consistency? Are we experiencing and promoting this in our relationships with the people? Do our processes support this? Is there room for this in our organizational purpose?

Jane and I met when I was working as the new Registrar of the college. Every year each student had to come to my office to have their documents signed, and she was in her third year when I first started in the role. I would notice her as she walked past my office on her way to the office where she and others graded papers for faculty. She always smiled on the way by. But it wasn't until one weekend when her roommate brought her along for moral support when she asked if I would be her Sadie Hawkins date for the weekend that our paths crossed more significantly. I was going away for the weekend, and when Jane heard this asked for a ride to Saskatoon. It was Valentine's weekend, and on the drive home, we both realized that there was a spark. Sometimes a seemingly insignificant moment, like saying yes to a ride, turns into a major milestone. I have seen this happen so often in life and leadership.

6.2 ENLISTMENT

"Enlistment involves inviting people into something bigger than themselves. It requires knowing your team well enough to know how to invite them into something that is important to them. Do you recall Josephs and Joiner's levels of leadership? True enlistment requires higher level leadership on our part; otherwise, our desire for others to join in is more like conscription than voluntary enlistment.

"Daniel Pink identifies people's three intrinsic motivators as autonomy, personal mastery, and purpose.[4] Do you know what your primary intrinsic motivator is? And just as importantly, do you know what your team members are?"

"I feel another homework assignment coming up," someone quipped.

"You know me too well. Make a note. Find out what motivates you, and make sure you build enough of that into your life to keep your tank full. Then find out what motivates your team and the key people in your life. This is especially important when you are working with volunteers."

---

4 Daniel Pink, *Drive: The Surprising Truth About What Motivates Us*, Riverhead Books, 2011.

Someone waved their hand with a question. "Apart from competency-specific criteria, what do you look for when you are recruiting people for a team Dr. Magnus?"

"I am so glad you asked that question. I like Patrick Lencioni's list of Humble, Hungry, and Smart."

As we began to write in our notebooks, he explained, "Humble refers to a healthy ego. Not too timid to speak up or so arrogant you think you know best. Hungry refers to a strong work ethic, something Lencioni says we need to develop early in life. It also refers to someone who is hungry to learn. His word Smart does not refer to our IQ but our EQ. Our ability to self-manage, to care for people and to read the room. The combination of all three makes what he calls an ideal team player. And we need all three. Missing one creates challenges. The person who is missing 'Smart' is a great person who makes lots of missteps relationally. The person missing 'Hungry' is fun to be with, but they don't get things done, so they can let down the team. Ouch, some of us are feeling these descriptions in our gut, aren't we? The most dangerous combination, according to Lencioni, is the person who is missing true 'Humility.' That person may excel at their job, get multiple promotions, and even *seem* humble. Yet they leave a trail of disaster in their wake. Amy, I see you nodding your head. Have you experienced one of these?"

"This has given language to something I experienced a few years ago. I had a co-worker that was always sitting with the right people, acting the right way, and saying the right thing. Yet somehow, there was something off about her. She was smart enough to act like the humblest person in the room—always speaking last and seeming to support others, but somehow using that to get what she wanted in the end. She was very politically savvy, and I didn't trust her. Sure enough, she left a trail of destruction and then left soon afterwards, leaving others to pick up the pieces."

After others had shared similar stories, Dr. Magnus said, "Lencioni suggests that we do the following exercise. Everyone is going to have one or two of these three attributes that we are stronger at and one that we are weaker at. If you had to choose one that you are not as good at as the other two—even if you are very good at all three—what would it be? This can be so helpful for developing self-awareness, as well as a personal development plan in the areas that really matter. Take a few moments and jot down your thoughts. Then discuss with a partner what the implications of this are and how you want to address this."

Tara, a leader in a college with a special heart for international students; Kalli, a leader in her Nation; Cam, a long-time police officer in special crimes; and Joel, a church leader who had recently moved from Ghana to Canada to study. These four sat together at a table. They were quickly becoming friends and had shared many laughs and insights already this week, but this conversation was different.

"Oh wow," Tara whispered as reality sunk in. "I know that I am strong in the 'Smart' and 'Hungry' pieces, so does that mean I must be weakest at 'Humility'?"

Cam added, "Well, I can't answer that for you, but if I'm honest, it is the humility piece I can manipulate when I'm not at my best. That's the 'evil Cam.' And that is scary because, according to Lencioni, and more importantly to Jesus, that is the worst of the three choices!"

Joel nodded in solidarity, then said, "There may be some cultural differences here, but I agree that many of the leaders I know are strongest on charisma and drive."

Tara asked, "Is charisma the same thing as EQ, do you think?"

"Hmmm, good question. I guess in my mind they were linked, but maybe they aren't?"

Just then, Dr. Magnus started to teach again. "Okay, let's talk about the impact we have as leaders. The more significant our leadership responsibility, the longer the shadow our influence casts. For good and for bad. What we say and do takes on more meaning because of our position. We are foolish if we don't acknowledge this. This is why it is so important that we are self-aware and managing ourselves, as well as building robust teams. Lencioni's grid can be a powerful tool for hiring and training, as well as gaining feedback for ourselves."

Eric put up his hand, "I love the simplicity of this model, but in the real world wouldn't it be fair to say that there are more layers of complexity than this?"

"Great insight Eric. And that would be true of any of the models we are looking at, isn't it? A model is, by design, simplified and will therefore leave out nuances and exceptions. We are wise to use them carefully and not to plug people into boxes that can be both limited and limiting. I'm so glad that you brought that up. What nuances do you see?"

Eric nodded and said, "Well, maybe it's just semantics, and this is already included in one of his categories but what about intellect? Don't you want that kind of 'smart' person on your team when you are facing complex issues? Or what about creativity? Is it possible that someone could be smart, hungry, and humble the way he describes them but not creative?"

"These are great questions, and I love that you are engaging critically with the resources we are considering." Dr. Magnus continued, "You have also pointed out how important it is when using a model to carefully clarify what you mean by the terms. Okay, stand up for a stretch and find two other people you haven't talked to yet today. What nuances may be missed in this model?"

After we had an animated conversation in cluster groups, we went back to our tables. Dr. Magnus had asked Cathie to share about the challenges of enlisting volunteers in the national ministry she led.

She began. "I can speak best to the challenges and strategies of engaging female leaders, and that is a significant resource since women make up more than half the church in Canada and around the world. You would think that because of that, the pool of volunteers would be deep. Yet women volunteers are under-represented at decision-making tables in many organizations. I think part of this is due to invitation and investment. Reversing this trend requires intentionality in both invitation and investment because, although women often score well on emotional intelligence and self-awareness, they also score lower on confidence, especially when it comes to working in professional or ministry contexts that are still largely built around strengths that tend to be attributed to men. I never cease to be astonished at the lack of confidence women have in their inherent strengths. In my experience, they assume the environment they are being invited to will punish failure and reward success. To overcome these challenges, leaders wishing to enlist volunteers should exhibit the EQ traits they want to attract. They should also be clear that the environment is designed to reward risk-taking and that failure is the fastest way to become a robust and resilient leader themselves."

6.3 ENABLEMENT

Our farm was four miles from town, just far enough to make it challenging for us to walk there and get into mischief, so we had to make mischief in other ways. My one brother, whose middle name could have been Mischief Maker, was often in the centre of this. He loved to drive our old truck at breakneck speeds even though he knew the brakes on it didn't work and his license wasn't current. And I was sometimes crazy enough to go with him. One time he was driving so fast he couldn't turn, and we drove through a closed gate. Another time he was trying to show off to friends, and he hit the gas, not realizing that the wheel was turned. He went down into a deep ditch, saved only from rolling over several times by the cattle rack on top of the old truck. Even so, we were on our side, him standing on top of me in his eagerness to get out before we fell into the slough. Fortunately, a neighbour came along and pulled us out and helped us to pound the dents out of the side of the truck. That was the day I told my brother I would never get in a vehicle with him again and started the long walk back to the farm. My dad never knew. Or at least never let on that he did, although sometime later, he did comment on the cattle rack being slightly crooked.

Despite all this craziness, my father was intent on setting each one of us up for success based on who we were and both the possibilities and the dangers he could foresee for us. He gave every one of us a piece of land. He coached us, taking a long-term approach to helping us discover what we wanted to do and ensuring we were ready to do it. He was very intentional about this. He did his best to ensure that seven very different kids went out into the world prepared for whatever they would meet and need.

―――

"When I use the word enablement, I'm not talking about enabling unhealthy behaviour, I am talking about helping people to be successful. I have talked about this one already because I think it is so important. Holding people *able*. Ensuring people can do what is being asked of them. We so often attribute a lack of will when it is actually a lack of skill. We have missed the importance of enabling. We thought we engage and then empower, but all that does is overpower people where we haven't taken a progressive path of enabling. We see this again and again in organizations." He smiled mischievously, "or at least in ineffective organizations. I love teaching leadership to already good leaders because we want to enable them to take it to the next level, so churches and organizations are led well.

"I owe a debt of gratitude to John Maxwell for helping me in my early years of senior leadership. His model of five levels of leadership influenced me to stay with something longer. And it shifted my focus. He talks about the difference between leaders who are followed because they get results and leaders who are followed because they reproduce themselves in others. I started building teams and developing others in the organization I was in at the time. I can't over-emphasize the importance of growing people's sense of confidence, competence, and capacity. This meant I needed to shift my focus from merely leading the organization to ensuring that people were co-leading the organization. And to do that I needed to invest more in the intentional development of people.

"Maxwell's 5 Levels of Leadership[5] is one of his most important contributions to the leadership landscape, in my opinion. There is the power of the position, and the position gives you a right to lead. We tend to dismiss this rather than understand that this gives us a platform. It doesn't give us people's loyalty, but it gives us the opportunity to earn it. We do this by building relationships with people so they follow because they want to. Being a well-loved leader is not the end goal, however. Although looking at some leaders, you would think so. Remember, we talked about the polarity of relationships *and* results. Leaders maximize the platform they have been given by also achieving results and investing in the development of people.

"Some leaders bemoan the fact that they just get someone 'trained up' and they leave to work somewhere else. If we have a Kingdom mentality, we shouldn't look at it that way. This kind of multiplication across organizations is healthy—as long as they are not leaving because they feel stifled or undervalued under your leadership. Maxwell calls level 5 leadership the pinnacle. That is lofty language, I know, but the concept is strong. We all know people that we follow out of respect for who they are and what they

---

5 John Maxwell, *5 Levels of Leadership: Proven Steps to Maximize Your Potential*, Center Street, 2013.

represent. These are people who encapsulate and surpass all the previous stages. They are getting results and developing people, but they are also raising the levels of ethics and motivation we talked about with Bass and Burns's Transformational Leadership. Their very presence elevates the conversation. They have massive influence—with or without a position."

Take a moment and reflect on these stages of leadership development. Where do you aspire to be? What needs to happen to enable you to move there? And how do these levels or stages overlap with Joseph and Joiner's or Clinton's stages of development?

People began to scribble in notebooks, and it was silent except for the occasional page-turning. As for me, I couldn't help wondering how much of my perspective of my personal leadership was aspirational rather than actualized. Our team deserved better than this, and as I slowly allowed myself to remember, our organizational purpose was something worth investing in. I made myself a note to talk to the team about what moving to another level of collaboration and investment in people might look like, preparing myself as I did for the naysayer and overly optimistic perspectives this kind of conversation might elicit. Thinking more about that, I added a note to reengage with a leadership coach and sign up for a Mastermind group for peer coaching. I knew I couldn't do this on my own.

After a while, Dr. Magnus said, "Jim Collins's research indicated that nine out of ten organizations that effectively moved from 'Good' to 'Great' were led by internally grown leaders.[6] In my experience, this is true. The best leaders in organizations are homegrown. They have been around long enough to understand the culture, learn the necessary skills, develop relationships, and prove their character in difficult times and good times. This means creating a culture that develops leaders. And that means both formal and informal opportunities to learn, lead and receive feedback.

"Nothing has been more helpful for me here than Ken Blanchard and Paul Hersey's Situational Leadership Model. It shows us *how* to develop people. I have an early 'nineties first edition, and it is still one of the most

---

[6] Jim Collins, *Good to Great: Why Some Companies Makes the Leap... and Others Don't*, Harper Collins, 2001.

helpful resources that we can build from. It answers the question, 'how can we actually influence people?' When people first start and have limited experience, they need lots of direction and encouragement. It can be challenging because people starting out don't know what they don't know. And we don't know what they don't know. They may have excelled in a different environment, but when they move to a new role or organization it is like they are starting over, at least for a short period of time. Our leadership must be more directive for them to excel in this season. Full autonomy would be over-empowering to them. They're unsure and need more clear direction, according to their readiness level.

"After a time, they may have run up against some walls and become discouraged. That is why more encouragement is needed to help them get over the hump. As they become more skilled and confident, they need less direction and encouragement, but they may still need you to be accessible to answer questions or help them think through unique scenarios. Eventually, as people become highly skilled and motivated, they are ready to take on new challenges.

"This is so important. And that is why I believe that coaching your team is something you can't really delegate to another department or to 'the professionals.' People needed to be guided close-up. Step by step based on their readiness. I am not dismissing the importance of receiving personal or even leadership coaching from a certified coach. I am actually a huge proponent of that. I am talking here about the supervisor's role in coaching for performance and character at work."

How intentional are you about ensuring people are ready for the role they have been given? Is there any work you would like to do there?

In my first year of college, we had to take communications, and one assignment entailed giving a speech in front of the whole class. I was so shy and nervous that this seemed impossible to me. I wrote my speech and went into the furnace room to practice it over and over and over. My professor was a stately gentleman named Homer Edwards. Three years later, after courses in homiletics and preaching with him I was chosen by my peers to preach the final sermon at Commencement. When I finished two thousand people jumped to their feet in a standing ovation. Homer Edwards, a man normally very difficult to read, came to me with tears in his eyes and said, "Now I can retire. To see someone as shy and withdrawn and afraid of speaking as you grow into someone whose sermon would open doors to any ministry setting. Remembering my own terror and recalling the impact this one gentleman had on my life helps me to be not only a better teacher but also a better leader and human being.

Enablement is not just about believing in someone; it is about believing in them enough that you help them to get where they can go. Even now I can get nervous speaking to a group of people until I remember to focus on them not myself. Leaders who are focused on looking good will never be effective enablers.

6.4 ENCULTURING

"Of course, there are times when bringing in someone from the outside is critical. Either because there is no one internally or a fresh approach is desired. However, in my experience, we do not do a very good job of enculturing people. When I was the President of the institution, I spent half a day a month with each new faculty. We started with how to write a syllabus. I wanted not just to empower them but also enable them to teach well. And I wanted to develop leaders. So, you can be sure there were a fair number of leadership lessons thrown in as we met together.

"Enculturing is the process by which we ensure that people understand not only the values and vision but also the nuances and unspoken norms of the organization. Who does what? And how do you get things done? In my experience, we are not very good at this."

Think about the recent hires on your team. How much time have you spent ensuring they understand how to be successful in your church or organization? Are there any gaps that should be filled?

6.5 ENCOURAGEMENT

I remember the day that I told my dad I was going to leave the farm. He was surprised, reminding me that of all the siblings, I was the one that loved it the most. And he was right, I loved the land, the horses, the lifestyle. Sensing my uncertainty and fear, he added, 'We will support you whatever you decide to do.' I have often reflected on that when a fearful leader stands in front of me. My father taught me to believe in people before they believe in themselves. I am not sure that you can lead well without this, I know I couldn't have.

"The research is staggering here, most people in organizations feel undervalued and overlooked. Understanding how to apply appreciative language is so important in organizations. We are getting better at understanding the love languages of our friends and family but don't necessarily know how to apply this on a broader scale in organizations. Some people need a lot more encouragement than others as a result of their confidence or competence level. Some people prefer public demonstrations of appreciation, and others prefer private. The key here is to not assume that what you need or prefer applies to others. And some people have been wounded and need extra care and affirmation.

"Ellen, I know you have done some research around the cost of women's low confidence and how to create environments where men and women can both thrive. If I recall, one of the pieces you help organizations with is the effect of mixed messages on someone, in this case, a woman's, willingness to speak up. Tell us more about that."

Ellen nodded and said, "Sure. Psychologist Robyn Goodman says that a woman's confidence peaks at age nine. While that is not true for every woman, of course, it is a concerning statistic that raises a lot of questions. The reasons are multi-layered, but as you mentioned, mixed messages are significant contributors. At a young age, many girls internalize the message that they shouldn't put their hands up too often or say too much.

James Detert[7] and others have done interesting work with 'Implicit Voice Theory' and the factors that make using our voice in social settings risky. The mixed messages we have received and our interpretation of them, impact us later in life. Imagine someone's invited to speak at a board table, where their opinion is genuinely sought and desired, but they clam up. Now imagine the train of messages, experiences, and responses that they have brought with them into the room and how much stronger that is than the invitation to speak they have just received. While these theories apply to all, they are especially prevalent among non-dominant groups. This is one of the reasons I appreciated our conversation about safe and brave spaces. It takes courage for people who have been trained to self-silence to speak, even in safe spaces."

Dr. Magnus added, "Thank you. So good. We don't always consider the impact of years of socialization on our influence and voice. This is part of the reason why encouragement is so important but also so difficult. See how the word includes 'courage'? Our goal in encouraging is more than helping someone feel good about themselves. To encourage is to help build someone's courage, so they are able to act on their convictions and bring their best self to the cause.

"Now, let's multiply what we have been discussing across organizations. It is difficult enough to create a healthy team when you are focused on six or eight people, but large organizations have multiple teams. Perhaps hundreds or thousands. So how do multiple teams become one? This is critical for the kind of systemic health we have been talking about. One factor is what I like to call entrustment. Let's take a break before we dive into that."

---

7 James R. Detert, "Implicit Voice Theories: Taken-for-Granted Rules of Self-Censorship at Work." *Academy of Management Journal,* 54(3), 461-488. DOI: 10.5465/AMJ.2011.61967925

6.6 ENTRUSTMENT

"We can't talk about trust without noting two seminal sources, *The Speed of Trust*[1] by Steven Covey and *The Five Dysfunctions of a Team*[2] by Patrick Lencioni. Covey describes trust as our most valuable asset, and suggests it is built through a combination of four credibility building traits: principles, motives, skills and track record. Would you agree that this is what builds credibility or add others?"

"Perhaps Covey is including this in skills, but I would add empathy or compassion to that list. I find that my team really needs to know that I hear them and care about them for them to trust me," Cam said.

Jacqueline agreed, "Absolutely, and I would add that one of the skills great leaders need to develop if they want to build trust on their team is coaching."

"And collaboration," Amy added.

"Great insights," Dr. Magnus said as he added them to his teaching notes. "Thank you. Has everyone read *Five Dysfunctions*? I was going to say that a copy should be on every leader's bookshelf, but let me change that to every leader's desk. It's that important. Lencioni imagines a pyramid with inattention to results at the pinnacle. Just underneath this is avoidance of accountability—which incidentally is apparently the number one problem teams will point to when asked which of the five dysfunctions is their weakest point. These two are supported by a lack of commitment and then fear of conflict. But the foundation of this pyramid of dysfunction is a lack of trust. Unless you build trust, you can never get to the robust discussions needed around diverse perspectives and the commitment that comes with that, let alone accountability and attention to results.

"We tend to focus on helping our teams trust us, but did you know that equally important to your teams' trust in you is your trust in them? People can tell when we trust them… and when we don't, they are less likely to be engaged or creative or to take positive risks. One global research study

---

[1] Steven R. Covey, *The Speed of Trust: The One Thing that Changes Everything*, Free Press, 2008.

[2] Patrick Lencioni, *The Five Dysfunctions of a Team,* Jossey-Bass, 2002.

recently showed that only thirty-two percent of leaders trust their senior leaders to do the right things. That is less than one in three! Fortunately, trust in immediate supervisors was a bit higher but still only at forty-six percent.[3] Then there is trust in our teammates and trust in ourselves!"

Ellen said, "I have been reading about adaptive teams and how important it is to build trust within the team's adaptive ability. Trust that we might not know what to do, but we have the right people on the team to figure it out. It's called adaptive confidence—the belief overall that we have the right people around the table to figure it out when the time comes. Could you speak to that a bit?"

"Yes, this is important, especially as we are on the cusp of another major shift in leadership complexity. And I think part of that shift will include movement from well-managed organizations to well-led networks where adaptive teams and adaptive confidence will be even more important. Dr. Gary Klein has done some interesting work here.[4] He says that in times of uncertainty, we need adaptive teams. He also says that while every team can learn to be adaptive, most won't. That is sobering, so I am going to let that sink in for a moment."

He paused and looked around the room, then went on. "Kline defines adaptive teams as those able to make the necessary modifications to meet new challenges. Anyone feel like they are experiencing new challenges these days? This definition makes it sound easy, but, in fact, we need to be both adaptive in our processes and priorities as well as adaptive in the way we think and interact. This requires a great deal of self-awareness, teachability, curiosity, and reduced ego, not to mention the ability to look at yourself and your system critically. No wonder so few teams are skilled at this. In my opinion, the most important factor is framing—the way we see ourselves and our role, the way we frame the world, and the way we frame the problems we encounter along the way. Adaptive teams consistently examine their own frames and monitor the forces and trends that are emerging within and outside their organization. They have a clear mandate but are not tied

---

3 Global Leadership Forecast, 2023,11. Development Dimensions International Inc. (www.ddiworld.com)

4 https://www.semanticscholar.org/paper/Adaptive-Teams-Klein-Pierce/639834c3172ba79c-94c25ef9afd13dd4bbfef509

to too many rules. They manage polarities like diverse perspectives—one voice. Adaptability and alignment. You can see how important high trust is to this kind of work. And how servant-like a leader must be to navigate this complexity humbly and well and attract high-quality people around important issues when they don't have to be there.

"Burns, who you may recall was a founder of the transformational leadership movement, often said, 'Leadership is when people follow you when they don't have to.' People didn't have to follow Jesus. And Jesus made no attempt to self-promote. He redefined greatness—read Mat. 20:26—and His followers have been seeking to walk in His footsteps of servant leadership ever since."

6.7 EMPOWERMENT

"Empowering those around you to be heard and valued makes the difference between a leader who simply instructs and one who inspires."
Adena Friedman

"Now we can finally talk meaningfully about empowerment. The first thing to note is that it must match readiness and need. I am talking about empowerment to match their growth. To match their level of readiness. When I was the President of an academic institution, we had three-hundred and fifty staff and our structure had become unwieldy. The Board and I knew that we needed to restructure. The book that gave me the most helpful guidance on how to do this was Ken Blanchard's *3 Keys to Empowerment*.[5]

---

5 Ken Blanchard, John Carlos & Alan Randolph, *The 3 Keys to Empowerment: Release the Power Within People for Astonishing Results.* Berrett-Koehler Publishers, 1999.

We adapted these keys to our setting like this," he went to the board and wrote:

- **CREATING AUTONOMY AND ALIGNMENT THROUGH SHARED INFORMATION AND EMPOWERING BOUNDARIES.**

- **PROMOTING INDIVIDUAL DEVELOPMENT THROUGH PERSONALIZED GROWTH PLANS.**

- **DEVELOPING ALIGNED AND INTERLINKING TEAMS.**

"Take some time at your tables to discuss how these three principles interact in your organization. Is there one that needs some more of your time and attention?"

Chairs were dragged into cluster groups, and the room was soon filled with conversation. It took some time for Dr. Magnus to get our attention, even after our time was up.

He began again, "In traditional hierarchies, responsibility and authority reside at the top—burning those people out and under-motivating and undervaluing the people who could share the load. And while it may sound counterintuitive that boundaries can empower, the right kind of boundaries do exactly that—like a sandbox that expands with our capacity and defines the area we can play within without constantly having to seek approvals or permissions. Let me tell you where I learned that.

"I was the Chair of the Board of a national ministry for several years. We changed the senior leader three times during my tenure. Those individuals had significant differences in their experience and leadership styles. We should have expanded and contracted the boundaries for their sake, to protect them and allow them to grow into the role. I wish I had known then what I know now. We may think you are empowering someone by letting them set their own boundaries, but in the end, we are not. Mistakes were made. People got hurt. There was a mismatch of expectations, and that inevitably leads to confusion and broken trust. This is another polarity I would like you to really wrestle with. How can we build personal and team autonomy and excellence with appropriate boundaries and developmental plans? There has to be both. You can't say, 'You can have more responsibility or authority once you grow,' if you aren't clear on the areas that need growth and build in the enablement process that is needed. Okay, enough said. I realize I get animated when talking about this. I have just seen so many people hurt and so many important missions undermined because of our inability to navigate this wisely."

6.8 ENCIRCLEMENT

"This is one I have been reflecting on recently. I think of it as providing an embrace of safety, inclusiveness, equitability, and accountability. It takes us back to God's modelling as outlined in John 14-17 and the beauty of healthy communities of learning and care.

"Here is some interesting research on that. 'Several recent peer-reviewed studies using simulation and past market performance support the theory that businesses with good employee well-being programs significantly outperform companies listed on the S&P 500 index. For example, portfolios composed of companies that scored highly in the Corporate Health Achievement Awards, which recognize North American companies, appreciated by 204% to 333% compared to the S&P 500 index appreciation of 105%.'[6]

"'In another study, forty-five companies that received high scores on a health and wellness assessment appreciated by 235%, compared to the S&P 500 Index appreciation of 159% over a six-year simulation period.'[7] Ensuring the overall well-being of our teams is incredibly important. Yet one global study revealed that 72% of leaders are experiencing signs of burnout and only 15% feel prepared to prevent employee burnout."[8]

---

[6] Fabius R, Loeppke RR, Hohn T, et al., "Tracking the Market Performance of Companies That Integrate a Culture of Health and Safety," J Occup Environ Med. 2016.

[7] Grossmeier J, Fabius R, Flynn JP, et al., "Linking Workplace Health Promotion Best Practices and Organizational Financial Performance," J Occup Environ Med, 2016.

[8] "Global Leadership Forecast," 2023, 11. Development Dimensions International Inc. (www.ddiworld.com)

Many heads nodded in agreement, but one person asked, "Where does that end, though? I work in a Christian non-profit, as you know. One of our biggest challenges is meeting the ever-increasing expectations of our staff with our limited resources. We aren't their local church or small group, yet it seems like, increasingly, people look to us for their spiritual development and pastoral care. Not to mention their physical and relational well-being. This sounds harsh, I know, but I am finding it challenging to balance all of that with our greater mission. Am I the only one?"

Others spoke up in agreement.

Adam asked, "Is everyone familiar with the Service Profit Chain?[9] No? Well, the gist of it is that organizations with higher employee satisfaction scores and loyalty are more likely to have higher customer satisfaction scores and loyalty. And therefore, higher profits. One thing that we have found really helpful in our organization is a deep dive into our scores to find out what levers affect our employee satisfaction. It is not always the things you think people will want that make the biggest difference."

"What do you mean by a deep dive? How did you find out what was most likely to make people feel cared for?" Dr. Magnus prodded.

"Well, we looked at the data, but to be honest, we learned the most by asking questions and listening carefully. Of course, you can't please everyone or meet everyone's expectations, but we were surprised that it was often the little things that made the most difference. Like providing some flexibility in work schedules for caregivers, ensuring there were healthy snacks available at meetings, and encouraging our supervisors to write personal notes to their team around special occasions."

I spoke up, "We experimented with something similar. We coached our supervisors to ask one simple question of each of their direct reports at the beginning of each quarter. The question was, 'What one thing can I reasonably do that would improve the workplace for you?' We were amazed at the answers and at the goodwill this simple act generated. At first, there was some skepticism, but we kept reinforcing to the supervisors how important it was to follow through on what they had committed to. As teams began to experience this consistency and came to expect the question each quarter, their requests became more and more insightful—both to them and to the

---

9 James, L. Heskett, W. Earl Sasser, Jr. & Leonard A. Schlesinger, *The Service Profit Chain: How leading Companies Link Profit and growth to Loyalty, Satisfaction and Value.* Free Press, 1997.

team. Some people began to plot together and come up with group requests. This resulted in us bringing puppies in for break time during tax season one year. That may seem over the top, but it relieved people's stress, cost next to nothing, and gave the people who came to play with the pups a boost of energy and, to our surprise, a more positive attitude toward our clients. I remember one person asked if she could move her desk closer to the window to get more natural light. That was an easy solve. Other times people asked for things that would benefit others—like asking if we could do a fundraiser for a team member who was going through a rough time. The point is that they chose what would be most helpful, and if we were reasonably able to accommodate the requests, we did them."

"I love it!"

"I'm going to try that."

Dr. Magnus waited until we were done, smiling encouragement at the way the conversation unfolded, then wrote the next word on the board.

6.9 EMBODIMENT

"This is a very important one. Modelling. Consistently showing how. John's Gospel shows us how Jesus embodied holistic leadership. Of course, I am not suggesting we can imitate Him perfectly. We're only human. However, we are being filled with the power of the Holy Spirit. I think we sometimes forget just how much God wants to move in and through His people. We forget that we truly are His hands and feet in our organizations. John Maxwell,[10] says that mentoring begins with modelling. People are influenced by what they observe, so modelling can be a powerful influence. However, according to Maxwell, true influence begins with the next step, motivating. This type of influence builds an emotional connection and builds their confidence. The next level or step is mentoring—where we pour ourselves into someone to help them reach their potential. Maxwell says the highest level of influence is multiplying—intentionally developing people who are developing others

---

10 John Maxwell and Jim Dornan, *Becoming a Person of Influence: How to Positively Impact the Lives of Others,* 1997.

in an organic but intentional ripple-out and trickle-down way. It all starts with modelling. And modelling leads to people wanting to be mentored and us mentoring them towards multiplication."

———

One of my greatest joys has been the opportunity to pour into high-calibre leaders. I could mention several, but let me highlight two. The greatest joy of mentoring Wayne was when he began to pour into Adam. When you begin to see this kind of generational transfer, you know that not only have you done a good job of choosing who to pour into, but they have risen to the challenge. Imagine the ripple effect of pouring into even a handful of people over your lifetime as they pour into others, who pour into others...

This transfer doesn't always happen. It takes a certain selflessness and generosity of spirit to give time to someone for their benefit. However, if even one of the people you invest in invests in someone else that is massive. We never know how God wants to use the people He sets in front of us. He chooses unlikely people. That is why I have tried to be careful not to rule people out. However, I do have two criteria. They must be teachable—they must want to learn and come prepared to do the hard work of personal change. And they must be honest to me and to themselves.

Another friend, Dwayne, would say that I mentored him for 17 years, yet at some point along the way, it became more of a peer mentoring relationship. With me learning as much from him as he from me, I am sure. However, one of my favourite methods of mentoring and coaching is in small groups. There is something about the accountability and diversity of insights of a group that magnifies the mentoring process exponentially. If you are not part of such a group, I cannot suggest strongly enough that you find one. One-on-one mentoring relationships and peer coaching groups have both been invaluable to my journey and to so many of the leaders I most respect.

———

Dr. Magnus took a deep breath and said, "My final word when it comes to thinking about the people doesn't start with an 'E.' It's the word alignment. We are back to the polarity of developing the individual and building momentum together. One of my favourite ways to think about this is interlinking teams. We could draw the difference between teams and interlinking teams like this."

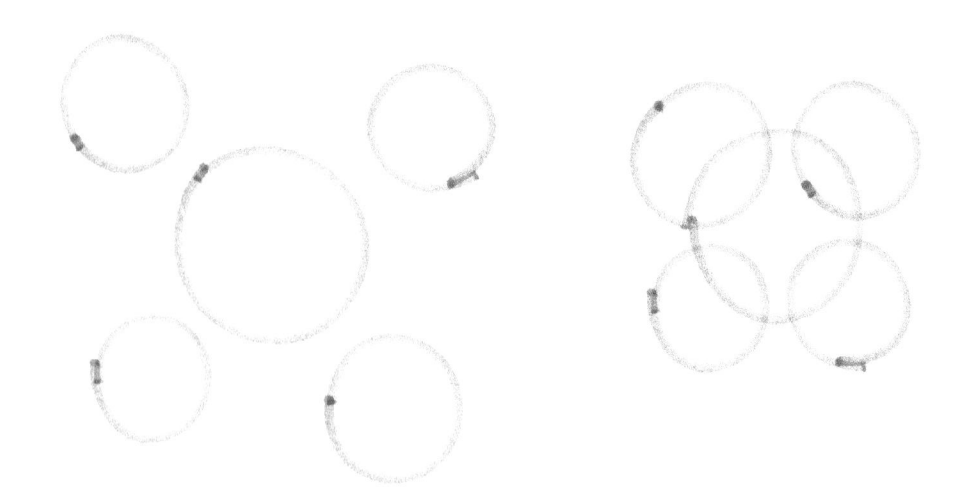

Dr. Magnus put down the marker and continued, "I prefer to lead from the centre. Maybe this is the place I am most used to from being the middle child. It is also the place—for pragmatic, philosophical, and theological reasons—that I think a Christian leader should seek to move to. In your opinion, where is alignment most needed in organizations?"

"Around vision and values, organizational culture."

"With standardized processes."

"I am not sure how to word this, but there should be equal opportunities for all employees to be well-led. Since a supervisor plays such a critical role in an employee's day-to-day experience and the trajectory of their careers, I feel strongly that there should be accountability and equity for all staff."

"In communication."

Dr. Magnus waited until everyone was finished, then said, "Great insights. I want to go back to the story I was telling you earlier. We organized the staff into teams to take the pressure off individuals who were carrying way too much responsibility. Then we had to find ways to keep those teams connected, communicating, and collaborating. That can be harder than it sounds. It takes longer to transition mindsets than to draw a new org. chart, but we kept coming back to the *3 Keys,* and they were profoundly helpful. And soon, our teams were becoming highly skilled and self-managing. Not everyone liked this new way of working, but many did. Motivation researcher Edward Lawler's work is interesting here. He found that when people are given additional control and responsibility, their companies achieve greater results. The work becomes its own intrinsic reward. This is increasingly true in our world today, in my opinion.

Now, of course, that can swing too far as well. If you have self-managing teams that become silos, that is a problem. If teams have too much or too little autonomy, they become unhealthy. If you overpower teams, you can underpower leadership—and vice versa. The art is to find and flex with the right balance."

Jay put up his hand, "As you know, Dr. Magnus, we have been collaborating on an initiative for people in multivocational ministry. The Evangelical Fellowship of Canada's 'Significant Church' research, that I alluded to earlier, found that thirty-two per cent of survey respondents' families had another income stream besides the salary they drew from their congregations.[11]

"That creates its own complexities for teams when you have not only multiple teams within an organization but people working on teams in multiple organizations. And, of course, this isn't the case just in churches. I read recently that fifty-eight percent of Gen Z Canadians are interested in gig work because of the flexibility it offers, and sixty-nine percent of Gen Z and Millennials are seriously considering a side project or business to earn extra money.[12] Can you comment on how this emerging trend impacts teams, and how teams can or should think differently in light of this?"

Dr. Magnus responded, "That is such a great question. When we have multiple teams in an organization, or when individuals are serving on different teams in different organizations the need for clarity grows exponentially. One area where this is especially true is with accountability—who is responsible for what, when, why, with whom, with what resources and within what parameters. A related area, of course, is communication. As a general rule, double or triple the amount of communication you think is necessary but find creative ways to ensure this communication is effective. None of us need more emails or ineffective meetings. Patrick Lencioni[13] teaches that we should communicate seven times in seven ways to ensure we have communicated well. And thirdly, another area worthy of serious

---

11 Rick Hiemstra and Lindsay Callaway, Faith Today Publications, 2023. "Significant Church: Understanding the Value of the Small Church in Canada," https://www.evangelical-fellowship.ca/SC, 11.

12 Stephen Harrington, "The Gig Economy is Here to Stay," Deloitte, https://www2.deloitte.com/ca/en/pages/consulting/articles/the-gig-economy-is-here-to-stay.html

13 Patrick Lencioni, *The Advantage: Why Organizational Health Trumps Everything Else in Business,* John Wiley and Sons, 2012

consideration is how to scale up or scale down as needed. Entrepreneurial enterprises tend to be nimbler, but increasingly organizations are needing to be more flexible and responsive to both workforce and client or congregant realities. The challenge for organizations is how to build community and belonging when so much is flexing and people are pulled in so many directions.

"That brings us full circle back to John 14-17 and especially Jesus' prayer for unity in chapter 17. We can have organizational alignment without unity. We can have order that is coercive or restrictive and that does not lead to unity. When I am talking about alignment, I am asking us to reflect on what it means to be the people of God, whether you work in a secular organization or a church or a mission—perhaps especially if you work in a secular organization. Our behaviour matters. We have stopped where a watching world is most ready to look. Our actions. Our unity. How was the early church known? By their loving actions toward the poor and the way they treated each other. The church at Antioch understood this in a way the church in Jerusalem had to learn the hard way. Acts 15 settled this dispute about inclusion in theory, but it took time for God's inclusiveness to be truly understood by the faithful then. And, if we are honest, the same is true for the faithful now.

"Returning to our model again, we see that centered leaders influence people. They ensure that engaging, empowering, and transforming processes are available. There is so much good stuff in this next segment. I am looking forward to the light you will bring as we unpack it together."

Journaling exercise: In your leadership context, who is within your circle of influence? How could you maximize your positive influence in and through their lives? What is the gap between your current level of influence and your ideal? What could you do to narrow that gap?

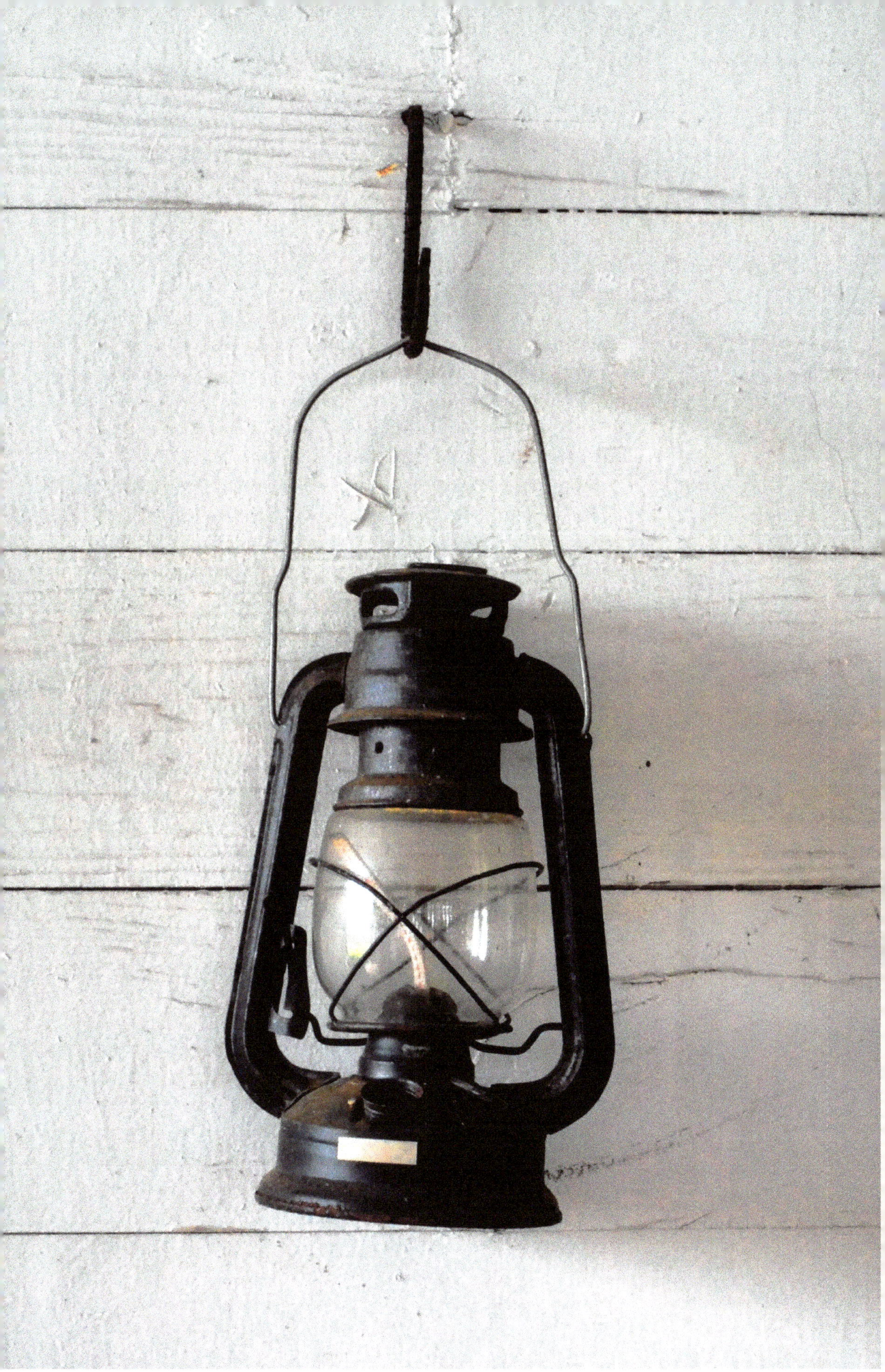

7. PROCESSES

Regulations were strict when I was in college. And strict regulations inevitably lead to regulation keepers who were chosen and required to enforce every rule. Anyone who returned to campus late would receive demerits. One of our classmates was assigned to Night Watch Duty. He had limited choice in this role, but it also felt like he enjoyed the opportunity of enforcement. This made it even more tempting to play some tricks on this fellow student.

In those days, young men and women were only allowed one date away from campus per semester. This classmate had asked my roommate if he could borrow his rather seasoned and well-used vehicle. My roommate agreed, and together we decided that our Night Watch classmate needed to experience what we planned.

Ironically, the reason we knew that our plan would work was that I had gained experience riding in the trunk of this same car the previous weekend. I had wanted to accompany my roommate as he took a carload of young women to a special church movie night. However, men and women were not allowed to be in Moose Jaw on the same weekend. As I had to 'help' my roommate, I did it from the trunk of his car. When we returned, we were marginally late, and this very same Night Watchman stepped out of a dormitory unexpectedly as my roommate pounded on the trunk and called me by my nickname, Pauly Wog, saying, "Get out." "Who are you talking to?" the Night Watchman asked. My roommate replied, "I am just beating on this old jalopy because it doesn't work as well as it should."

As a consequence, on the very next weekend, when this classmate Night Watchman and his fine girlfriend were going to use my roommate's car, we hatched our plan. My roommate let me into the trunk to accompany this couple and chaperone them in secret. I was enjoying the ride but knew I should let them know I was there, so I lifted the seat out of the way, reached in from the trunk and tapped our friendly classmate Night Watchman on the shoulder. I was careful to tell him he had better watch the road because he spun and looked back, and I was convinced he would take us all into the ditch. His dear girlfriend, who had been sitting next to him, swiftly slid across the seat to the door while I smiled and told them we thought they needed a chaperone.

When it appeared that they were feeling uncomfortable about spending the evening with me, I let them know that they could drop me off, as my roommate was coming in another car to pick me up. We told him that we had planned this as a prank when we knew he didn't have the opportunity to give us a demerit point. When we stopped, I wished them a very nice evening together and encouraged her to slide back to where she was sitting before.

Suffice it to say if we build our regulations and rules too tightly, we should expect people to find a way around the boundary. I think my roommate and I were attempting to offer a "gift in kind," and we are both pleased that the couple took it so well and ended up as husband and wife.

There is an important place for policies and procedures, but not for the kind that elicits frustration or workarounds. Policies and processes that are designed to protect can restrict creativity, engagement, uniqueness and potential if not carefully managed.

———

The coffee was on as we came into the room, and Dr. Magnus was eager to get started again. As soon as we were seated, he said, "In the last several years, there has been an increasing understanding of the need to ensure processes are highly engaging, empowering and multiplying. Why are the right processes so important? They enable us to come together and go together more seamlessly," he paused and pointed to the model on the board, "toward a purpose that really matters."

I sat up straighter in my chair as Dr. Magnus moved again to the whiteboard. This was another area where I knew I needed help.

"So, let's look at the kind of progressive, transforming, multiplying processes that enable:

1. The design and delivery of great and godly leadership
2. Leaders and teams to be strategic learners
3. The wise navigation of both problem-solving and polarity management
4. Coaching of self, individuals, teams, and teams of teams
5. Caring candour
6. Co-creation
7. Planning wisely
8. Measuring and celebrating forward movement

9. Managing change well
10. Handling power and conflict well
11. Fluency in system design, development, and re-design
12. Governance
13. Self-awareness and self-leadership toward God-glorifying resilience
14. Personal mastery and high-performing teams

"I could go on and on, but I think that gives us an idea of just how important good processes are. When we talk about people, the key word is 'together.'" He took one step across the room to punctuate the following comments.

"We can accomplish so much more together. It can be so much more enjoyable when we work well together. To follow in the footsteps of the Trinity's style of leading and relating means to be in step with each other.

"To move toward our higher purpose requires alignment. We know this at one level, but what we haven't done well is build a system to support this. How do we create genuine co-envisioning, co-creation, co-owning, co-delivering, and co-measuring in our shared pursuit of a compelling higher purpose? That is a really important question, with many layers."

"Another homework assignment?" someone joked.

"Now that you mention it, that is a great idea!"

"I'm excited about that exercise. In fact, I can already envision how that might change the way I have been thinking about a few things. Exploring that with our team could build significant synergy."

Dr. Magnus beamed, "Excellent. Synergy is an important word in leadership literature these days. I am interested in how to create and measure that synergy in real time in real organizations. Angie, as an executive leader, what have you discovered about how best to bring functional alignment in organizations?"

Angie smiled and said, "That is such a great question Dr. Magnus, and not an easy one to answer. The two parts of your question are important, how to create synergy and then how to measure it in real-time. I think the creating part is easier because of all we have learned about co-creating with our teams. If we truly create a clear process that engages the whole organization from the front line to the board, and we ensure that everyone understands how decisions will be made, then it is possible to realize synergy around a co-created plan.

"The challenge lies in the measuring, especially in missional organizations where financial reports are not the dominant indicator of impact. It is also challenging because sustaining momentum and synergy around the plan requires constant attention and good processes, something that many of us don't like to create or adhere to. I'm not sure I know the answer to this part yet, but I think it lies, in part, in engaging others in the design of the metrics that matter and how this information will be captured, reported, and even interpreted. The whole team needs to understand and embrace the importance of this and its connectedness to the success of the plan that we created together in the first place.

"Needless to say, effective, consistent, and bi-directional communication is the key to creating and measuring synergy."

"Thank you, Angie, that is really helpful." Then turning to the rest of the class, Dr. Magnus said, "I am sure some of you will want to talk further to Angie later, but for now, let's use my Co's as a frame to hang our learning on."

Finding a clear spot on the board, he wrote:

CO-ENVISIONING
CO-MMUNICATION
CO-LEARNING
CO-CREATION
CO-OWNING
CO-DELIVERING
CO-MEASURING
CO-CHANGING

"Okay, so the communication is stretching the pattern, I admit, but after all these years of preaching, I couldn't help myself. Before we jump into them, I want to make a few general comments. This may seem self-evident, but why are well-designed processes important?"

Joshua answered right away, "Without purpose, the people flounder. Without process, it is all just a dream."

"Well stated. Processes are designed to help us move to a particular end. A purpose worth dedicating our time to. Together. Here is the important thing to remember: when they stop doing that, it is time to change them!"

Opening his hands to indicate this was not a rhetorical question, Dr. Magnus asked, "How do leaders know when it is time to change processes?"

"When it is obvious that they aren't working anymore?" someone tentatively asked.

"Yes, and how do we know when they aren't working?"

"When people start working below the line."

"Yes, exactly. When you see the system struggling and/or people getting frustrated and bogged down, that is often a signal for you to take a hard look at the processes you have in place. Can anyone think of a time when people on their team were pointing fingers at each other, and it turned out to be a process problem?"

"After our third pastor in a row left within a year of arriving, we clued into the fact that maybe it wasn't the people but something bigger."

"When several of our teams were encountering the same roadblocks. They were pointing fingers at each other, but we soon realized it was a process problem that was causing the siloing, not the other way around."

"We had huge communication break-downs that we were blaming on key players. It turned out that the systems and structures we had built were no longer working."

Dr. Magnus acknowledged each answer and then said, "At your table, create a list of core processes that every organization must build to create greater synergy."

Sometime later, after each group had presented their findings, we had a compiled list on the board that included:

Recruitment, hiring, orientation, and training
Communication
Strategic Learning and Thinking
Decision making and Polarity Management
Problem-Solving
Planning and Appreciative Inquiry
Team Building and Personal Development
Health and Safety and Risk Management
Governance and Compliance
Assessment—both lead and lag measures
Finance
Marketing…

Dr. Magnus examined the list to see if any important ones were missing, finding none, he continued. "Effective processes should help people to be more agile—not less. They are like the edges of a river or the sides of a sandbox. They contain and give direction while still providing space to play. Are there other times when processes might need to be updated?"

"When there are technological advances."

"When the organization grows or shrinks."

"Sometimes, when there is a change of leadership."

"A change in any one of the four parts of the model," some added exuberantly.

"Move to the head of the class! That is thinking holistically. Do you see? A change or a challenge in any of the four lenses of our mind map is a reminder to look at the whole. To address whatever needs tending in each area. A technological or cultural shift, a significant change in sales or the size of our workforce, a change in leadership or strategy. All of these should serve as flags alerting us to pay attention to every part of the model. Our leadership. Our people. Our processes. Our purpose."

Take a moment and reflect. Is there anything happening inside your organization, or any forces from outside your organization that are impacting you, that suggest it is time for a closer look at your processes?

He waited while we reflected, then began again. "Another thing I wanted to mention about engaging processes before I give you some time to think about this. Processes are best developed experimentally and refined as needed. However, it is important that processes are uniquely interwoven, which means that sometimes changing one will have a domino effect on others. We must look at this systemically.

"And the last thing I want to mention is that, for processes to be helpful, people must be both empowered and enabled to use them well. Okay, now, going back to the list of processes that we generated. I am going to assign one per small group, and I would like you to discuss what would need to be in place for that process to be engaging, empowering and have a multiplier effect. The alternative is a process that is counterproductive and polarizing. And secondly, please discuss what the upstream and downstream implications of this might be. By that, I mean what domino effect—intended or unintended—might it have on other processes and departments in the organization.

Any questions?" He paused and looked around. Then with a twinkle in his eye added, "Take your time and map this out. This will be good practice for the homework you will do when you apply this to your own context."

After a lengthy discussion and a short break, we gathered back to share our insights. Tara said, "Our small group discussed the challenge of strategic thinking and planning in a VUCA[1] world. That is a very real tension for us in our context."

"Yes, good insight. How to stay focused on the big picture when the day-to-day feels so urgent. How to look and plan ahead when there is so much uncertainty. That leads us beautifully into the first of the Co's I want us to think about."

> *"By failing to prepare, you are preparing to fail."*
> Benjamin Franklin

7.1 CO-ENVISIONING

> *"I'm no longer accepting the things I cannot change.
> I am changing the things I cannot accept."*
> Angela Davis

Dr. Magnus leaned on a stool. "We could cluster Appreciative Inquiry, Strategic Thinking, Learning and Planning, and Systems Thinking as processes that enable us to co-envision."

STRATEGIC THINKING

"You may recall I mentioned earlier that Dorie Clark addresses the polarity you raised Tara in her book, *The Long Game*.[2] She says that '97% of leaders identify strategic thinking as key to their success, yet 96% say they do not have time to do so.' Those are staggering statistics. Even if a

---

[1] VUCA stands for Volatile, Uncertain, Complex and Ambiguous

[2] Dorie Clark, *The Long Game: How to be a Long Term Thinker in a Short Term World*, Harvard Business Review Press, 2021.

percentage of that is true in your organization, that should alert us to the importance of carving out space, which of course, is what this course is all about, creating space for you to think! There are so many good books out there for this. For example, in *Seeing Around Corners*,[3] Columbia University professor Rita McGrath claims that with the right processes, it's possible to predict what is coming."

APPRECIATIVE INQUIRY

"In these times of uncertainty, when people are unhappy with what is but don't necessarily know how to move to what is better, leaders need to step in rather than out. One of the most helpful processes I have found for this is Appreciative Inquiry. I was working with a church one time that had dropped drastically in numbers. Hardly anyone came Sunday mornings, but when we announced an optional gathering where we would facilitate a collaborative listening, learning, and discovery process, we had hundreds of people show up. We had to bring out extra tables and chairs. This is so important because the first and most important piece when it comes to change is identifying what needs to change! And that can be a lot harder than it sounds. And secondly, why it must be changed.

"Then, of course, how to measure what moves us towards that desired change. I always mix people up at the tables so they get the chance to hear from people very different from themselves. That is very important. And, of course, we want to be sure these times are saturated with prayer—if we are working in a setting where that is permitted—and with the kind of questions that will enable us to treat each other with relentless respect as people made in the image of God. These times inevitably become sacred as we reflect not only on what we see but what we sense God may be seeing or dreaming of for us. It's about who God is calling us to be and what He is inviting us to do. You may recall when we were talking about Nehemiah, I mentioned that one of the tools that I have developed over the years is something called the Wall of Wonder. I draw it like this," he said, sketching a model on the whiteboard.

---

3 Rita McGrath, *Seeing Around Corners: How to Spot Inflection Points in Business Before They Happen.* Harper Business, 2019.

WONDERFUL

WONDERING IF

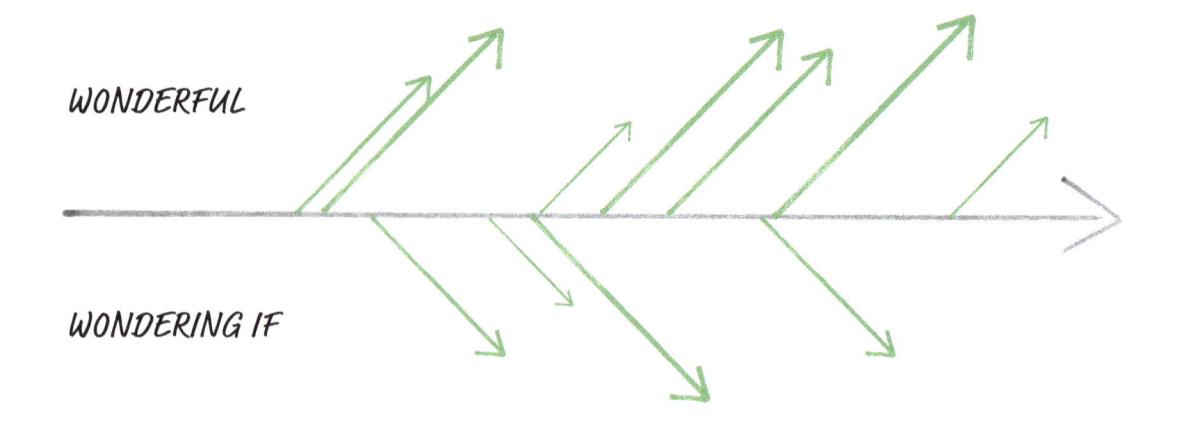

"We begin by identifying a timeline. This could be by decade for a well-established organization, or it might be by season or even by week if that is more helpful for the context. Then we fill in the top half of the wall with things that we are amazed at. Gifts that God has given, things that are wonderful about what happened or what was accomplished or built. The arrows that we create can be different colors, or I prefer to use different lengths to demonstrate the big things and little things that all contributed and that we want to celebrate.

"Only then do we reflect on our 'wondering ifs,' which we record on the bottom half of the board in response to what is above. These could be questions raised or alternative ways of thinking or acting. They could also be dreams for moving forward. We look for the commonality between what is above the line and what is below the line and discuss what these patterns suggest to us. We also look for chronological patterns, for example 'during times of leadership transition we tend to see this happen,' or 'during times of growth we seem to forget to focus on this.' Well facilitated, this minimizes conflict and builds clarity about how we got where we are, what we can build on and what adjustments we want to make. Here is a simple rule to remember… when tackling something big, go narrow. When there is increased possibility of confusion or conflict focus on a limited number of specifics. That principle has helped me in more situations than I care to remember."

*"A wise woman wishes to be no one's enemy. A wise woman
refuses to be anyone's victim."*
Maya Angelou

"I love the idea of building a wall together, each of us doing our part and building on the work of those who have gone before. And I love that this is not a wall that is stagnant in time or space. Notice that we have drawn an arrow that helps us to keep moving forward, building toward a higher purpose and with a renewed sense of how far we have come. Together. We are building together!

"While we are talking about this, I would like to make one comment about Problem Statements. There is a time for carefully crafted Problem Statements. A problem well stated is a problem half solved, as they say. However, I also find that reframing problems as Opportunity Statements, or even Closing the Gap Statements, as in 'what would it take to close the gap between where we are and where we want to be?' can sometimes unleash different kinds of fruitful conversations with forward energy.

"Graham, you have mastered using Appreciative Inquiry to enable groups of people to move toward purpose and alignment. Can you tell us about some of your most important insights from this work?"

Graham laughed and said, "Well, first of all, I wouldn't say I've 'mastered' this. I have become a certified AI facilitator and have worked with various groups such as churches, staff teams and boards. I find that the AI process and principles focus on discovering and building on strengths that are currently part of a system. Usually, people focus on what is not working, and while that should not be ignored, it doesn't actually tell us anything about how to address the issue. While AI is strengths-focused, the process naturally leads the group toward innovating and then overcoming weaknesses. Focusing on strengths can often provide us with the clarity and momentum to help overcome weaknesses.

"AI also addresses whole system change that requires a change in thinking and behaviour. Rather than the leader introducing and implementing change, the AI process invites everyone in the system to co-create, co-own, and co-deliver change. Once someone has had the opportunity to shape change, they are much more likely to embrace it.

"The AI process unifies people in a way that I have never seen in classic strategic planning or change management. When people have an opportunity to walk through the process together, they tend to unify around the plan. I think this occurs because their voice has been heard, and the process leads the group toward a collective decision. It seems that people are willing to lay down their ideas if stronger ideas emerge and the group, through the process, decides to embrace these.

"As a leader, I find AI remarkably helpful in the change process. Once the group has had the opportunity to co-shape a vision, the leader no longer has to sell them on the vision. A leader can now act as a steward of the vision that the group has developed. Rather than having to sell and motivate, the leader can remind, share, communicate, and implement without the pressure of having to convince people or win them over. Really, AI takes a lot of the pressure out of leading change."

Personalize it: In what ways might an Appreciative Inquiry or community discernment process be helpful for your organization or church?

Eric had been listening carefully. "Lesslie Newbigin describes a church congregation as a hermeneutic of the Gospel—the Gospel contextualized in and through community.[4] Is community discernment another process that could be helpful here?"

"Yes, good. Tell us more."

Eric continued, "I just find that too many leaders that I have encountered view spirituality, and discernment about vision, as an almost exclusively personal pursuit. They might not say that, or even think they believe that, but their actions demonstrate it."

Ellen agreed, "This is where the issue of power and power plays can be so dangerous, isn't it? I have seen leaders who assume they have more insight into God's will because of their position. However, I have also seen the divisiveness that can occur when people who have perhaps not matured into their gifting yet, claim to hear from God—perhaps with good intentions, but I also think, sometimes to manipulate—and use their gift inappropriately to try to influence leaders or whole faith communities. No wonder God stresses humility so much throughout the scriptures, and employees across all sectors rate humility and integrity as such important attributes for leaders."

---

[4] See for example, Lesslie Newbigin, *The Gospel in a Pluralist Society.* Eerdmans, 1989.

Several people began to speak at once, "Imagine that very scenario and the person who purported to hear from God also happens to be the biggest financial contributor and ties their giving for the upcoming year to us listening to what they are saying," one person said as others jumped in with similar stories about situations in churches and organizations they had been connected to.

After a few moments, Dr. Magnus raised his hand and responded, "I have had my own share of people coming to tell me what God said I should do. This is where wisdom and godly leadership comes in. Only God can help us navigate these challenging situations."

SYSTEMS THINKING

"The biggest problems facing our organizations, and arguably the biggest challenges facing the world—war, hunger, poverty, human trafficking, and environmental issues—are essentially system failures.

"Systems thinking is the discipline of stepping back from the day-to-day to look at how the various people and parts of our organization are interacting with each other and with the broader community. Think, for example, about the complexity and interconnectedness of the Amazon rainforest or the internet. They are ecosystems, and as such, affecting one piece in one part can create disequilibrium in the whole. They are also adaptive, meaning they respond to feedback loops and can learn and change. The same is true in an economic system, a town, a grocery store chain or a hospital or a church. Many organizations find it helpful to map out the system in which they function to identify trends and patterns and consider what levers they could pull that would lead to positive impact and what their inbuilt feedback systems are indicating. Peter Senge has done some great work in this area. I especially like his book *The Fifth Discipline*.[5]

"Bottom line: you can't have a healthy whole without healthy parts. And you can't have healthy parts without a healthy whole. So, we need to be working on the system and its parts at the same time. Some leaders prefer the macro. Others get bogged in the micro. You need both.

---

5 Peter Senge *The Fifth Discipline: The art and practice of the learning organization,* Currency, 2006.

"We spoke about crisis earlier. Sometimes we are creating our own crisis without meaning to, by doing the very things that worked in the past. John Kotter explains this so simply but brilliantly in *Our Iceberg is Melting*.[6] Have you seen this cute little book. It looks like a children's book which makes the insights it offers so disarming and powerful. The characters in the story are all penguins who have moved to an iceberg because of the abundance of fish in the area. Of course, as more penguins arrive the number of fish is depleted, which is to be expected, but they experience unexpected consequences as well. With so many penguins on the iceberg it begins to sink, making living conditions increasingly constricted and increasing conflict among the birds. It is so clever. There are several important insights given, but I want to focus on two. First, thinking at a systems level enables us to uncover unexpected contributing factors, find unconventional ways to track what is happening and find creative solutions. And secondly, sometimes doing the same thing we were doing before that led to success is the very thing that now contributes to our failure or stuck-ness. Here is another small homework piece for you," he finished with a sideways smile to show he realized it was anything but small.

If you were going to map your system with key people and pieces, interconnecting linkages and positive and negative feedback loops, what would it look like? What insights does this mapping exercise afford? Who else should you invite into this systems conversation?

I have often been asked to help groups who have become divided to move back together. In some cases, this was a full-time job that took months to accomplish. In others, we were able to gather for a series of weekends to re-envision and re-engage. In one of these contexts, it was one of the largest churches in their city. A series of unexpected and unfortunate circumstances had resulted in a church of well over a thousand dropping to about thirty. We did an appreciative process to help the church redirect their energy, focus, and engagement. In the morning service, there were thirty people. In the afternoon appreciative

---

6 John Kotter, *Our Iceberg is Melting: Changing and Succeeding Under Any Circumstances,* Portfolio, 2016.

inquiry session, there were typically around two hundred, and those numbers grew each time we gathered for the next step of the appreciative journey. First, with the board and then the whole group, we reviewed their shared history. Participants were randomly seated in groups of ten to mix people together.

We began with a Wall of Wonder, asking them to identify what was wonderful decade by decade. Then we asked not what was bad or unproductive but what their "wonder ifs" were that could have contributed in some way to the current challenges—again, decade by decade.

Each table identified what was wonderful, what they would love to see again, and what they are wondering could have been otherwise. This encouraged hope and revealed patterns that should be considered. Then we asked the table groups to discuss, "What do you really love about this church, and what do you long to see enhanced?" and then, "What do you long to see that isn't in place or that that you'd love to see more of?" This gave everyone a chance to contribute and minimized the voices of those who might take over. The energy in the room rose as tables were invited to speak.

Then we asked a series of "dream" questions that grew out of what people had shared. We said, "Dream about what would need to be in place for you to fully engage," then "What do you dream about leadership for the future?" and "What are your dreams for the church's role in the community?"

Normally to get to this point takes two to three two-hour sessions. The next step is to ask, "Having heard each other's dreams, what needs to be prioritized?" After they have come up with a short list, we ask each table to choose one top priority. Within about four sessions in every environment where we have gathered people, we have seen significant breakthroughs. This encourages people to keep going.

I am a believer in using processes like this to co-create a better future for teams and entire organizations. Co-envisioning often moves into co-designing.

To finish out my story, once we have co-prioritized, we have clarity and momentum for the Board to establish SMART Goals. They can be accomplished over time in pursuit of the priorities and the staff and volunteers to carry on co-designing the future. Now you have the community coming back together.

———

7.2 CO-MMUNICATION

Picking up his bible, Dr. Magnus said, "John 1:14 has been so helpful for me when it comes to Jesus' modelling of God's way for us to relate. He came full of grace and truth. We tend to think of these as two different things. In fact, we could draw them as a polarity with grace at one end and truth at the other."

GRACE ——————————————— TRUTH

"Many of us have been socialized to be nice. Not kind, but nice. To not rock the boat or say anything that others might disagree with or be hurt by. And we think this is peacekeeping, and we think it is unity, but it isn't. Not true unity anyway. Jesus suggests a third way. A way of grace *and* truth. We see this in his encounter with the woman at the well. Great compassion and great truth-telling.

"Kim Scott,[7] uses the language of challenge and care. Her model has forcefully driven home to me the fact that our most common and serious flaw—the worst thing that we can do—is offer grace without truth. She calls this ruinous empathy. It's ruinous because our false sense of compassion perpetuates a pattern of denial or ignores something that needs to be tended to. That reframes things, doesn't it?

"Ruinous because we are not telling them the truth, and as people of faith, we know that it is the truth that sets us free, but truth balanced by grace and compassion. If we think of the truth-grace continuum again, we can see how we may need to slide toward grace in some situations and toward clarity and truth in others. It is situational and depends on the circumstance, the person's teachability and track record, and our discernment.

"We could think of further progressive continuums of caring collaboration, caring conversations, caring confrontation, and caring accountability.

"Scott's work is so helpful when it comes to wise confrontation. She advises that we become more specific to help limit both lack of clarity and resistance. You can apply her principles to teams and organizations as well. For example, when working with senior leaders, I ask, 'What is the one thing

---

[7] Kim Scott, Ra*dical Candor: How to Get What You Want by Saying What you Mean,* St Martin's Press, 2019.

you need that individual or team to do in this situation?' If we can't become that specific, we tend to overwhelm people.

"Conflict is a result of broken expectations, differences of opinion, and misunderstandings. There can be power differences, rights differences, communication differences, cultural differences—and perhaps the most interesting—cumulative differences that build to create a disconnect. And these differences can be between individuals, teams, departments, institutions, and nations... no wonder Jesus prayed so fervently for us to have unity!

"I want to stress that unity is not the same thing as avoidance for the sake of 'keeping the peace.' This quickly develops into resentment or passive aggression. We can imagine conflict as a continuum that moves from productive conflict about ideas and perspectives—something every healthy team should actively seek out—to unproductive conflict. When conflict turns personal or polarizing, we are in trouble. This should signal to us that we need to do some work. And of course, we can think of conflict as being between individuals, but it can also take on structural and systemic components over time.

"This is where I find Appreciative Conversation to be so helpful. Processes that enable us to unearth what we hold in common, dream together about what could be, and then deliver on what we dreamt. In my experience, this kind of approach changes negatively charged situations into opportunities for both deeper understanding and forward movement. Leading those kinds of conversations takes practice. The skill of creating respectful settings and establishing shared outcomes, not to mention the ability to show up as a non-anxious presence in spaces where that may be difficult. While no word adequately describes this for the sake of our conversation here, I am calling that a centered leader.

"Jay W., you have done some really interesting work in this area. What are your reflections on how truth and grace interact in the life and teachings of Jesus, and how this informs the way His people speak to each other?"

"Sure. As you already mentioned, in John 1:14, we read, in my opinion, one of the most important verses in all of Scripture, 'And the Word became flesh and dwelt among us, and we have seen His glory, glory as of the only Son from the Father, full of grace and truth' (ESV). To say that Jesus was full of truth is to recognize that He is the mind behind the created order. He spoke into existence every salient detail that He envisioned throughout the cosmos (Jn 1:3; 1 Cor 8:6; Heb 1:2). To say He is full of grace is to recognize that His favour to a hostile creation is unmerited. The coming of our Lord into a world that would ultimately nail Him to a Roman cross reflects the clearest picture of the human heart toward a holy and just God—yet He came. As the whole is always the sum of its parts, as the eternal Word of God, every word that Jesus spoke was perfectly true (Jn 14:6). As a vessel of grace, every action that Jesus took was an example of unmerited favour toward sinners—even unto death. Christ's mission and life inform our communication with one another centrally in the same way. Truth orientates our minds to the mind of God—truth enables us to think like God and to seek truth with one another. Grace orientates our hearts and posture toward one another, for the good of the other, and the glory of God, even when we or our neighbor may not deserve it."

"So beautifully said, Jay. Thank you." Dr. Magnus said, smiling with delight. Then turning to us, he added:

"Identify a conversation that you know you need to have that will require both truth and grace, both challenge and compassion. Where would you plot it on the continuum, and how will you approach it to ensure you get the right mix of specificity and support? What might you need to script and practice to be more balanced when that conversation occurs?"

As the middle child of seven siblings, growing up, I often found myself mediating and organizing. This taught me to lead from the middle. I often felt that we were wasting time and energy trying to organize the lot of us to get work done around the farm, and my father graciously accepted the many suggestions I would bring about how to streamline processes and designate roles according to strengths. Leading from the middle is very different from leading from the top. Leadership from the middle is earned slowly—through earning trust, offering wise suggestions, and being willing to do what is needed to ensure everyone has both input and influence. An older brother doesn't listen to you because they have to. You have to earn that. The same thing is true with our teams. We have to earn their trust and respect.

Dr. Magnus gave us a few minutes to begin scripting a conversation. It was easy for most of us to think of a conversation we had been avoiding. People leaned forward in their chairs and began to write. I did a mental scan of our team at work, and an example soon became clear. The problem was that I was avoiding it for a reason. It could go very wrong. I was concerned my emotions might get the better of me, and I thought it likely that those of the other person might too. Everything that Dr. Magnus had described. Plotting it on the continuum gave some clarity on how to approach it more thoughtfully.

After some time, Dr. Magnus asked what was challenging about the exercise.

I spoke up right away, "Being specific enough in my own thinking to be able to know how to articulate that to someone else."

"Not allowing my relationship with the person to change the fact that there are issues that need to be addressed."

"Fear about my ability to stay 'on script' when it comes time to have this actual conversation."

Dr. Magnus acknowledged our insights and then said, "I have come to realize that one of the reasons people don't grow as much as they could is because we, their supervisors, don't gracefully—yet with clarity and specificity—tell them the truth. And the same is true the other way around. The more authority and power you have in an organization, the harder it will be for you to hear the truth. I would say that one of the hardest things for a leader to do is to get honest feedback about her or his performance. Why do you think that is?"

"We don't want to hurt people's feelings?"

"We are uncomfortable in that role."

"It doesn't feel safe."

Dr. Magnus took notes as we spoke. "All great answers, yes. It can be uncomfortable; we are concerned about hurting others, and/or it doesn't feel safe to tell the unvarnished truth. But think about the cost! I am deprived of the opportunity to grow. My team won't grow. Therefore, one of the most important things we can do is to create the kinds of safe cultures and supporting processes that not only allow for but almost require caring candour.

"Here is the thing, emotions always go up when we perceive important differences. This means we probably won't be at our best, and the other person won't be either. Sometimes we must bring in a third party, but there is a lot we can do too. The first conversation we need is with God. Asking for a clean heart and for wisdom. The second conversation is with ourselves. This takes us back to being centered, doesn't it? We are probably coming with all kinds of assumptions, exaggerations, and preconceptions. We need to remove these from the story we are telling ourselves. Then we set a reasonable goal. Scale back from 'all or nothing.' Our goals are often unrealistic and maybe even unfair. I have found it helpful to always have an alternative to best-case resolution, a reasonable alternative in mind in case the conversation doesn't take as straight a path as you were hoping. All of this will help you to relax a bit and show up in a healthier, less anxious way. Develop a plan but be aware the conversation may take unexpected turns. Then when you are talking to the person, you are more able to tend them well. Be fully present and listen to God's guiding voice and the insights they will bring that you had not considered.

"Pay attention to body language. Tell your unexaggerated story calmly with the absolutes and excess emotion taken out so it is a bit more tenable to someone who thinks differently than you do. Don't assume that they aren't ready to move. They may be more desirous of help than you realize. Speak tentatively. Give room for clarification and conversation. And take the long view. Keep in mind the big picture of what is needed. Then, when you ask them to tell their story, it should feel safer. Hopefully, theirs will change because you told yours differently. This approach forces us to slow things down rather than react and regret it. Adam, in your line of work, you must have several of these kinds of conversations. What insights do you have to add?"

Adam thought for a moment then answered, "I agree that the tentative piece is so important. I try to use I statements like 'here is what I observed' or 'here is what I think happened.' And I try to test my assumptions with questions like, 'how did it feel when I said…,' or 'is your perception of that different?' I always want to check my own perceptions because it helps me to remember that my perception is not necessarily reality, or at least not the whole reality."

"Yes, good. Perception is not reality, but it becomes that. For them and for us." He looked around the room and asked, "Helpful?"

"Very," we all said, thinking of recent situations where we wished we had applied even a fraction of this wisdom.

"I do have a question," one person offered.

"Good. Yes?"

"Brené Brown has moved away from the language of safe spaces and talks about brave spaces[8] instead. I like this as it helps us to realize that courage is needed, often by all parties involved."

"So glad you raised that, and again a perfect segue. Her language reminds us that we are not talking about 'nice spaces.' That truth and grace can and must co-exist and that this will take courage for all involved. My favourite way of thinking about this is creating spaces of relentless respect. Let's talk about that. What makes you feel respected?"

"Being heard."

"Being treated as a whole person."

"Having input."

"Yeah, being invited."

Dr. Magnus nodded with each addition and then asked, "When I use the term 'relentless respect,' what does that suggest to you?"

"Remembering that people are made in God's image."

"Yes," I agreed, "and building on that, I think of it as treating someone with dignity."

"The addition of the word 'relentless' suggests perseverance and commitment beyond what we might normally give to this value."

Dr. Magnus smiled. "I like that. Seeing the dignity in someone else regardless of the situation. There is dignity under the dust so to speak. Treating people with the dignity that humans deserve. What is the hardest part of relentless respect for you?"

"Being genuine."

"Yes, good. It isn't real if it isn't real, is it? And people know when it is real."

Pointing to the centre of the model on the board, Dr. Magnus said, "Do you see how we are incorporating several of the intelligences we discussed earlier? It is exactly in these kinds of situations that we are thankful we have been intentional about our Mindset, Emotional Quotient, and Soul care."

---

8 See for example https://brenebrown.com/podcast/building-brave-spaces/

Look at the list of intelligences that we have discussed and consider: Does the quality of the conversations you have been having, or avoiding, recently give you any insights into an area where you or your team need some extra tending? Do your processes support these guiding principles? How may the quality of your conversations be impacting your purpose as an organization?

After a few minutes Dr. Magnus continued, "Shola Richards has done some interesting work around civility in the workplace. He talks about the insanity of inaction. Sitting around waiting for happiness to happen at work. High percentages of employees in his research admitted to taking their frustration for a supervisor out on customers, intentionally decreasing the quality of their work, or leaving because of them. Seventy-eight percent said their commitment to the organization declined because of one person's consistent thoughtlessness and incivility.[9] This one person was normally their boss. And that kind of leader soon creates clones."

Jan put his hand up. "I agree with his point that it is insane to sit back and wait for this kind of toxicity to just go away, but that is exactly the kind of unsafe environment where people are least likely to speak up."

"Yes, right. So, people speak in other ways, don't they? Excess sick days. Reduced productivity. Unwillingness to go the extra mile. Passive aggression."

"It's a form of bullying, really."

"Yes, and Richards would say that although there are people intentionally perpetrating this culture, everyone is responsible for addressing it. We must keep uncovering and rooting out what is negative, as well as intentionally developing a positive culture. That takes courage and persistence.

"And that is harder than it sounds when the negativity is really entrenched or when those in power choose to look the other way in spite of being made aware of what is going on."

"Yes, very challenging. We have a biblical principle here, though, don't we? 'As much as it is possible with you, be at peace with all men.'[10] As much as it is possible with *you!* Do your part no matter what. Then you can either stay or leave with dignity and integrity. And pay attention to the shadow you are casting. It is always easier to point the finger at someone else.

---

9 Shola Richards *Making Work Work: The Positivity Solution for Any Work Environment* Stirling Publishing, 2016.

10 Romans 12:18

Richards says that many of the words or actions that add up to these toxic cultures are 'seemingly inconsequential' at the time. We may not even be aware that we are doing it!"

Adam sighed and said, "In my experience, these kinds of toxic or borderline toxic situations are as common or are even *more* common in the church and overtly Christian organizations than in so-called secular workplaces."

"I don't have any data on that, but that may be true because, in those environments, we might not have the processes in place for people to voice concerns. Plus, many Christian organizations focus on keeping the peace over dealing with issues."

"A false peace."

"Oh, absolutely a false peace. A hurtful peace. A contrary-to-God's-version-of-peace, fake peace. So, to clarify, relentless respect does not negate candour and holding people accountable. We are talking about relentless respect *as* we practice candour and holding people accountable."

Stan put up his hand and said, "This applies so well to the work we do with athletes. I read recently that the Chicago Bulls didn't start winning until they brought in Bill Cartwright because he wasn't afraid to take on one of their key player's toxic behaviour on the team. You can have a phenomenal player who still holds the team back if their behaviour on and off the court isn't addressed by someone who cares enough about them and the team to take it on. Before Cartwright, even with all the talent they had, they didn't win. After they got him, they started winning championships. They needed to have someone come in to create that environment where bullies weren't tolerated."

Dr. Magnus nodded, "This is a great example, Stan, thank you. We need to address conflict in a timely, mature fashion and with appropriate processes and transparency. Okay, turn to a neighbour and describe a time when you saw this handled well."

There was a moment of silence as people thought then multiple conversations broke out. After a few minutes, Dr. Magnus interrupted us, saying, "I have noticed that teams often have one or more people who ensure the team is respectful. They are like the glue. Often, they are someone other than the designated leader. Have you noticed that? The leader can exhibit power disproportionately, so it may be more helpful to have peers hold each other accountable. This is true kindness where we tell the truth with respect and wisdom, even when it is uncomfortable."

Stan spoke up, "This reminds me of Jesus' redemptive conversation with Peter after he had denied Him three times. He didn't wait for Peter to come to him. He sought him out. It's that kind of kindness you are talking about, right? Where the leader goes out of their way to find the person who has failed and doesn't just shove what has happened under the rug but helps them find a way back. It's a picture of a leader who has the courage to tell someone what they need from them while giving them a sense of belonging. It cracks me up that in the moment of vulnerability, Peter asks, 'What about John?' He is still trying to deflect, but Jesus keeps the conversation focused on the real issue."

"That is a great example. Following in Jesus' footsteps, it is critical that we take seriously our responsibility for creating civil workspaces where both truth and grace are practiced. This is a place where we are going to have to work even harder than ever because our world seems to be endorsing incivility and polarization. Not everyone is moving in that direction, of course. Carlie Fiorina said something like, and I'm paraphrasing here, 'We need to assume that most people want a better world, want a better team and workplace culture. And set out to create it together.'

"Okay, let's think at an organizational level. Mathieu, you have devoted yourself to helping organizations communicate more effectively. What are the one or two things you think churches and organizations could do differently that would help them to elevate their external communications strategies?"

"Well, I can tell you what I say to clients who ask a similar question. Churches and organizations need to think very specifically about who their ideal audience is and then talk to them." Mat said. "Let's talk about churches first. This runs counter-intuitive because naturally, we think, 'Everyone needs Jesus!' And yes, this is true, but every church or organization should look at who they are best built to serve. What age and stage of life are they? Where do they live? What do they care about? What do they need? Who do they listen to, and why? Who do they hang out with? When are they available? Then speak to that person.

"Clarity cures frustration. Make it easy for someone to look at your messaging and say, 'Hey, that sounds like me.' This makes it much easier for them to engage with you.

"If you're not sure what you're built for, ask the people who attend your church or purchase your product. Why do they drive past dozens of other options to come to you? What do you offer that makes them choose what you offer over what others do?

"If you're still unsure, ask someone gifted in facilitation to help you articulate what you uniquely excel in."

Dr. Magnus continued, "Thank you, Mathieu. That is so helpful and also a perfect segue, as I'd like us to talk about co-learning next—something very close to my heart. But before we do that, let's take a short break."

"If [we are] through learning, [we are] through."
John Wooden

7.3 CO-LEARNING

Coming back from break, Dr. Magnus approached the whiteboard. "Global research reveals that the most important factor influencing whether high-potential employees stay and grow with their companies is having opportunities to develop. Eighty-five percent want coaching. Seventy-one percent want in-person, instructor-led training to strengthen their leadership skills. Staff under the age of thirty-five are even more desirous of these intentional developmental opportunities. In an age when finding and retaining quality staff is both challenging and critical, this research identifies what should be non-negotiable. Of course, we could build a business case for this as well. Organizations that offer effective development opportunities across all levels of leadership are more than two and half times more likely to be performing in the top ten percent of their industry.[11] Additionally, the study showed that turnover rates are skyrocketing, the top concern of fifty-nine percent of CEOs is attracting and retaining top talent, and here is the important piece for our conversation, ineffective leaders are the number one reason leaders want to leave their company.[12]

---

11 Global Leadership Forecast, 2023,6, 22-24. Development Dimensions International Inc. (www.ddiworld.com)

12 Global Leadership Forecast, 5. 2023, Development Dimensions International Inc. (www.ddiworld.com)

"Organizations with high-quality leadership cultures develop leaders across all levels in critical skills, implement a common leadership model and strategy across the organization, and they focus on promoting internal leaders. Organizations that follow these practices have an average of forty-two more high-quality leaders than their peers and are three point four times more likely to be rated a top place to work by their leaders.[13]

"We've talked about strategic learning already, but I would like to revisit it here. When it comes to strategic learning, the leader needs to learn ahead. The organization won't learn if the leader isn't. Now having said that, it is impossible for one leader to learn all that is needed, so the people must also be provided with the opportunity for real-time, strategic learning and a way to share their learning. This is a co-learning process we are talking about, not a top-down, single-focused one.

"Are you familiar with double loop learning? It's double loop learning that enables an organization to be agile and adaptable. We can think of single loop learning as learning or practicing a skill, for example, how to lead an effective meeting. Over time we will develop tools and strategies that work well. Then one day, things start to fall apart. The problem is that we have become locked into one way of thinking about meetings that may have served us in the past but is not serving us now. Our tendency is to try harder, make the meeting longer, or blame people for not contributing more. We are locked in a cycle and can't see our way out. Double loop learning requires us to step outside that circle. I like to think of it as a figure eight where we turn our backs on the assumptions and practices of what we were doing for a while to explore those assumptions and ask questions like 'What do we need to achieve in this season that is different from previous ones?' and 'What are other ways of thinking about this?'

"After we have spent sufficient time in that second loop, we are now ready to circle back to the first one, but this time with new insights, strategies, and questions to apply."

Mini-Case Study: ABCD Ltd. was facing an interesting problem. Client numbers were dropping, and previously best-selling products were no longer in demand. What questions should the leadership team be asking, and of whom?

---

13 Global Leadership Forecast, 2023,12. Development Dimensions International Inc. (www.ddiworld.com)

Personalize it: Think of a situation you are currently facing that could benefit from a double loop learning approach to co-learning. What is needed to create space for this?

"It is important for us to think of strategic learning in both the short- and long-term. Let's look at this through the lenses of our model, starting with the leader.

"When I was young, I thought primarily in terms of monthly or annual rhythms and progress. Then, when I reached a certain stage in life, I started thinking in decades. Now I think in quarters, dividing my life into twenty- or twenty-five-year segments and focusing on how to maximize the impact I have at this stage of life! The other options were too short and too detailed by that time.

"Here is another important question: What happens when something outgrows you as a leader? What do you do then?"

Animated conversation broke out. "It seems like that is easier to identify in someone else than yourself. How do you know when that is happening?" Josie admitted.

"This is one of my biggest fears as a leader and part of the reason I take my own growth so intentionally, but how do you know when it is time to move on for the sake of the organization?" Bonnie asked.

Dr. Magnus smiled. "Seems like my question generated more questions than answers for us. We will talk about succession later but let me remind you of a few things that I know you already know:

1. Surround yourself with a diverse group of smart people. Develop adaptive confidence in your team. Then when you don't have the capacity for what is needed, you have processes and norms in place for the team to figure it out together.
2. Make it safe for people to tell you when you are missing the mark.
3. Keep learning but stay humble enough to know that you are in your role for a season. Your most important work will include raising up other leaders and setting them up for success. Simon Sinek says the greatest contribution of leadership is making other leaders.[14]

---

14 Simon Sinek, *Find Your Why: A Practical Guide for Discovering Purpose for You and Your Team,* Portfolio 2017, 152, 206.

"That leads us nicely to thinking about the next lens. People. When we think about influencing and developing people, we need to take the long view. I am amazed at the number of leaders who have taken years to get to the level of competence or the ability to think system-wide, yet they expect their direct reports to pick it up right away. I am dismayed by the number of organizations that don't have long-term developmental plans for their employees to step up as needed or desired. It boggles my mind. Or alternatively, the organizations that have developmental pathways in place but take such a rigid approach to it that many people don't make the cut. Often the reason is simply that they don't fit the model. The people who do 'get in' don't have the kind of personalized pathway that enables them to grow into their fullest capacity. Adam, you have a unique way of reminding yourself to take the long view with the high school students you serve. Can you tell us about that?"

Adam nodded and said, "At Cornerstone, one of the ways that we think about the long game—and acknowledge that development is a process—is by keeping a jar of marbles. There are nine hundred and thirty-six weeks from the time a child is born to the time a child graduates from high school. I keep a jar of nine hundred and thirty-six marbles on my desk to remind us that we need to be intentional about each week available to invest in the lives of our students. However, it also serves as a reminder when I work with parents and teachers, the moment we're in is not all there is.

"When parents come to visit our school to explore kindergarten, I bring this jar of marbles. I express that I'm delighted they're here to explore what the next ten months and their child's first experience of school will be like. However, that only represents a few dozen marbles in the jar. I ask, 'What do you want to be true when your child is eighteen and walking the graduation stage?'

"This powerful illustration reminds me that in every interaction, I'm not just focused on the seven days ahead of me. We are also in the grand story of our students and families as we equip and empower citizens to leave our school and engage the world."

"I love it. Thank you, Adam. Bonnie, as an Executive Leadership Coach, you have coached many teams and leaders to greater wholeness and success. Can you talk about coaching as part of the co-learning process in organizations?"

"Leaders often speak to me about the difficulty of setting aside time to focus on their professional growth, and that's where coaching comes in. I honestly believe that coaching is an integral tool for achieving greater effectiveness as a leader. The benefits are far-reaching, with a cascading effect on direct reports, teams, and the organization. Leadership coaching allows people to learn about themselves as leaders. They gain a greater understanding of their strengths as well as the behaviours that may be limiting their success. In coaching, I work with the leaders to help them identify goals for personal development and increasing leadership effectiveness.

"Leadership can be lonely and coaching also provides a safe and confidential space for leaders to speak candidly about tough decisions or pressing challenges. I find leaders often gain greater clarity when they can step back and assess the situation from different perspectives. My role as coach is to serve as a trusted thinking partner to help leaders consider other ideas and viewpoints to open new possibilities and opportunities for more informed decision making.

"The benefits of coaching are so wide ranging. My clients often speak of increased emotional intelligence and more insight into how they impact others, enhanced leadership skills, bolstered confidence, more effective communication skills and overall improved performance.

"Many leaders benefit from finding a good coach. Especially those who are transitioning into new roles, taking on new responsibilities, or those who want to explore other ways of thinking about challenges and opportunities."

7.4 CO-CREATING

*"If you don't have time to do it right
when will you have time to do it over?"*
John Wooden

After a short discussion about coaching, Dr. Magnus began again. "Co-creation and co-delivery are deeply linked, but let me differentiate the way I am using them like this. I think of co-creation as the opportunity for everyone to innovate and inform. And I define co-delivery as the opportunity for everyone to act according to their strengths and in alignment with the needs of the organization and its clients. With that in mind, let's talk about co-creation.

"Greg Satell, the author of *Mapping Innovation*,[15] busts some myths. He says that innovation is not about ideas. It is about solving problems. Helping your team understand that one distinction can greatly increase their ability to improve things. Secondly, the goal is not to hire innovative people but to hire a diverse group of people. That, along with psychological safety and intrinsic motivation, has been proven to greatly increase levels of creativity, problem-solving and fresh approaches to maximizing opportunities. And thirdly, encouraging a culture of generosity—sharing ideas, sharing success, knowing who to ask for help with what and letting others improve on your ideas all contribute to a culture of co-creation."[16]

I am here to this day because of one man. Henry Budd. He was a brilliant professor and I learned so much from his classes, but he reached into my heart when he invited me to come co-create. Twice. The first time was when he was both directing and teaching at a kids' camp that ended up with twice the registrations they were expecting. He asked if I would come and set up a system of registration for them and help them get organized, so I did. A couple of years

---

15 Greg Satell, *Mapping Innovation: A Playbook for Navigating a Disruptive Age*, McGraw Hill, 2017.

16 https://digitaltonto.com/2017/generosity-can-be-a-competitive-advantage/

later when I was at university, he contacted me to say that they were looking for someone to set up a Registrar's Office at the school, and he wondered if I would come. Not long afterwards, one of my university professors told me that every year the philosophy department chose one student to go directly into the Doctoral Department at U of T, and they had chosen me. When people you respect and care about see things in you and invite you into important opportunities, that does something to you. Both were amazing opportunities.

I chose Briercrest, and that co-creation opportunity led to other opportunities until soon I had held twenty different roles in this organization and ten elsewhere. When Henry Budd, a man greatly deserving of so much more credit than I am able to give here, was stepping down as President of the institution, he looked at me and said, "Now it is your turn." He saw something in me and gave me a chance. I give him a lot of credit for helping a young guy grow into leadership. That is the beauty of co-creation. When we see the potential in someone and invite them into something important, when we enable them to build it with us, we give them a great gift, and we end up with something better than we could have done on our own. That is what leadership is.

7.5 CO-OWNING

"It can be challenging to create the kind of environment where employees feel a sense of ownership," Dr. Magnus admitted.

Mini-case study: Employee morale is at an all-time low, and you notice that people are slacking off at work, taking liberties and failing to bring any innovative ideas. What could be some of the underlying causes of this?

Personalize it: What strategies have you found helpful in building a sense of co-ownership with your team(s)?

A short while later Dr. Magnus held up a book and said, "*Extreme Ownership*[17] by Joko Willink and Leif Babin has some good insights for us here. They suggest that ownership is something that can be both taught and expected but is mainly learned through modelling. This requires leaders who understand and are committed to the mission, who have their egos in check, who take responsibility for their own failures, and who come alongside weak members to coach and train them toward greater success. The authors take leadership so seriously that they claim there are no bad teams, only bad leaders. Do you agree?"

I reacted immediately, saying, "That puts a lot of responsibility on the team leader."

"I wonder if this works better in the military due to the nature of their work and the way they are trained?"

"That feels like a cop-out to me."

A robust conversation broke out again as people wrestled with the issue of healthy ownership and how to create it. After a time, Dr. Magnus spoke up. "One of the principles that Willink and Babin explain is the polarity between clarity of outcome and flexibility of delivery. I have sometimes called this a statement of leader's intent. Officers know that there is no way of predicting what will happen in the field, so giving orders can be challenging. The soldiers in the trenches know *what* needs to happen and *why*, but they have latitude in *how*. This builds ownership and success. Would you agree with that principle?"

"That makes a lot of sense to me."

"So, by now you know what I am going to suggest next," Dr. Magnus said with a smile.

Could your team articulate your statement of intent with regards to their key priorities? And do they perceive themselves to have sufficient latitude with the how to feel a sense of ownership about the outcomes?

---

17 Joko Willink &Leif Babin, *Extreme Ownership: How US Navy Seals Lead+ Win*, St Martin's Press, 2017.

7.6 CO-DELIVERING

"While co-delivering may sound chaotic, it is anything but. Like a choreographed dance or the way a pit crew team explodes over a wall. They never run into each other or get in each other's way. High-performing teams are increasingly skilled at both personal and team excellence.

"The fact is that execution and complexity don't play well together. To execute, we need clarity and a commitment to translate strategy into the fewest number of targets possible and to communicate frequently and transparently so people have the information they need to be successful. As Chris McChesney, author of *The 4 Disciplines of Execution*,[18] reminds us, the first discipline is to focus on the wildly important.

"His biggest insight from fifteen years of research and practice across thousands of interactions is that the number one driver of engagement is when people feel they are being successful. When they are winning. No one wants to feel like they are losing, especially if they don't know why. Therefore, I keep coming back to enabling, not just empowering. Enabling includes ensuring people have what they need to be successful.

"In all my years, this is only the second book that I know of that focuses exclusively on execution."

"What is the other book about execution?" someone asked, ready to take notes.

"It's easy to remember because it is called exactly that. *Execution*.[19] So helpful. Business-focused, mind you, and Western in worldview perspective as many of these resources are, but with lots of transferrable principles that you could customize to your setting. When it comes to both strategy setting and execution, the hardest thing for leaders to do is change human behaviour. The *4 Disciplines* gives us guidance in the very place where it is hard for leaders—setting the strategy and executing it in ways that change behaviour. Leaders are always asking, 'What are the fewest battles we need

---

[18] Chris McChesney, Sean Covey, Jim Huling, Scott Thele & Beverly Walker. *The 4 Disciplines of Execution: Achieving Your Wildly Important Goals,* Revised and Updated, Simon and Schuster, 2021.

[19] Larry Bossidy and Ram Charan, *Execution: The Discipline of Getting Things Done*, Currency, 2002.

to win to win the war?' and 'What are the most achievable things we can do that will have the most impact' and 'How can we make it more likely that there will be significant, lasting change?'

"This is where execution and change overlap with systems thinking—seeing the big picture and making changes at that level. Edwards Deming's often said, 'If the majority of people behave a particular way the majority of the time, it is probably not the people who are at fault.'

"See? It's all related. That is why we are trying to paint a holistic view of leadership. And this is why it's so important for us to be always learning and always God-dependent in our leadership. Thank goodness for the Holy Spirit, who Jesus promised would lead us into all truth. There are so many situations where we need both great and godly wisdom to navigate well. Any thoughts before we move on?"

"I find it interesting that both books about execution have the word discipline in the title."

"Ha. Yes. That tells you something doesn't it. Both books complement Patrick Lencioni's *Five Dysfunctions of a Team*[20] so beautifully. Especially *The 4 Disciplines*. When we have a compelling scoreboard and a cadence of accountability—especially peer accountability—we can move in unison toward previously set SMART Goals. Enabling people and using empowering processes, as we move together toward a compelling purpose.

"Co-delivering is dependent on every member of the team and every team doing their part toward a greater goal. And that means that everyone needs to know that we need to move from y to z and by when. That sounds simple but it requires that everyone needs to understand the starting line—our current reality—the finish line—our desired end—and how to get from one to the other. Together! Engagement, morale, and accountability all go up when we have a high level of clarity."

Joel put his hand up and asked, "Can we talk about shared leadership at some point? We have been experimenting with that in our church, and it comes with its own set of strengths and weaknesses."

"Let's talk about it right now. Angie, you have been intentional about developing your leadership team. What stands out to you as having been crucial to your approach?"

---

[20] Patrick Lencioni, *The Five Dysfunctions of a Team,* Jossey-Bass, 2002.

"One of the most powerful ways you have challenged my thinking is in this area of how to create a leadership team that leads together. Ideally, a leader supports the team that leads the organization. Together this team makes decisions and shares accountability. If done well the leader rarely needs to make a final call. This is very different from teams where direct reports relate to the leader but not each other. I loved this nuanced way of thinking about leadership teams and have sought to embody it in how I lead."

Dr. Magnus turned to another table and said, "Sharon, you have some experience of this in your academic setting. Can you speak to the way collegial governance works?"

"At its best collegial governance," Sharon answered, "at least as practiced in our university setting, allows for diverse voices to be given equal representation. It requires the full engagement of every faculty in making academic decisions and not only ensures all stakeholders are included but also invites those stakeholders to think at an institutional rather than departmental level. A framework of rules, relationships, and responsibilities creates structure. I am always fascinated that participation in this process is described as service, not voice or rights. This helps the conscientious participant to not politicize the process or minimize the importance of respectful engagement."

Dr. Magnus thanked Sharon and then continued. "Participation in a leadership process should always be envisioned as service, but I agree that so often this is not the case. And service is a good framework to keep front of mind whether you are a solo leader or part of a team. Both come with their own challenges and opportunities. When it comes to thinking about a plurality of leaders, Gene Getz did some interesting work many years ago in a book called, *Elders and Leaders: God's Plan for Leading the Church*.[21] Like any resource, there may be parts you agree with and others you don't, but one of his suggestions is that, even with a team of leaders, there must be a primary leader. Is that how you function Joel?"

"I'm not sure we would call them a primary leader. We use the term 'team leader,' and that person is chosen not to suggest hierarchy, but rather job function. They need to be someone skilled at facilitating conversations

---

21 Gene Getz, *Elders and Leaders: God's Plan for Leading the Church- A Biblical, Historical and Cultural Perspective.* Moody Publishers, 2003.

where there are differences of opinion, making sure everyone has a voice, helping the team have the processes in place that enable us to move forward together. That kind of thing."

"How is that person selected?"

"It is a team decision that is based on everyone's perception of their ability to be fair, to lead effective meetings, and most importantly to have the faith to trust God and the moral courage to do the right thing, even when it is hard. That is what our team respects and knows we need."

"That is an important distinction. Patrick Lencioni has a great book called *The Motive*.[22] It is very helpful. Among other things, he identifies two types of leaders. Those who think their role has been earned and comes with rewards, and those who think their role is an opportunity that comes with responsibility. One of the most helpful parts of his book is his description of the types of things that a reward-oriented leader doesn't do. When you read the list, it can be convicting because none of us wants to think we are this kind of leader. However, he says that if you aren't developing people, managing your team and ensuring they are managing theirs, having the difficult conversations and ensuring good communication, and leading the kind of meetings that people come away from with clarity and conviction…well…"

"Ouch," someone whispered.

"Yeah," Dr. Magnus added and let the silence hang in the air for a moment as we all self-assessed. "However, that does not address the other part of your question, which is 'How does a team of leaders, with a facilitative team leader, not get bogged down in decision-making or diverted down all kinds of rabbit trails of ideas and opportunities?'"

"Exactly."

"Let's use our model to think that through. Everyone sitting at these tables here, I'd like you to think through: When this kind of team-led structure is in place, what attributes would be needed in the team leader? These tables here: What differences might this structure create for the people in the church or organization? Tables at the back: How might the processes need to be different? And the rest of you: Might there be any impact on the way that purpose is defined or carried out?"

After a lengthy conversation and time of sharing between groups, we gathered together again. Dr. Magnus began.

---

22 Patrick Lencioni, *The Motive: Why So Many Leaders Abdicate Their Most Important Responsibility*, Jossey Bass, 2020.

"Here is another way to think about navigating the complexities of current organizations: a dual operating system. Hierarchies provide a backbone to an organization but make it difficult to truly innovate and respond to customer or client needs in a timely fashion. John Kotter's book *Accelerate, XLR8*,[23] offers insights into how to set this up. Drake, your church has been intentionally experimenting with this. Can you tell us some of your key learnings?"

Drake answered, "I have developed a deep conviction that for any organization to accomplish their grander vision and the strategy that accompanies it, we need a dual operating system. This means a more traditional 'command structure' that holds the organization accountable to the vision, values, and strategies operates alongside a 'team of teams' system where those closest to the problems and opportunities of the day-to-day details, plans and tactics are authorized to make decisions in that realm. This requires great trust in each other and protects the organization from the bottleneck of the command structure needing to make or be involved in every decision.

"When our second born son was much younger, he loved to play in the sandbox, but he had the notorious habit of taking the sand out of the box and building things all around our yard. I needed to remind him that there was one rule to the sandbox, keep the sand inside it. In the same way the command structure provides the walls of the sandbox in the form of vision, values, and strategy, and their goal is to remind, coach, inspire, and clarify these elements. If you have done this well, the clarity you have brought becomes the main source of accountability for your team. But it's free from the tyranny and temptation of micromanaging. The interconnected 'teams of teams' within the organization now have lots of space to function freely within, bounded by the clarity set by the 'command structure.' It works really well for us."

Dr. Magnus thanked Drake and added, "In some respects, the organization had to become bi-lingual. Robert Quinn speaks to this.[24] It is difficult to do some of the things you are talking about here without clarity on that. That is another challenging context to govern in. Any questions or responses to Drake's story?"

---

23 John Kotter, *XLR8, Accelerate*, Harvard Business Review Press, 2014.

24 Robert Quinn, *The Positive Organization: Breaking Free from Conventional Cultures, Constraints, and Beliefs*, Berrett-Koehler, 2015.

Several hands went up with questions. After a lengthy discussion, Dr. Magnus shifted the conversation saying, "I'd like us to talk about Robert Quinn's *Beyond Rational Management*.[25] This is another oldy but goody. Kim Cameron and Robert Quinn also developed a competing values culture model that I found so helpful. Their team looked at high-performing organizations to discover what kind of culture was most likely to lead to success. To their surprise, they found that there was no one culture that fits all but rather sets of competing priorities that, when properly understood, enabled different types of cultures to work for different organizations and organizational seasons.

"The two most important poles they identified were an organization's internal-external focus and how decentralized-centralized the organization was. You can draw these as two x-y coordinates yielding four possible operational systems.

"Organizations functioning in the internally focused, decentralized quadrant are described as Collaborative or Clan Cultures. Decentralized and externally focused cultures function with an innovative, breakthrough focus Cameron and Quinn call Ad Hocracy. Opposite the Clan is the competitive, client-oriented world of the Market Culture, where sales and responsiveness to client needs are key. And the remaining quadrant is a Bureaucracy, where internal focus and centralization create well run but less innovative or customer responsive organizational cultures.

"Now, the interesting thing is that there is not a right or wrong operating system. It depends on what is needed for the health of the organization in its context and the stage of development the organization is in—organizations often move from Ad Hoc startups to comfortable Clan Cultures until they sense the need for more standardized and streamlined processes and move to Bureaucracy before realizing their policies have become restrictive and no longer serve the actual end user. As you can imagine, each culture attracts a different kind of person, and this both strengthens and ingrains that culture.

"The challenge comes when we choose our culture based on personal preference. For example, many people prefer the Clan Culture because it is inward-focused. It meets our need to know what is going on and be part of every decision. However, it might not be what the organization, or the beneficiaries of that organization, need.

---

25 Robert Quinn, *Beyond Rational Management: Mastering the Paradoxes and Competing Demands of High Performance*, Jossey Bass, 1992.

"Highly creative or entrepreneurial people may prefer an Ad hoc Culture, while their more process-oriented peers may be sure that a Bureaucracy Culture is necessary. My point is that it doesn't depend on our preferences. It depends on what is best for the organization and its constituents. Many organizations, and certainly many growing churches, struggle with this."

"Yes," a few voices chimed in as people scribbled notes in their books.

Mini-case study: Your church or organization has been functioning as a family-like Clan Culture and people are used to having a voice in all decisions; long, shared coffee breaks; and the boss knowing everyone and their dog by name. However, a growing need to be more responsive to clients has caused you to sense that it's time to move towards a more lean and outward focus. How will you determine the way to become more entrepreneurial and market-oriented without losing the relational quality your team has come to appreciate?

Personalize it: Which culture quadrant do you think your organization is currently primarily functioning out of? Is this the culture needed for the next step in your shared journey?

7.7 CO-MEASURING

"Three of the four disciplines McChesney outlines in *The 4 Disciplines of Execution*[26] are related to measurement and accountability. That percentage demonstrates how important measurement is and how it is something we must do together. Of course, these depend on and build on identifying and focusing on the wildly important—which is a co-design piece.

Focusing on the wildly important.
Acting on lead measures.
Keeping a compelling scoreboard.
Creating a cadence of accountability.

---

[26] Chris McChesney, Sean Covey, Jim Huling, Scott Thele & Beverly Walker. *The 4 Disciplines of Execution: Achieving Your Wildly Important Goals,* Revised and Updated, Simon and Schuster, 2021.

"The one point I want to stress is the importance of keeping a compelling team scorecard. Teams love to see what each team member reports on. This creates a sense of momentum and a cadence of accountability. Do you see how these four disciplines are interconnected? Discover and prioritize the wildly important. Choose the lead measures that will predict movement toward these outcomes. Keep a compelling scoreboard. I love that. A compelling scoreboard. Something dynamic and helpful and motivating. I also love the idea of a cadence of accountability. A rhythm and process whereby we hold each other accountable to what we have committed to be and do."

7.8 CO-CHANGING

"Okay, let's talk about change. Anyone experienced any of that these last few years?" Dr. Magnus asked with a halfhearted chuckle.

Stan admitted, "The biggest challenge I face as a leader is the amount and speed of change. I am expected to make decisions quickly—with no precedent, limited context, and sometimes massive implications. Important things that I will be held accountable for. Is anyone else experiencing that? At a level that is unprecedented in our lifetime?"

Several heads were nodding in agreement, and side conversations started about similar challenges.

Dr. Magnus let us talk for a few minutes, then stepped in. "The challenge of leadership is that normally we will be lacking something. Budget. Time. Information. People. Authority. Direction. Experience. The problem recently is that we may be lacking many or even all of these things and need to make massive changes in less-than-optimal circumstances. When a crisis first hits, people expect changes and are more open to them. You can sometimes get more changed in the three days after a crisis than in three normal years. This is part of the reason organizations sometimes artificially create a crisis—but that's a conversation for another day. In the last few years, we have seen massive global disruption, uncertainty, and change. Mindsets are changing. Realities are changing. Opportunities are changing."

Stan jumped back in, "And everyone is tired of it."

"Say more."

"Well, it seems like there is so much change going on everywhere that people are growing weary of it. So, when we introduce another one at work, there is either more resignation or resistance than normal."

Dr. Magnus nodded his head. "So true. And even more so in the church, perhaps. The one place we want to remain constant in the craziness of our personal and work worlds."

Adam disagreed. "Although it seems like people in the church are crying out for change too. Or perhaps I should say the people who used to be in the church but aren't now."

"True again. How are we feeling about that?"

"Discouraged."

"Confused."

"Saddened."

Sharon shifted the focus, saying, "I understand those emotions and don't mean to minimize them in any way, but I also feel a sense of excitement, like the stage is set for the changes many have been longing for, for years."

Jay agreed. "Jamie Robertson's book *Overlooked*[27] gives a great snapshot into the historical context and current reality of the church in Canada. He says something similar, Sarah, that the church can do whatever it wants now because no one in the watching world cares. God cares, of course, and I don't think he is saying anything goes, but this is a unique time for churches to go back to the heart of the Gospel."

The room started to get animated.

"Such an important conversation," Dr. Magnus agreed, "How about you, Joshua? Your mission has seen tremendous growth and change under your leadership. Can you tell us a bit about that?"

Joshua nodded and then said, "When I started, we served in sixty-five countries. Now we are in ninety. To accommodate that growth, we needed to not only restructure our leadership team but also think differently about issues like centralization and decentralization and, in our context, how to align diverse, multicultural contexts. We are in another season of change now as individuals and organizations rethink both priorities and processes."

Dr. Magnus continued, "During seasons of change, people may feel frightened, confused, defensive or threatened. That is normal, but it can lead to

---

27 James T. Robertson, *Overlooked: The Forgotten Stories of Canadian Christianity,* New Leaf Network Press, 2022.

the breakdown of trust in relationships and the ability to co-create and move forward. Somehow, we have to rebuild a sense that 'we are in this together' and we will 'figure it out together.'

"Have you read Kerry Patterson's book *Influencer: The New Science of Leading Change*[28]? Such a brilliant book. They describe how important it is to find the few vital behaviours that will make the most positive impact and then apply six lenses to reinforce those changed behaviours. Understanding that change requires both will and skill, they assign three complementary and well-documented ways to increase motivation and three ways to tangibly reinforce the skills. This is a book you should have on your shelf. Their holistic framework enables you to not only plan an effective change process but also ensure that you and your team are reading and learning across the six lenses.

"Of course, as people of faith, we could add two or more additional circles to their model to show the role of the Trinity in guiding us, training us, and moving on our behalf.

"Okay, I am going to say something that may be a bit controversial. In Christian communities, we can cling to one polarity or the other when it comes to change. Leaving all the hard stuff up to God or taking on hard changes without consulting God. In my experience, churches are more likely to do the former, especially with the hardest changes. We have a bias towards prayer and fasting and leaving it with God instead of noticing that oftentimes in the Bible, when the people prayed, God gave *them* instructions of what to *do* or sent a leader to guide them in what to do. In those situations, we seek to delegate to God the very things God has delegated to us to do.

"I love the book of Acts. It is so practical. It shows us how. How to deal with problems. How to deal with growth and scaling up. How to mentor young leaders. How to handle conflict. The people pray, and they act. They discern, and they make decisions. They say things like, 'It seemed good to the Holy Spirit and to us.' They understood that God was always at work on their behalf, *and* they understood what they had signed up for. Service. Which sometimes means dealing with the hard stuff. And leading change. Drake, we talked earlier about the dual operating system your church instituted because of a season of change. Can you tell us more about that?"

---

28 Joseph Grenny, Kerry Patterson, David Maxfield, Ron McMillan, Al Switzler, *Influencer: The New Science of Leading Change,* McGraw Hill, 2nd Ed. 2013.

Drake chuckled and said, "On February 25th, 2020, I accepted a job as the Executive Pastor of Ministries at a church with sixty-plus staff and three locations. It was coming up to its one-hundredth anniversary and was in the beginning stages of a Lead Pastor succession. Three weeks later, COVID hit. Suddenly I became the COVID crisis manager for the entire organization.

"I mean, I was brand new. I had so much to learn, people to get to know, and ministries and systems to understand. And in a blink of an eye, it all changed. To be clear, I joined an amazing staff team and was part of an executive team that could help shoulder this burden. But in short, I went from the new guy still being onboarded to having people looking to me for answers.

"It was in this landscape that being able to deploy a dual operating system was so crucial. There would have been no way we would have been able to navigate COVID effectively without both a solid command structure and the freedom to release people through a team of teams model.

"Since things were constantly changing and the stakes were high, as an executive team, we met daily to discuss the opportunities and challenges before us as an organization. We were doing a daily SWOT analysis for the entire organization. What we didn't do, though, was have a daily all-staff meeting, and during our daily executive team meetings, we didn't get into the weeds of every ministry or operations decision. Instead, we sought to bring the high-level clarity and declarations that were needed by our different departments.

"From here, we would be able to work our next level of strategic thinking and equip and empower those teams to go down another layer, work with their staff and volunteers, and make daily decisions. This posture allowed us to settle the higher-level strategic needs that would give clarity and conviction across all our teams and trusted our department heads and ministry leads to take that information and make the decisions they needed.

"Since things were changing on a sometimes-daily basis, we needed to develop systems of decision-making, budgeting, planning, and communication that could adapt to the system's changes. We adjusted from a yearly ministry plan cycle to a seasonal one and focused on the basics.

"This enabled the authority of accountability to vision, values, and strategy to stay firm at the executive level while the authority of decision--making was pushed even more so to those closest to the problem. As you can imagine, this required a very high level of trust, healthy conflict, an entrepreneurial spirit, and for communication to flow freely. This posture didn't always work perfectly, and it took a lot of work to keep people focused on the most important things. But in the end, what we learned in COVID has helped us find new processes and systems that have continued this dual operating system long past COVID.

"Though we don't do daily executive team meetings anymore, and plans are a little more stable, we continue to operate a dual operating system. Now we have a hybrid ministry planning model that allows us to do yearly planning with seasonal check-ins to gather new intel on shifts or starts and stops.

"This model has allowed us to stay nimble when needed and still do good thinking, planning, and executing that is anchored in shared convictions.

"Building this kind of system enabled us to sustain a culture amid incredible change."

Mini-case study: Imagine you were in Drake's position. What are the first three things you would do in response to this escalation of responsibility?

Personalize it: How did a recent crisis impact your church or organization? What system changes did you make that enabled you to navigate the crisis more effectively? Looking back now with the advantage of hindsight, what changes could you have made? Are there any changes you need to make now? What are you personally doing to prepare yourself for possible escalations in your level of responsibility?

I was scribbling notes. Were we still focused on the most important things? Did our measures and subsequent conversations reflect these? And perhaps most importantly of all: Had I allowed our culture to deteriorate so much that we no longer had a genuine cadence of peer accountability? I made myself a list: Order these books… Arrange for a team offsite to discuss these concepts… Spend more time in the lunchroom. Ask more pointed questions to find out what is really going on.

Dr. Magnus stood to indicate it was time for a break and said, "I am excited to dig into the next section together. Co-governing. Leaders so often forget that there are multiple governing teams in an organization and that they are normally linked and leading both up and down."

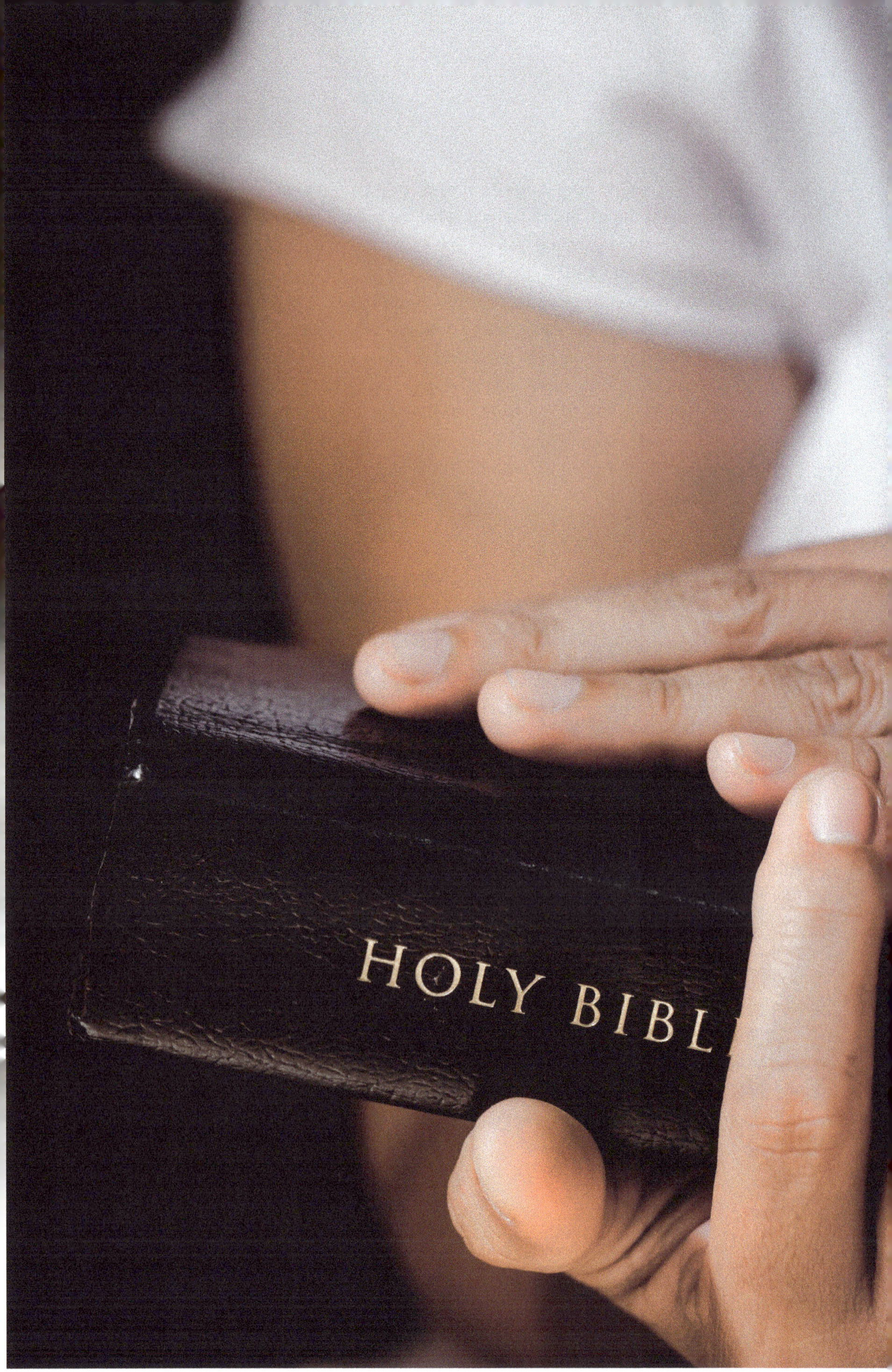
HOLY BIBL

8. PURPOSE

> "Where there is no vision, the people perish."
> Proverbs 29:18

Dr. Magnus pulled open his notes and began, "Many leaders are lacking a sense of purpose in their work, and this trickles out through the rest of the organization. One study found that 63% of global C-suite leaders felt a strong sense of purpose in their work but fewer mid-level executives (47%) and frontline workers (41%) said the same.[1] That is concerning on several fronts."

I sat back in my chair. Concerning was right. And I was one of the leaders who had lost any semblance of a strong sense of purpose. I didn't know if I should lament or take comfort in the fact that I was not alone. As a Christian leader, lament seemed like the more viable response. I was just wondering how I had allowed myself to get to this point when Dr. Magnus said, "Joshua, I am going to pick on you again. As you draw near to the end of this chapter of your leadership in a large, multicultural, and global organization, what are your reflections on what is critical for organizational health?"

Joshua responded, "That is a big question, but perhaps I could answer it with a few life learnings. The first thing that comes to mind is how important it is for the whole organization to know the purpose for which we exist. Knowing what we do and why we do it creates a sense of belonging and meaning.

"Secondly, I would say that everyone, and I mean everyone, must feel that their part is important to the whole. Again, this helps build a sense of belonging as well as value. A sense that 'I am contributing to something bigger than myself and what I do matters.'

"Thirdly, we all need to know that people care about us. That our leaders care about us as people, that the team around us has our back.

"And finally, what holds all of this together—what makes it possible—is good leadership and effective governance. Governance that understands the

---

[1] Global Leadership Forecast, 2023,15. Development Dimensions International Inc. (www.ddiworld.com)

scope and responsibility of their role and gives the leaders the freedom and information they need to do their job well. And leaders who understand that the freedom and information that they have been given comes with the responsibility of acting on it wisely and in a timely fashion in support of their mission and their team."

Dr. Magnus agreed, "Yes! Knowing the purpose for which we exist and how we fit into that is so important. Charles Taylor's conclusion after mammoth research is that humanity is longing for meaning and higher purpose. Everyone has hunger, and this may be expressed in diverse ways. Thank you, Joshua. Graham, let me ask you. What role has clarity of purpose played in congregational settings in this season of uncertainty?"

Graham thought for a moment, then answered, "Churches that understand their compelling 'why' had something to organize around during the pandemic. They were less reactive and more intentional in seeking innovative ways to continue. That doesn't mean it was easy for them, nor that changes didn't have to be made. It did mean that they had done the important work of discerning, communicating, and prioritizing their purpose, so when a crisis came, they were more ready to address it in a healthier and less divisive way. You know, prior to the pandemic, most leaders I know said they thrive on change. We are learning that it is actually only when *we* introduce it into the system that we feel that way. Yet even there, having a clear sense of purpose enabled leaders to engage their people in more intentional ways, even in light of imposed changes."

Dr. Magnus pulled up a slide showing the progression of leadership and management thought since the mid-1900s. "Look at where we are. For the past decade or more, we have been in the era of holistic leadership and meaning. Our current culture is looking for meaning and whole-person engagement. We ignore this to our peril."

"I agree. During Covid, people were expecting to be more engaged and consulted than they were. I think that is why we saw some of the extreme reactions we did. The same thing can happen in organizations. The broader culture expects involvement, dialogue, and engagement. It is now counter-culture not to provide this."

"Did everyone have a chance to read Robert Quinn's *The Economics of Higher Purpose*[2]? What did you think of it?"

Amy spoke up, "I was interested in the underlying assumption we have come to believe, that we can be profitable or purposeful but not both. His research really debunks that myth."

Jacqueline added, "I totally agreed with his premise that leaders have been socialized to believe that their employees, especially younger employees, are self-seeking, self-interested and unmotivated, so they need to create systems of control to ensure work gets done. Of course, staff resent this coercion, so it becomes a self-fulfilling prophecy. You would think we have moved away from that way of thinking but in my consulting work I see this all the time."

Dr. Magnus waited to see if anyone else had a comment, then said, "Quinn's antidote to these misconceptions is ensuring that there is a compelling higher purpose and aligning the organization around that purpose rather than restrictive policies or regulations. Let's look at this against the backdrop of our model. Our irresistible purpose—whether it is ensuring clean water or safe homes or education or fair wages; or whether it is preaching the gospel and discipling people—must be supported by great and godly co-created processes and tended by ennobled and enabled people. Do you see? It is holistic. It must be seen holistically."

Dr. Magnus' voice rose with passion, and he looked at each of us in turn. Then taking a sip of coffee, he went on, "One of the things I love about Daniel Pink's work[3] on purpose is that he helps us identify the difference between what he calls 'capital P Purpose' and 'small p purpose.' Capital 'P' Purpose is the compelling, overarching vision. He calls this a charismatic vision because it attracts people. In fact, he says that we have thought we need charismatic leaders when in fact, what we really need is effective leaders serving a charismatic purpose. Did you catch that? This is important. This kind of purpose is deeply motivating. Yet studies show that when asked why they left an organization, many people answered, 'I felt like I wasn't making a [blank].'"

He paused on the last word, "What do you think goes in that blank?"

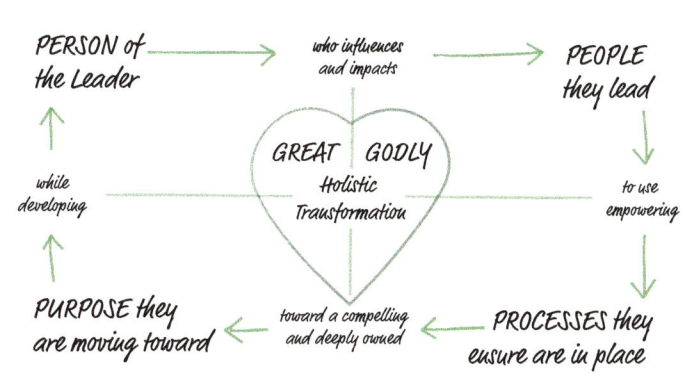

---

2 Robert Quinn, *The Economics of Higher Purpose: Eight Counterintuitive Steps for Creating a Purpose Driven Organization*, Berrett-Koehler, 2019.

3 Daniel Pink, *Drive, The Surprising Truth Behind What Motivates Us*, Riverhead Books, 2011.

We answered in unison, "Difference."

"You would think so, wouldn't you? However, the most common answer was 'contribution.' That is our small 'p' purpose. Our personal contribution. People need to know how *they* are contributing.

"The corporate purpose is the compelling vision that the whole organization gathers around. People who align with it are hired. Processes are designed to move us progressively toward it. It is our overarching purpose. In recent days there has been a great emphasis on the importance of this being a higher purpose worth devoting your work life to.

"Historically, the leader who brought the highest corporate purpose was considered the epitome of leadership. And often selected to lead the enterprise. Jim Collins' research revealed that corporate entities do not move from good to great when led by leaders with this kind of all-consuming, self-designed, and self-proclaimed vision. He described this kind of leader as functioning at level four. Good at their jobs but not able to move the organization toward greatness. His thorough research identified that level five leadership was marked by personal humility—including the willingness to listen, grow, and consult—and a relentless focus on the co-created, co-understood high purpose. Many Christian readers see Jesus as the supreme example of this. His humility and relentless pursuit of a higher purpose took Him all the way to the cross!

"Collins demonstrates how, over time, even good leaders can become proud, and as a consequence, their organizations fall into irrelevance, decline, and even death.

"More recently, additional research by Joseph and Joiner[4] identifies people's longing to participate in co-creating that macro purpose. Then it has meaning for them. Sadly, their research indicated that only 4% had the agility and mastery to co-create that purpose. We could envision this as level 6 leadership, where leaders utilize creative processes to lead their teams in co-creation. So, my challenge to every leader is this. Please ensure that your big macro purpose isn't just yours and that it becomes compelling for every person you are privileged to lead.

"Daniel Pink reminds us that all humans need a purpose. We desire to contribute and know that we are contributing. Tom Rath explores this further in his book *Life's Greatest Question: Discover How You Contribute to*

---

4 Joseph and Joiner, *Leadership Agility*

the World. I really like the books Rath has authored or co-authored.[5] In this one, he describes how, at sixteen, he learned he had a genetic mutation that would lead to multiple cancers that could escalate at any point in his life. The things he heard shared at funerals gave him a sense of urgency about how important identifying and maximizing our contributions are. Over time he observed that helping people lean into their strengths could be misapplied, leading to self-focus or an unwillingness to step outside one's comfort zone for the sake of something greater than themselves. He discovered that people who know their personal purpose and are committed to a compelling higher purpose are willing to grow and develop in service of this higher vision. Rath developed a 'Contribify' assessment that I highly recommend.

"Colossians 3:17 reads, 'and whatever you do, whether in word or deed, do it all in the name of the Lord Jesus, giving thanks to God the Father through Him.'[6] This is a life-guiding verse for me. We sometimes think of the Venn Diagram that points to our personal sweet spot. The key for me is that I live my life for the glory of God, making a difference in benefiting His world and His creation.

"Having celebrated my 80th birthday, I am even more convinced of the importance of the contribution we make to our families and places of service.

"And having reached this milestone, I am even more aware that our sense of large P and small p becomes increasingly challenging when we no longer need to work for a living. However, it does not matter where you are on the journey. Rising in the morning and knowing that we are on this earth to contribute—with a formal assignment or not—is part of what it means to be human.

"We talked earlier about *The 4 Disciplines of Execution*. It teaches us that out of all the information on our scorecard, Team Engagement is key. How do we build this? Tom Rath, in his great book, *Vital Friends*,[7] reminds us that people want to have good work relationships. We just discussed how people want to contribute. Relationships and results. People want to be part of a healthy team that is making an important difference.

---

5 *Strengths Finder 2.0, Strengths Based Leadership: Great Leaders, Teams and Why People Follow Them, Fully Charged: The 3 Keys to Energizing Your Work and Life.*

6 Colossians 3:17 NIV

7 Tom Rath, *Vital Friends: The People You Can't Afford to Live Without*, Gallup Press, 2006.

"Purpose is linked to more than a compelling vision, though. Development Dimensions International did research with 1,827 HR professionals and 13,695 global leaders. They found that young, high-potential workers are much more likely to feel a sense of purpose if they receive key developmental opportunities.[8]

"Have you read Duffield's book about Thriving[9]? What were the three crucial areas she pulled from Genesis 1:26-28?"

He moved to the board, drew a triangle, and labelled the three sides as we shouted them out. Belonging. Being. Contributing.

Then he continued, "Do you see, we are created for community, identity, and contribution. According to Tom Rath 'A growing body of evidence suggests that the single greatest driver of both achievement and wellbeing is understanding how your daily efforts enhance the lives of others.'[10] While you may have been encouraged to follow your passions, Rath offers what I consider to be a more Christlike approach: ask what you can give. This takes us out of the centre of the picture and makes service the objective.[11]

---

[8] Global Leadership Forecast, 2023, Development Dimensions International Inc. (www.ddiworld.com)

[9] Ellen Duffield, *A Theology of Thriving: Belonging, Being, Contributing,* Shadow River Ink, 2023.

[10] Tom Rath, *Life's Great Question: Discover How you Contribute to The World,* Silicon Guild Books, 2020, 12.

[11] Tom Rath, *Life's Great Question: Discover How you Contribute to The World,* Silicon Guild Books, 2020, 48.

"Duffield labels the triangle with different language for organizations: People, Purpose, and Product or Process. Thriving organizations ensure all three are front and centre.

[Triangle diagram with "THRIVE" in the centre, labelled PURPOSE, PRODUCT, and PEOPLE on its three sides]

"The purpose attracts and motivates the kind of people you want on your team. And it gives focus to the contribution. Here's where another piece of Daniel Pink's research is helpful. He discovered that people are more likely to do the right thing *because it is the right thing* than for personal reward. If we layer these findings, we see that people are motivated by belonging, big picture purpose, the opportunity to do the right thing and small p contribution. Fascinating. Okay, break into groups and discuss."

Where have you seen this being played out and what insights does that afford you for moving forward?

I had a hard time engaging in the table conversation because my mind was racing. These insights enabled me to think differently about this important part of leadership. Someone might work in education because they believed in the capital P purpose of giving kids a good start, but if small p personal purpose didn't have opportunities for regular expression, they would still lack purpose. In our industry that was huge. What was my small p purpose? And did I know that for other members of our team? Did they? I made myself a note to spend time reflecting on this.

Several moments later Dr. Magnus asked for insights from our conversations.

Joel spoke up, "We were discussing how leaders' underestimate the importance of purpose and how crucial it is for us to help people know both the capital 'P' and small 'p' purpose for their context."

Cam agreed, "Yes, and adding to that, we chatted about the times when we have felt most engaged. Generally, they were while working on something that mattered to us as well as to the organization."

Bonnie added, "Our group said the same thing. Going back to the language you used earlier Dr. Magnus; we talked about co-creation and co-delivery. Making mistakes and learning from them together and having agreed upon measures that were motivating because they showed progress toward a goal that mattered. These are all so important and so rare."

"Yes, good," Dr. Magnus smiled, "But why so rare?"

There was silence for a moment then someone hazarded an answer, "I think for me because I get so wrapped up in the task I forget to—or maybe think I don't have time to—focus on helping my team see how their small 'p' personal purpose aligns with our capital 'P' purpose."

"Yes. So important. People are looking for a higher purpose than mere existence. I would even say that some think our culture is Godless, but I think our culture is God-hungry and in many ways looking to be their own god to fill that vacuum."

For me, one of the issues that I hope more contexts take seriously is the issue of incivility. We have polarized on everything. We just can't stay here. We can't be constantly casting doubt on people on 'the other side.' We must converge our energy to owning the compelling purpose of going forward and building together as opposed to using every opportunity to polarize with such incivility and seeming deception that there is so little trust left in our world.

"Simon Sinek, in his excellent book, *Find Your Why*,[12] says the greatest contribution of leaders is to help other leaders find their why. Here is the problem. Leaders tend to focus on 'their vision' instead of discovering the shared

---

12 Simon Sinek, *Find Your Why: A Practical Guide for Discovering Purpose for You and Your Team*, Portfolio, 2017.

vision God is giving the people. That is why I love Appreciative Inquiry. It is co-creative and draws out what God is saying. In secular settings, it is still important to co-create and design with the dreams and uniqueness of the team in mind. If you look at hiring practices, we often ask the candidates what their vision for our organization is. The person with the most vision, the biggest vision, will often be the person we choose. Sadly, envisioning and achieving are not the same thing—and may even require different skill sets. Plus, the person who comes with a well-developed vision is not going to be open to reading the culture, listening to other people, and being collaborative in establishing it. Not only does this undermine shared ownership—in the West, at least, people expect to be part of the envisioning process—but it also increases the likelihood that we have missed something important. Or imported something we saw work elsewhere that won't work here. One of my favourite quotes from Sinek's book is: 'Happiness comes from what we do. Fulfillment comes from why we do it.' Co-envisioning and co-creating are a gift to our team, as well as to the world. They make it more likely that people will feel fulfilled and more likely that we will achieve what God is calling us to do. I cannot stress this enough."

Dr. Magnus paused and looked around the room, "I am interested in hearing from others with other worldviews. Are there different ways of thinking about this? Jan, what differences, if any, have you observed in the way people in different countries think about purpose as it relates to work?"

Jan nodded and said, "The common denominator I see across many cultures is that the idea of a strong connection between purpose and work is weakening. In countries where people have money, resources, and options, the language of work is usually focused on what we are 'wired for,' or called or destined to do. Work in that context is a means to get where one wants to go, a stepping-stone toward greater things or an obstacle to overcome. Purpose is no longer to be found in work but in pursuing one's dream.

"In some countries, work has become like a god, especially in the bigger cities where it seems that the harder you work, the more you are 'seen.'

"In countries with less resources or opportunities, a job is seen as a gift from heaven. Young people may share the same dreams as those from more affluent countries, but the obstacles they face are often insurmountable."

"Thank you, Jan. Our perspective can be so limited to what we have experienced. How about you, Joel, what differences, if any, have you observed in the way people in Ghana think about purpose in churches and organizations?"

"Ghana is still a very traditional country," Joel answered, "and while this bears several advantages, it also impedes the possibility of co-envisioning and co-creation. In a hierarchical system where age and position are considered over inclusivity, sharing opinions can be a very arduous task. This leaves people feeling drained and less interested in the process. In that scenario, the people are just there to help achieve someone else's goal. Or alternatively, some members remain part of the ministry or organization because it serves their personal goals and not because of the purpose of the organization. Both these situations are concerning.

"The trend is changing with more and more people gaining education on how to build organizations that involve members in co-owning and/or co-creation. These organizations and ministries have honed the skill of articulating their purpose well to their members. The result of this is that leaders garner a strong loyalty and contribution from members who feel they are a part of something greater than themselves. However, I wish we could do this without sacrificing the benefits of our traditions and culture to the alternative of progressiveness."

Dr. Magnus nodded and said, "You have articulated such an important polarity. How do we maintain the benefits of cultural traditions while updating processes and perspectives? Thank you for bringing this to light for us. So interesting.

"I have placed purpose where I have on the model because purpose is something that draws us, not something that drives us. There is a big difference.

"We, the people, and the processes we put in place, act in service of this end purpose, but the purpose must also be inspiring to the people asked to support it. This capital P Purpose must be clear, but it also must be updated as the world changes and as we grow toward understanding our role in it. When did Jesus assign the purpose for the disciples? I have been thinking about that. He was clear about His purpose from the beginning, but He didn't explain what that would mean for them until near the end of the Gospels when He said, 'now it's your turn' and sent them out. We are getting close to the end of our time together and I hope you are sensing an increased call on your life to go in Jesus' Name to lead.

"To apply great and godly principles.

"To think holistically and systemically.

"To remember that people are made in the image of God and the calling of stewarding people and resources in an important work that should both drive us to our knees and cause us to want to bring our very best."

Dr. Magnus paused and took a sip of coffee, once again looking at us as if to invite us to take this in. Then he said, "Jim Collins talks about the Hedgehog Principle.[13] He contrasts a hedgehog, who has one proven strategy for survival, with a fox, who has many strategies for attacking his prey. The hedgehog knows what works for him or her and does that. Consistently. Repeatedly. Applying this concept to organizations, he demonstrates how great organizations focus on their own sweet spot rather than trying to imitate what others are doing or being all things to all people. He calls this their 'Hedgehog.'"

Do you know what your hedgehog is? What does the world need, and what is your organization wired to do? And do you know why this matters? That is your why.

―――

I was asked recently to describe a capstone leadership experience when I felt God gave breakthrough and joy. A time when I was working within my personal 'Hedgehog." This caused me to reflect on how God used who I am to set me in spaces where I could have the most impact. It took me a while to learn where those spaces were.

When Marcus Buckingham's, Standout 2.0: Assess Your Strengths *2005 instrument was first released, I used it in looking back and forward over my journey, and it clarified that I worked best as a "pioneer connector." It describes me as the type of person who "sees the world as a friendly place where, around every corner, good things will happen." This distinct advantage starts with optimism in the face of uncertainty and enables me to act as a catalyst. It also described my craving to put two or more things and/or people together to make something bigger and better than it is now.*

What amazes me most as I look back over my life, is the number of occasions and places where I was invited to do this. Likely the time I was most amazed

―――

13 Jim Collins, *Good to Great: Why Some Companies Make the Leap and Others Don't*, Harper Business, 2001.

was when I was invited to serve as the President of Briercrest, given what the board perceived it needed in that role at the time.

I took the position with the promise that I would not step away from the challenge until five major targets had been realized. The most challenging goal was that we would be out of debt and have a financial surplus across all budgets. The other goals were very significant but this one was especially challenging. At that time the institution owed over $5 million, a very large sum in that day.

I was away, and when I returned, the Leadership Team questioned me. It was obvious that they were in serious doubt about my ability to achieve such a challenging goal, especially since I had mostly held academic leadership roles in the institution up until then. Although I didn't have Buckingham's language or tools at that time, I knew that I was going to have to both access my unique strengths and develop new skills if we were going to be successful.

Fortunately, our prior President, a widely connected leader, dear friend, and our chief fundraiser, was willing to stay and help us. Unfortunately, he had to leave two years later. Yet, amazingly and by God's incredible grace, we not only got out of debt but were able to establish a surplus of $750,000 to give the incoming President a good start.

This sense of success was a significant benefit in some of the following ways:

1. It influenced my definition of success in life and service to describe it as having clarity of what you do best and doing it, liking what you do enough that you stay with it, and knowing whose glory you do it for.
2. It deepened my sense of calling to be a hungry learner and invest my next chapter in fully engaging, enabling, and empowering hungry learners to lead where they are best within whatever context they were serving or invited to serve in.
3. It freed me to own what God has given me and invest my days in seeking to deliver it with a deep sense of gratitude.
4. It helped me increasingly become a team player, equip teams, and team players who become "one" at whatever level they serve in an organizational system.

After a time of reflection, Dr. Magnus went back to the front of the room and said, "Hopefully, by now, we are beginning to see that purpose is not a 'feel good,' 'fluffy,' or 'would be nice if we had the luxury of time for it' component to leadership. It is one of the critical lenses that leaders must keep. A clear and compelling purpose answers why we do what we do every day. Then if we want to help people be able to run toward that vision, we need to provide goals that are actionable, as reflected in the action plan they generate and that we execute on."

Moving to the whiteboard and pointing to his model, he said, "There is a useful resource for ensuring that you have a clear and compelling purpose that will enable you to move toward results in the delivery of a higher purpose. It is Andy Stanley *Visioneering*.[14] He identifies that a vision is an attempt to solve a significant, unaddressed, and unmet problem. It becomes so compelling that people move toward it together.

"In addition, I so love Robert Quinn's book *The Economics of Higher Purpose*.[15] I love that resource because it is research-based, and for those trying to build for Kingdom purposes, it is gold.

"Our sense of purpose may grow from a picture of a better future state or in response to a current challenge. It must create such a sense of discontent about a condition or situation that makes us agree that 'we just can't stay here.'"

This book is co-written in the hopes that your whole system has clarity about who you are and what you do—starting with "Why do we exist?" That big purpose is your why. What difference are you trying to make for what people with what?

---

[14] Andy Stanley, *Visioneering: Your Guide to Discovering and Maintaining Personal Vision* Multnoman Books, 1999.

[15] Robert Quinn, *The Economics of Higher Purpose*, Berrett-Koehler, 2019.

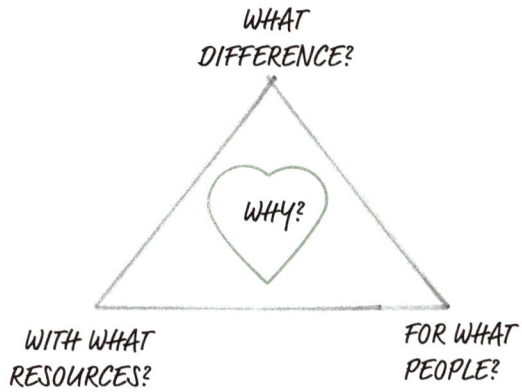

WHAT DIFFERENCE?

WHY?

WITH WHAT RESOURCES?

FOR WHAT PEOPLE?

Copyright 2023, Paul E. Magnus

"In the centre of that triangle that I use over and over to keep myself on track is the question 'why.' Answer that, and you have a mission statement to anchor you.

"On the heels of that, I have always loved the *4 Disciplines of Execution* and as it helps us remember that we are acting on wildly important goals. Wildly important. Worthy of our time and energy. Important enough to track on a compelling scorecard that will motivate the team to carry on during difficult times.

"There are so many great tools, but never forget that our purpose is higher and worthy of 100% commitment and engagement—together as believers across our world and as leaders nationally and globally. It is my longing and prayer, and the reason we are doing this resource, that you will perceive your leadership's higher, noble calling."

Personalize it: What is the purpose that you would stay up all night for? What is your "enough is enough?"

Apply *The 4 Disciplines of Execution* to create a path to your big picture purpose that is actionable, aligned, and measurable, and that includes enabling and ennobling people, and intentionally developing the heart, mind, and soul of your leadership.

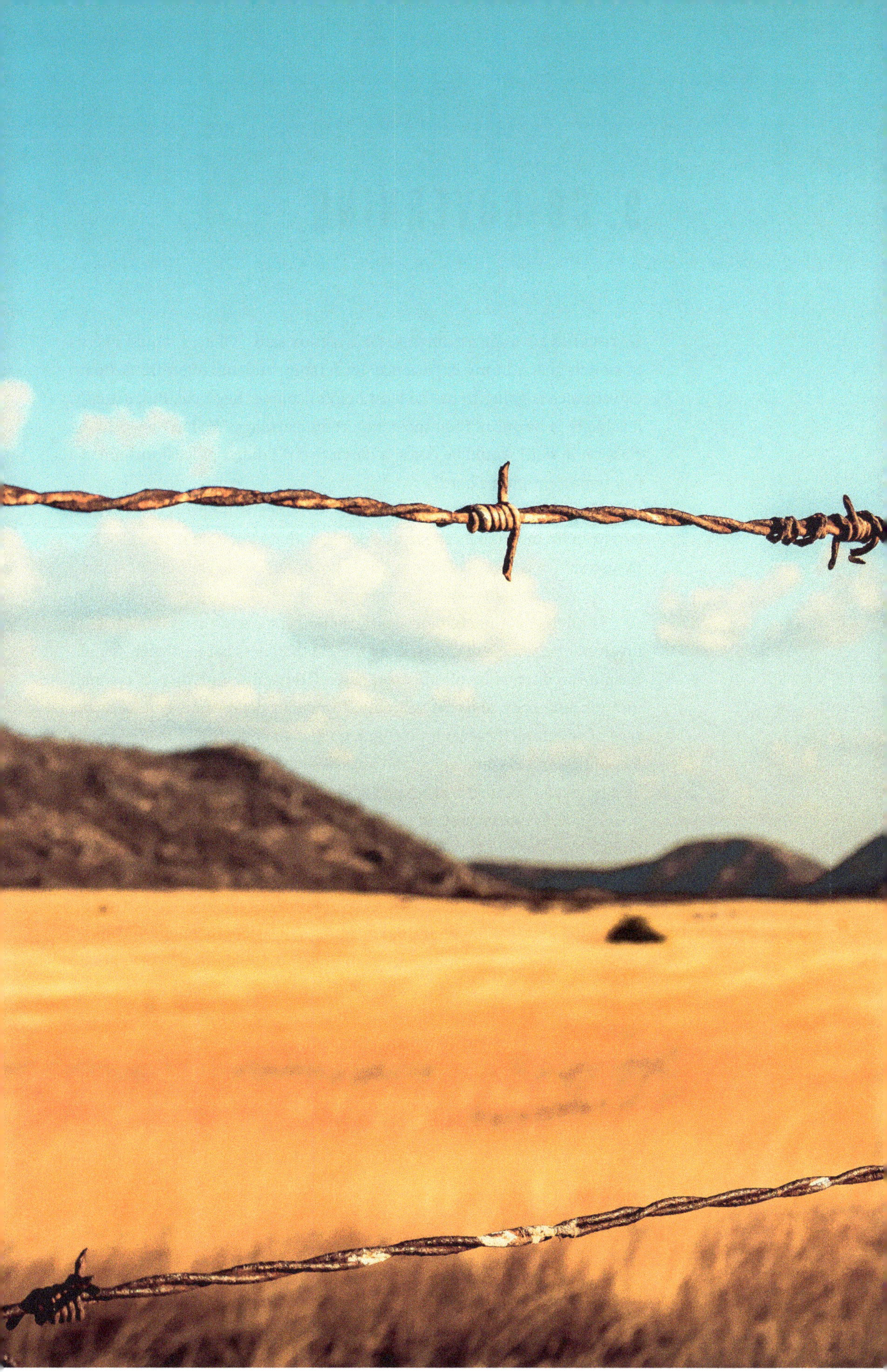

9. CO-GOVERNING

Gathering us back together, Dr. Magnus said, "Okay, I would like us to switch gears. In my experience, leadership students often think Board Governance is going to be the least helpful course they take. But, actually, it is likely to be one of their most important learnings. We have a weeklong class on it, but I would be doing a disservice if I didn't at least introduce a few important pieces here."

He read aloud, "Organizational governance is the process by which two or more individuals arrive at a decision that affects an organization or ministry. When we speak about board governance, we are talking about a very specialized policy-based governing system for an entire organization.

"Building alignment between the various pieces of the system that are involved in making and carrying out these decisions is harder than it sounds. Imagine an interaction of processes and relationships with lines of communication, authority, and responsibility. To varying degrees, depending on the type of structure, these lines flow both up and down to ensure that everyone has clarity and is empowered and able (we have been using the word enabled to mean equipped and supported) to act as one body with many parts.

"And yet ninety percent of the people that I have worked with don't realize that the board of directors works on behalf of what is called the moral owners. The moral owners may not always financially "own" the organization, but they are the people for whom the organization exists. The stakeholders. Depending on the type of organization, this might mean the investors, the constituents, or the congregation. They have expectations. The board is accountable for whatever the moral owners entrust them to do. "Note that the board is in the middle and influences up, but the moral owners exercise authority towards the board.

The board has a responsibility of *Caritas*, which is the Latin form of the Greek word *agape*. *Caritas* refers to both the care the moral owners have for organizations and the duty of the board to care about the interests and values of the moral owners. There is a mutual concern. This is both a relational and an ethical component to this. Many people forget this.

MORAL OWNERS

Insight
Entrust and Expect
Feedback
Full Engagement

C.G.O.

BOARD

Governance Process
Strategic Direction
Board & Leader connection
Empowering Boundaries

Primary Leader

STAFF LEADERSHIP TEAM

DELIVERY TEAM

DELIVERY TEAM

DELIVERY TEAM

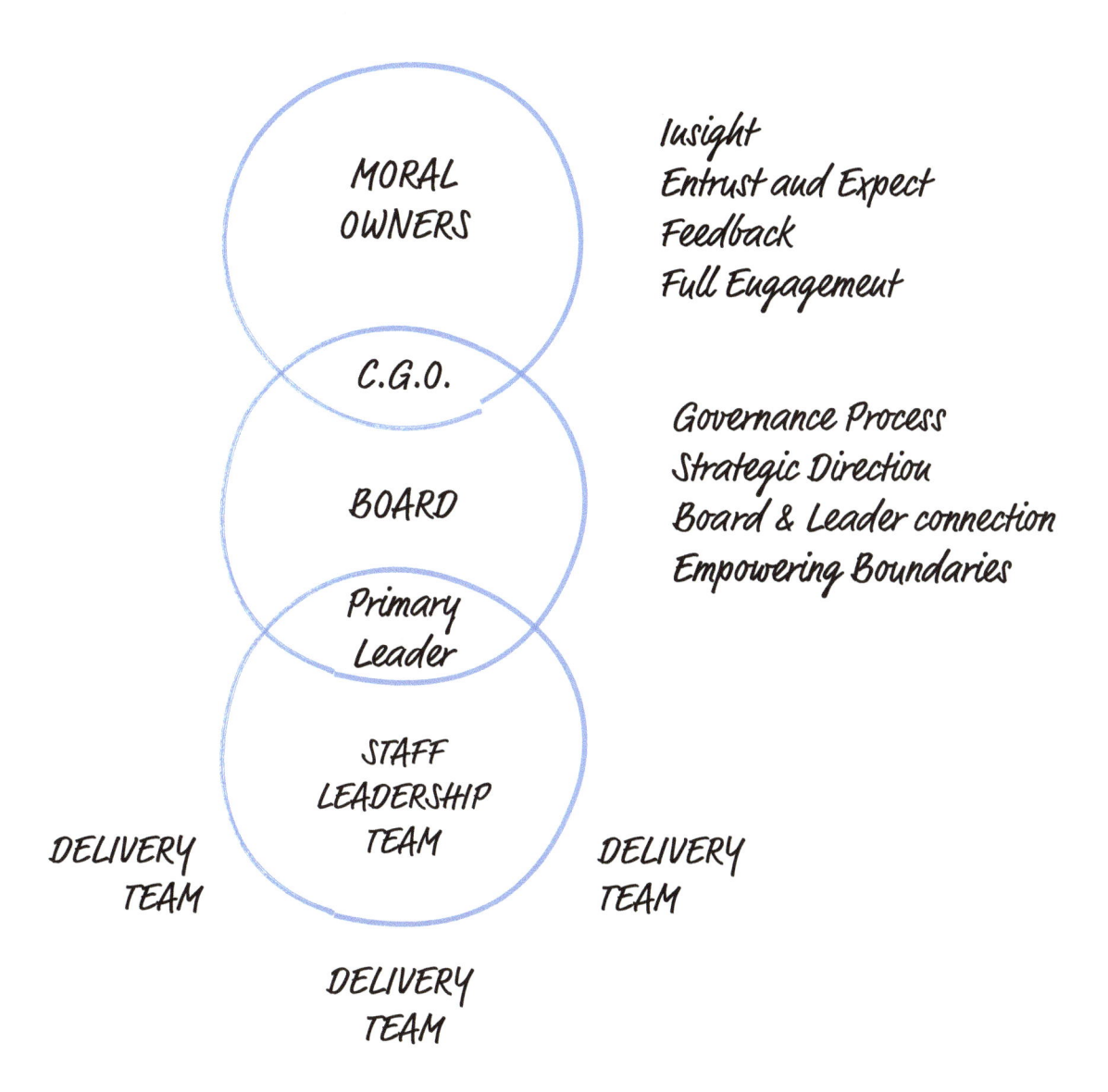

Copyright 2023, Paul E. Magnus

Notice in this model that the Chief Governing Officer (CGO) or Board Chair links the board to the moral owners. She or he are the conduit of communication in both directions.

The board is entrusted with the responsibility to set direction for the organization. In most organizations, they are linked in the other direction to the staff leadership team via the primary or prominent leader (PL). Depending on the organization this person may be called a CEO, Executive Director, lead pastor or other.

The PL is the connection to the staff, and through them, the beneficiaries. It is the responsibility of the key leader(s) to execute the direction set by the board. In other words, while the Board is accountable to direct and protect, the staff leaders are accountable to deliver. And they do this through the delivery teams that link them to the customers, clients, constituents, or congregants.

"The governing board sits in the centre to ensure good governance for the *entire* organization. What is most frequently misunderstood is that the board delegates responsibility for action and designated decision-making to their Prominent Leader.

"We are addressing this as co-governance. Each of the three interconnecting circles holds a certain level of governance. Each must be held accountable and held able. Significant confusion comes when we fail to clarify what each level needs to govern and how they will remain aligned.

"The visual here shows what is needed for any organization to be smoothly governed."

		DOCUMENT:
↑↓ RELATIONSHIPS	DIVINE AUTHORITY	Bible
↑↓ COMMUNICATION	LEGAL AUTHORITY	Letters of Patent or Articles of Incorporation
↑↓ RESPONSIBILITY	MORAL OWNERS	Constitution / Bylaws
↑↓ AUTHORITY	BOARD	Board Policies Manual
↑↓ ACCOUNTABILITY	P.L.	Team Handbook
	STAFF	Staff Handbook
	BENEFICIARIES	

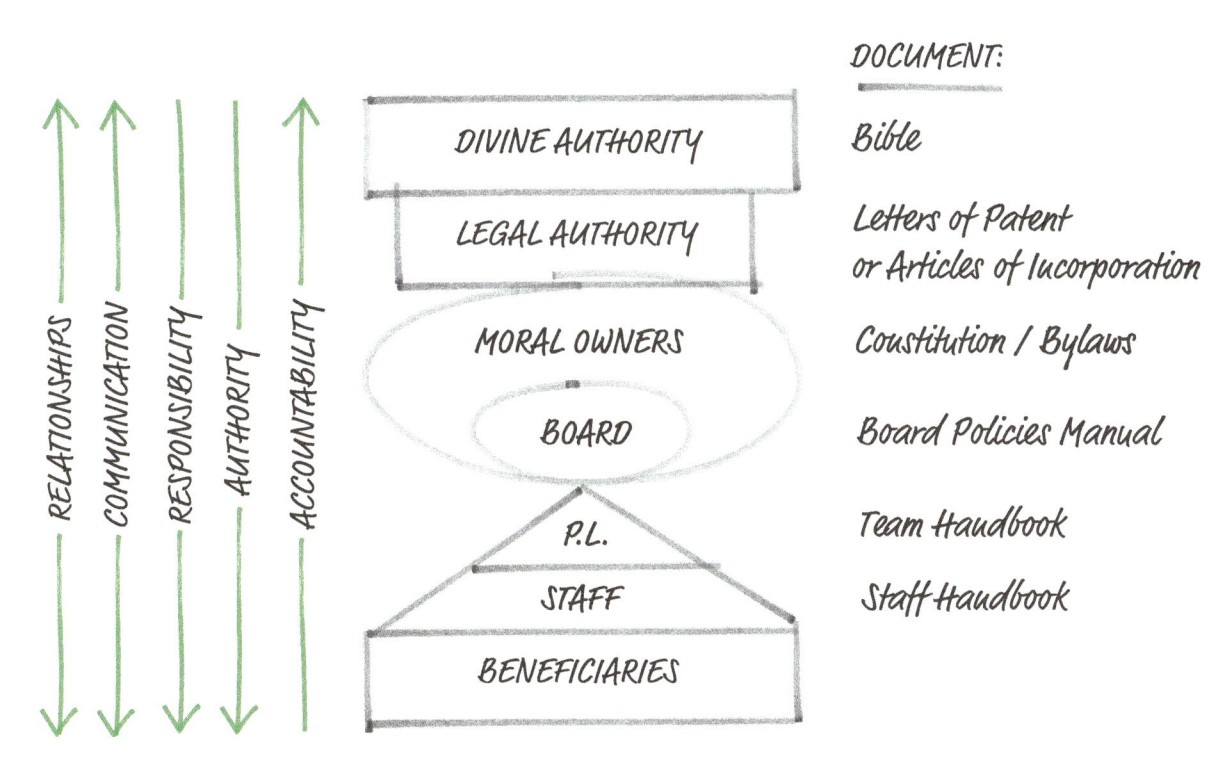

Adapted from Jim Brown's model in *The Imperfect Boardmember: Discovering the Seven Disciplines of Governance Excellence*, Jossey-Bass, 2006.

"The Board Chair speaks on behalf of the board. The PL speaks on behalf of the staff. This is another piece people often forget. The board chair builds the network and takes the heat from the moral owners, not the PL.

"Richard, you have given oversight to the finance departments of large corporations as well as your own public accounting firm, and you have served on and advised many institutional boards. Can you tell us a story of one where you saw this break down?"

Richard responded, "Dr. Magnus, I appreciate your model of an aligned co-leadership that clarifies responsibility, authority, and accountability. When leadership is aligned, the board—on behalf of the moral ownership—ensures that the Prominent Leader is accountable for achieving objective, measurable results and avoids what is unacceptable. No board can fully exercise their fiduciary responsibility without this clarity.

"It has been my experience that most board members need help understanding this co-leadership role. Each person brings a different experience from other boards, and often they have learned from a bad example.

"Let me draw recent examples from two Canadian universities. A colleague of mine shared her board experience. During one meeting, a board member (a CPA) asked the vice president of finance a financial question. The question was entirely reasonable. However, the VP told him the question was getting too far into the weeds. She was astonished to see other board members shaking their heads in agreement. Not long afterwards, this university had to apply for emergency funding. The VP of Finance told the board that enrolments had dropped precipitously for many years. Not one board member was aware of this. This is an unfortunate example of the breakdown of a system meant to protect from exactly this kind of situation.

"Late last year, another university came out of creditor protection. The board was unaware that reserve funds had been used for years until the school could not meet payroll. The university was forced to fire over a hundred faculty and staff and close seventy programs. In a scathing report, the provincial auditor blamed the board for not meeting their fiduciary responsibilities. Perhaps both universities should have been getting into the weeds.

"If there had been an alignment of leadership, the board would have held the university President responsible for reporting financial solvency and avoided the ensuing economic calamity. They would have had the information to take corrective action."

Dr. Magnus nodded. "Thank you, Richard. These examples powerfully demonstrate just how important it is to have alignment and accountability. Sadly, this kind of thing happens much too frequently.

"Of course, the other extreme can be true as well. Boards sometimes hold too tight a reign and have unrealistic expectations for their Primary Leader. I often ask the board how they want the leader to treat the staff. Then I ask them if this is the same way they treat their PL. If the key leader is not coming out of board meetings feeling more resilient and with greater clarity than when they went in, the meeting has been diminishing rather than enabling. The board has failed.

"It changes everything when a board realizes that they exist to support and direct one leader. Nothing helped me understand this more than Jim Brown's book *The Imperfect Board Member*.[1] Max De Pree's *Called to Serve*[2] was also very helpful. Both books are older, but still excellent resources. Okay, we have covered a lot of ground. Take a few minutes and discuss this at your tables. Where have you seen this functioning well?"

Several minutes later, we reconvened. Many agreed that their board could use some help. Some told horror stories of demoralizing meetings, other of divisiveness, and still others of confusion about roles. A few were surprised to learn that their very positive board experience was not as common as they thought.

Dr. Magnus got our attention back and said, "I had a student once who wrote guidelines for both the board and the Moral Owners. I have not heard of anyone else doing this and thought this was very wise."

Matthew asked a question. "Our camp board is made up of volunteers, hardworking and good-hearted people, but they are not necessarily trained in board governance. If I understood you correctly, you said that it is the board's job to set direction, but our board is very hands-on. They would describe themselves as a working board."

---

1 Jim Brown, *The Imperfect Board Member: Discovering the Seven Disciplines of Governance Excellence*, Jossey- Bass, 2006.

2 Max De Pree, *Called to Serve: Creating and Nurturing the Effective Volunteer Board*. Eerdmans, 2001.

"Yes, good. That brings us to our next important topic. There is a continuum of ways a board may do their job of influencing the organization and still call it governing. Some ways are more effective than others at different stages in the organization's history. I like to envision it like this," he said drawing on the whiteboard.

BOARDMANSHIP CONTINUUM

GOVERNANCE BOARD

- Govern by establishing all-embracing policy
- Govern by setting policy
- Govern by giving advice
- Govern by responding to management problems and proposals on a case-by-case basis
- Govern by committee representation or by an individual (Founder-like)

"In my experience, a board moves toward more hands-on leadership when they don't trust the leader and toward more hands-off leadership when they do. Sometimes it is based on preference or precedence, but often it is based on their perception of the leader's effectiveness, as noted in the visual to follow. Fortunately, or unfortunately, camp boards can think they are a working board that is working on behalf of the leader. It may be that they are a management board that wants to rule on certain things but not the whole. A governing board is best described as a board that governs based on a clearly developed and designed job description. It has four major assignments, as we will discuss in a moment. In this visual, boards become overly engaged toward one end of the continuum and disengaged towards the other end. Managing or working boards can become overly engaged in what isn't their real job. So often, they think all governing is the purview of the PL, and they are just rubber-stamping things, and then they disengage. They don't perceive that they are making a difference big enough to matter.

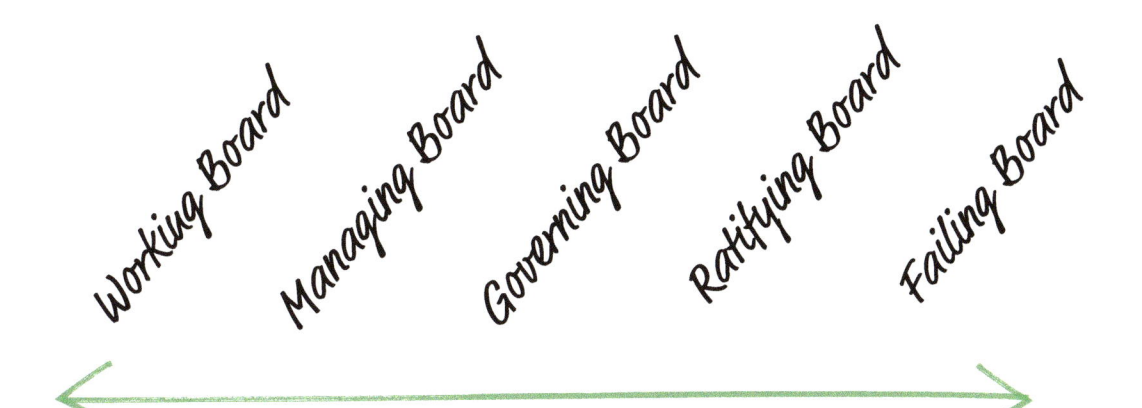

Working Board — *Managing Board* — *Governing Board* — *Ratifying Board* — *Failing Board*

⟵──────────────────────────────⟶

OPERATIONAL ENGAGEMENT

INCREASING DISENGAGEMENT

Above: The result of a joint research project guided by the Evangelical Fellowship of Canada.

Linda, whose ministry supported Christian camps across the country, spoke up, "Like Matthew, many of our boards began as hands-on, working boards and have been transitioning to governing boards as their ministries grew and became more established. What advice can we offer board chairs as they seek to lead this process?"

D. Magnus smiled at the class and said, "you are now the experts. What do you think?"

How would you answer Linda?

Personalize it: Using the language of this continuum, how would you describe your board? Is this the style of leadership needed from this team in this season, or is a change needed in order to move forward well?

Looking at the options on the continuum, Richard said, "I am guessing that by a Ratifying Board, you mean one that rubber stamps whatever the Primary Leader does? Your continuum shows this as one step away from a failing board. Many of the small non-profits I have supported would fall into this category, and I imagine that is not uncommon. This raises some questions for us."

What are some of the red flags that could help a board know if they had moved from governance towards an unhealthy level of lack of accountability?

"Is this continuum true for churches as well? Is it different for volunteers?" Carmen asked.

"Volunteer boards are more likely to think that they are not capable of giving guidance to leaders—especially competent or articulate leaders. Yet, this is one of the board's four jobs: Strategic Direction, Empowering Boundaries, Board to Leader Connection, and Governance Process."

Wayne interjected, "Do the scriptures talk about volunteers? Or differentiate levels of responsibility based on remuneration?"

"No, Wayne, it does not. Good point, and point taken. However, I do find though that elders boards don't think of themselves as boards. They don't perceive themselves as having authority over their pastor. And that can lead to many abuses and missteps. And on top of that our seminaries are turning out pastors who aren't trained to work with boards."

Matthew asked, "Are there any other books written specifically to help with this?"

"Robert Andringa's *Good Governance for Non-Profits*[3] is another very helpful resource. Robert and I have worked together, and he knows what he is talking about. Boards, including elders' boards, are responsible to their moral owners, which ultimately includes God in a Christian organization or church. They are responsible to identify the Ends—or SMART Goals, as I prefer them to be called—because that forces us to move toward greater clarity in terms of what they expect from their leader.

"If you find yourself in this kind of situation where trust needs to be rebuilt, one of the tools you might want to revisit is conversational intelligence. Our goal, remember, is to move towards co-creation, co-delivery, and co-measurement. Working together as one entity made up of interlinked, motivated, enabled, and healthy teams of teams. The board is one of these teams—linked to the others through the Primary Leader."

He went to the whiteboard and redrew the model.

---

[3] Fredric L. Laughlin and Robert C. Andringa, *Good Governance for Non-Profits: Developing Principles and Policies for an Effective Board,* AMACOM, 2007.

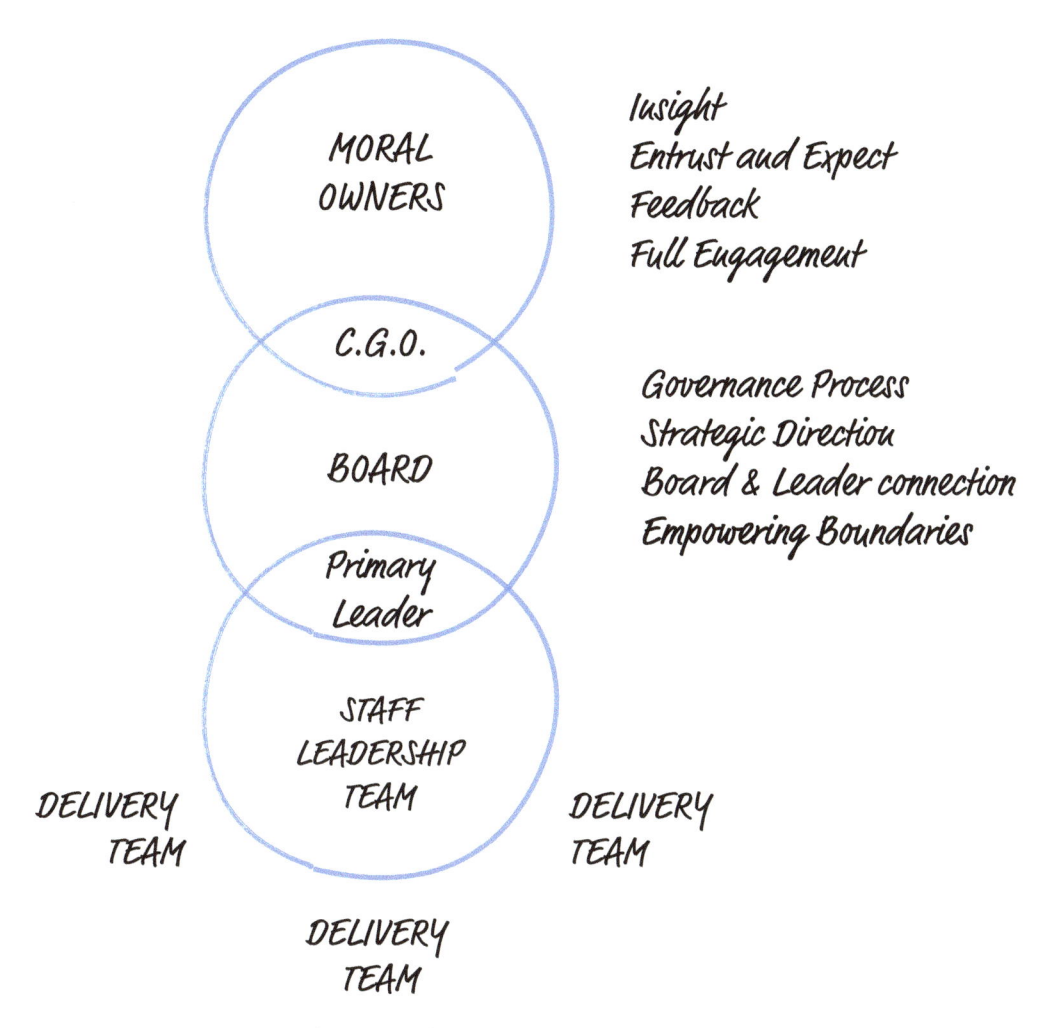

```
MORAL
OWNERS                    Insight
                          Entrust and Expect
                          Feedback
                          Full Engagement
    C.G.O.

    BOARD                 Governance Process
                          Strategic Direction
                          Board & Leader connection
    Primary               Empowering Boundaries
    Leader

    STAFF
    LEADERSHIP
    TEAM
DELIVERY          DELIVERY
 TEAM              TEAM

    DELIVERY
     TEAM
```

Copyright 2023, Paul E. Magnus

"Going back to your comments about ineffective boards. I want to acknowledge that it is much harder to build an effective board than it sounds. As John Carver[4] once said, 'Boards are made up of individually competent people who are incompetent as a board.' Many boards have lots of passion and good people, but lack the discipline of a system and structure, or the practice of accountability needed to get traction. Good governance holds the leader responsible and on the path that holds everyone together. And, good governance holds itself responsible to work wisely within its mandate."

Wayne added, "I agree that discipline is a big challenge for boards. People need to know what is expected of them. The board's job is to speak in one voice to give direction, set protective boundaries, and ensure accountability. I often say to boards, 'Everything is fine until it's not.'

---

[4] John Carver, author of the seminal work *Boards That Make a Difference: A New Design for Leadership in Nonprofit and Public Organizations*, Jossey-Bass; 3rd ed. 2006.

"This happened not too long ago on a board that I am a part of. We brought on a new leader and thought we were giving him time to get his feet under him before holding him accountable for some of the things his job required. It is amazing how quickly he took us off the rails—and that was our fault. Holding leaders accountable is challenging. Especially in ministries. In business, it's a bit easier because everyone knows what the bottom line is, and you either achieve it or you don't. In ministry, it is more challenging to identify how to assess the achievement of the board ends or goals. There is sometimes more room for interpretation, and whenever that happens, there is a lack of clarity and the potential for problems."

AN INTEGRATED BOARD POLICY GOVERNANCE MODEL

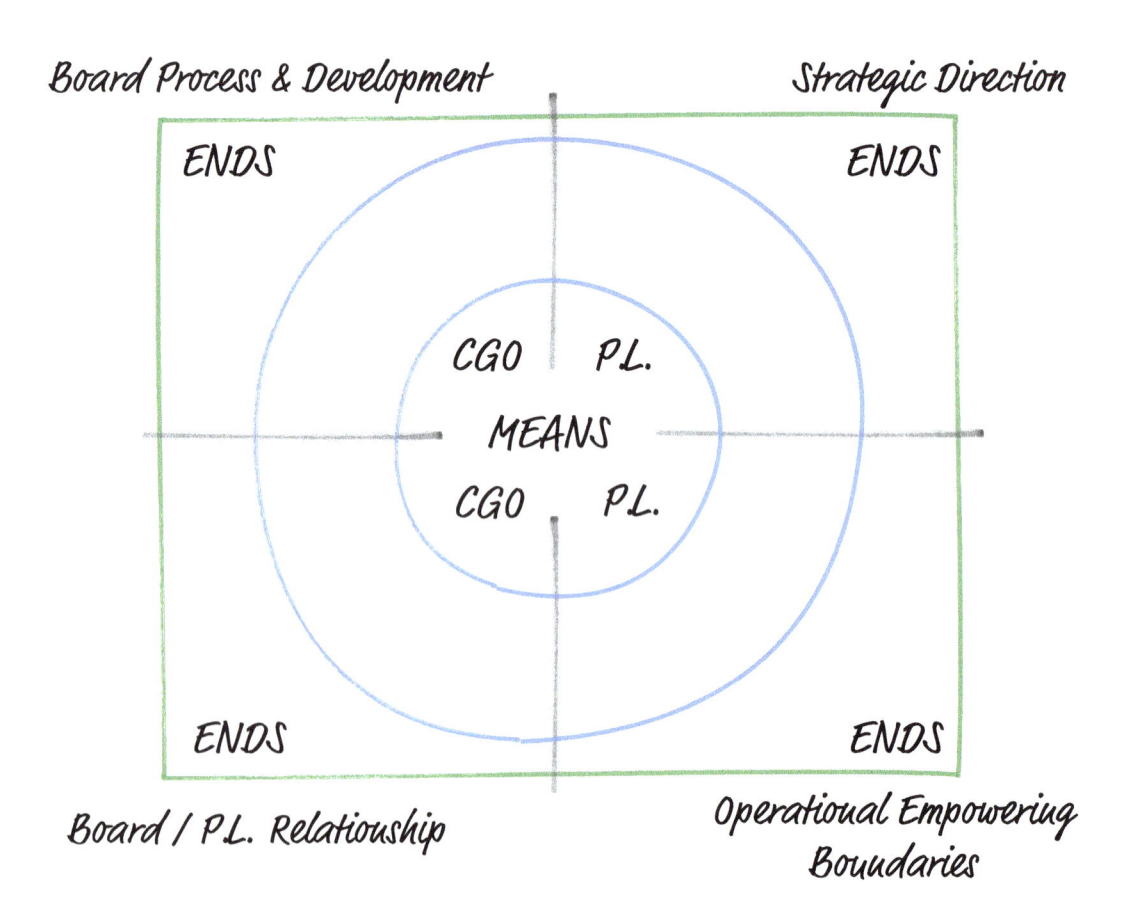

Board Process & Development — ENDS

Strategic Direction — ENDS

Board / P.L. Relationship — ENDS

Operational Empowering Boundaries — ENDS

MEANS: CGO, P.L., CGO, P.L.

Adapted from John Carver and Miriam Carver (see *The Policy Governance Model and the Role of the Board Member,* Jossey-Bass, 2009)

Dr. Magnus agreed, "That is an unfortunate but good example. Appropriate boundaries and appropriate support. I never let a board hold someone accountable if they don't also hold them able. What about the challenge of ensuring the board chair is speaking on behalf of the board? A board chair must do what the board has decided, or cohesiveness breaks down. They are out of compliance if they don't. Yet, I have worked with so many boards where this is the case."

Wayne agreed, then added, "In times of transition or crisis, the board must study their own documents and be very disciplined about following them. These tell them what must happen and what must not happen. In fact, we often need to tighten up on what must not happen during seasons of transition or crisis. These kinds of boundaries and guidelines are crucial for the protection of all involved. That is why current and comprehensive board documents are so important. The Constitution and bylaws of so many organizations and churches are obsolete. Often written when the enterprise was much smaller and simpler and not updated. No one goes to them until there is a problem. Then they are pulled out and weaponized, even if outdated. They should be reviewed every three months and adjusted as needed."

Dr. Magnus intervened, "Let's go back for a moment. I like what you said about business leaders sometimes being easier to hold accountable because the bottom line is clearer. In the social sector, you don't have as many definitive measures. That may cause some people to think that it is impossible to set ends or measure progress toward them. However, it is possible to measure anything. Here is a good resource on that," he said, holding up *How To Measure Anything: Finding the Value of Intangibles in Business*[5] by Douglas Hubbard.

I also really like Patrick Lencioni's focus on having three strategic anchors.[6] These are the distinctive and strategic things that define how we will succeed. When we have this level of clarity about our key priorities, it empowers people to make decisions and removes so many bottlenecks. Boards need to know what they are asking the Primary Leader to execute

---

5 Douglas Hubbard, *How To Measure Anything: Finding the Value of Intangibles in Business.* Wiley; 3rd edition, 2014.

6 Patrick Lencioni, *The Advantage: Why Organizational Health Trumps Everything Else in Business.* John Wiley and Sons, 2012.

on and how to measure progress. They should be asking if this leader is on target with the action plan that emerges from this big-picture clarity. And, of course, I am not just speaking about getting things done. How we do them is equally, and sometimes more important. An organization's values must be operationalized."

Richard jumped in, "In my opinion, this is one of the greatest challenges. Boards are not clear on what success looks like."

Jack agreed, "Especially in Christian organizations where even that word is suspect. Call it ministry indicators, or commitments or desired results. Whatever you call it, build clarity around this. If you don't, you are doing a disservice to your senior leader and the organization. How can you move towards something if you don't know where you are headed?"

Dr. Magnus nodded and then added, "We need to work harder at being clear on both what and the who. In Christian settings, almost no one is clear about who is responsible for what. Even if people know what they are personally responsible for—and even that isn't always the case—they don't know how this aligns with the bigger picture, and they don't know who is doing what in the organization. So much time is wasted with overlap and gaps, not to mention how long it can take to get an answer on something because no one knows who to even talk to about what. Related to that, there is the issue of authority. So often, congregations think they have more authority than the board. This creates the potential for serious conflict and loss of control.

"Alternatively, the Prominent Leader can believe they have more authority than the board, and again this can create conflicting tensions. The system lacks clarity either between the circles or within the circles. Unfortunately, energy is wasted because no one is clearly focusing on organizational results. Instead, they are debating who is responsible to establish the desired results or who is responsible to deliver them or veto them or throw overboard someone who isn't producing what they should. Organizations need great clarity on the roles, responsibilities, and authority of the board and the senior leaders.

"Adam, you chair an influential national board. What have you discovered about the importance of effective board governance in this role?"

Adam answered, "I agree with everything that has been said, and I would like to add the importance of personal growth. If the Primary Leader and the board are committed to personal growth, they will be much more open and teachable, and much more likely to be responsive to the data and feedback that will enable the organization to respond and become increasingly healthy and agile."

Wayne agreed, "This is so important. Right next to character and leadership skills in my books. When people are not growing, and know that they are falling behind, they are more likely to become scared or insecure, and that can lead to autocratic behaviors at the worst times."

"Oh wow," I exclaimed involuntarily. "Oh, sorry. I just had a huge realization about something that happened a few years ago in my workplace. You just gave it words." I began to scribble some notes.

Barb interjected, "You mention character, and this is such an important part of leadership and governance. Good governance requires ethical and legal conduct, as well as, sound policy, and accountability."

"That is a great description," said one student scribbling it in their notebook, as a conversation broke out about whether this was comprehensive enough for all contexts.

Notice that this list may include and go beyond stated values. What shared and deeply owned list governs your team or board?

Dr. Magnus continued, "I mentioned earlier that one of the greatest challenges that organizations face is that people don't know who is responsible for what. In my experience, the executive leader assumes that they are responsible for everything. Everything! No wonder they are burning out, resigning, or underperforming. Add to this that the CEO is often expected to do the board's job, or the board's ends are so unclear they cannot be measured with any degree of accuracy. How does the board know if the senior leader is accomplishing them if they can't even define them? When I am working with boards I always ask them to define their mission using this triangle."

WHAT DIFFERENCE?

WHY?

WITH WHAT RESOURCES?

FOR WHAT PEOPLE?

Copyright 2023, Paul E. Magnus

"Next, I ask them to determine the five measurable things they need their CEO to do. Many boards struggle with this. It is hard work. It means doing your research and praying for wisdom. It may mean looking at some uncomfortable truths or challenges. Or making changes to some sacred cows. However, in the end, it will create clarity. And, as we read in Lencioni's *The Advantage*,[7] creating and reinforcing clarity is one of the most important parts of good leadership and management.

"In *Procrastinate on Purpose: 5 Permissions to Multiply Your Time*[8] by Rory Vaden we find light on how to focus on what matters most. Vaden describes a Focus Funnel that includes five choices and five permissions. We need these to make these important decisions about what tasks to focus on and those we can no longer keep.

"If we need to:
- Eliminate some tasks. We will need to give ourselves permission to Ignore some things
- Automate some tasks. We will need to give ourselves permission to Invest in some things
- Delegate some tasks. We will need to give ourselves permission to allow some things to be Imperfect.
- Procrastinate on some tasks. Do it later—this is an interesting one—we will need to concentrate. Procrastinate on purpose
- Leave some things incomplete. We will need to give ourselves permission to let go.

"Every board should engage in retraining every three years if they want to stay current and truly serve their organization or church. One of the biggest problems I see on boards is insufficient orientation and the subsequent challenges this creates.

"Okay, before we move on, I want to make one further observation. I never talk about governance without reading John 14-17. We talked about this earlier, but I want to stress it again here. The Trinity's modelling is so

---

[7] Patrick Lencioni, *The Advantage: Why Organizational Health Trumps Everything Else in Business.* John Wiley and Sons, 2012.

[8] Rory Vaden, P*rocrastinate on Purpose: 5 Permissions to Multiply Your Time, 2015,* Tarcher-Perigee.

helpful. Many voices acting as one. The integrity of the whole. Clarity of roles and honouring of the other.

"And that leads us to the final part of our interconnecting, integrated roadmap.

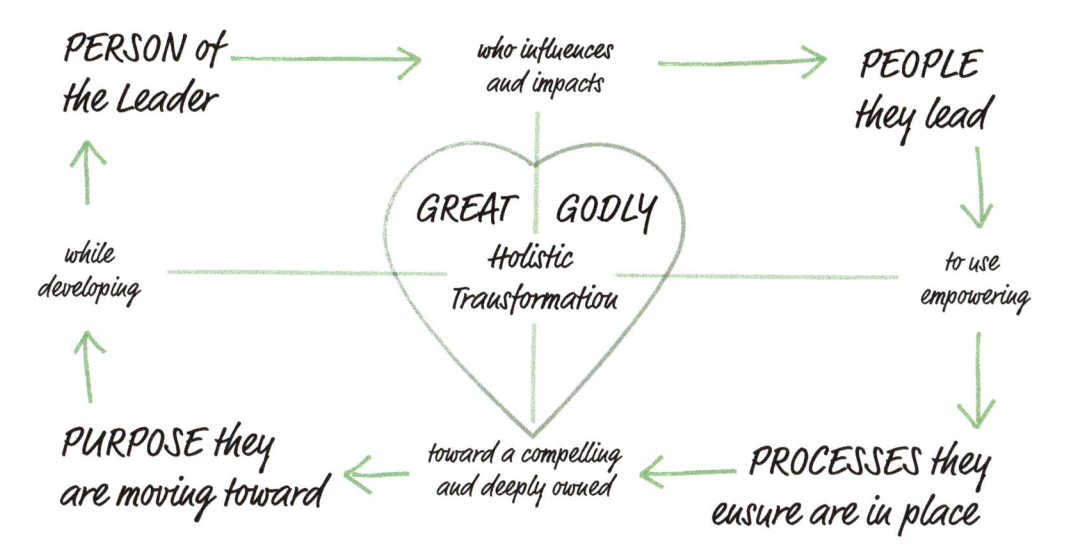

PERSON of the Leader → *who influences and impacts* → **PEOPLE they lead**

while developing ↑ ↓ *to use empowering*

GREAT GODLY *Holistic Transformation*

PURPOSE they are moving toward ← *toward a compelling and deeply owned* ← **PROCESSES they ensure are in place**

See these connecting words 'while developing'? The leader we have been describing here is thinking long-term. About their own future and about the future of their team or organization. They are wisely developing themselves to either be the person needed for the next chapter of the organization's history or wisely planning a transition strategy for themselves and the organization. One of the greatest gifts of my work has been the privilege of journeying long enough with some of my students that I saw them enter their places of influence, faithfully serve their places of influence, and now reach out for counsel on how to finish well. Ok Wayne, lead us through a Case Study."

Wayne moved to the front of the room and said, "By now, we see that organizational effectiveness begins at the board level with good Policy Governance, intentional, disciplined implementation, and accountability. In my experience, much focus is given to the leadership and management of the CEO, but it seems less common to focus on the board with the same intentional, disciplined implementation and accountability. Let's consider a few common situations. Team one you will work on the first scenario, team two the second and team three the last."

SCENARIO 1: BOARD GOVERNANCE

A CGO is tasked with executing board directives, yet not everyone abides by them.

Example:

The board just conducted an in-camera session. At the end of the session, a clear board directive was issued to the CGO for execution. Within ten days of the board meeting, the CGO circulated an email stating that they decided, upon advice from a few of their "personal advisors," that the board directive was poorly processed and ill-advised. They then informed the board that they had decided on a very different directive and approach.

There is high empathy among some members who would like to ignore the CGO's disregard of a board directive, even though the Policy Governance document speaks clearly to the role and boundaries of the CGO.

- How should this be addressed, by whom, and when?
- Why is this important?

SCENARIO 2: MONITORING

Organizational effectiveness is contingent upon accomplishing board-stated ends, within board-stated boundaries. Yet things can quickly go wrong.

Example:

A CEO is hired and tasked with accomplishing board-stated ends, within board-stated boundaries. Nine months later, the organization is facing a significant and shocking fiscal deficit. All along, the CEO implied compliance with expectations, yet it is now evident that the fiscal deficit is threatening the future of the organization. The board is taken completely by surprise, although the CEO had technically passed their performance review and had each of their carefully edited board reports approved.

- What should the board do at this point?
- How should the board have taken proactive action to monitor organizational effectiveness rather than assuming a wait-and-see approach?

SCENARIO 3: CONTROL & ACCOUNTABILITY

While organizations and boards have existed for centuries, Policy Governance is a relatively new concept or process. It requires an owner to be identified. The values and expectations of the owner must be preserved and honoured at every level of the organization.

Example:

Boards establish organizational ends and boundaries to be honoured and adhered to. Once the Policy Governance document has been carefully prepared, the board hires a CEO, entrusting the entire organization to that CEO. Imagine you are consulting with two boards

Precisely how will you advise the first to give their new CEO the power to lead while ensuring desired outcomes with full confidence?

Knowing that organizational drift is not uncommon. How will you advise a volunteer board to ensure both existing and new members keep responsibly oriented to the Policy Governance process that they have committed to?

RESOURCES TO ASSIST WITH CO-GOVERNING

After our groups reported back Dr. Magnus continued, "One final thought about governance before we move on. There is tremendous organizational pressure to change and develop quickly. There is a common perception that the governing system, with its clear lines of alignment and accountability, is too cumbersome and slow to change with sufficient ease. This is especially true in seasons of complexity, change, transition, succession, and such. One way to address this is by considering a dual operating system.

"There are increasing numbers of resources emerging about this. Robert Quinn[9] clarifies the key ingredients in a positive organization and contends that we may need to consider proceeding as a bi-lingual organization. The two languages we need to be able to speak are those of control and constraint; and possibility and emergence. I highly recommend Quinn's resource. He offers key characteristics that mark a positive organization, such as a growth focus, self-organizing teams, intrinsic motivation, positive contagion, full engagement, individual accountability, decisive action, and constructive

---

[9] Robert Quinn, *The Positive Organization: Breaking Free from Conventional Cultures, Constraints, & Beliefs,* Berrett-Koehler, 2015.

confrontation. These contribute to a visionary, innovative, and productive team of self-actualizing and high-performing individuals. Few organizations achieve this.

"Yet, his list does not stop there. He goes on to include cost control, organizational predictability, procedural compliance, and a list of other wise practices. This is where we most see Quinn's brilliance. As I have sought to stress throughout, it is not one or the other; it is both-and. Another polarity. Stable governance and generative opportunities. Consistency and rapid iterations of innovation. If you have too much on one side of the pole, you may see flourishing for a while, but soon there will be chaos. If the organization swings too deeply into a bureaucratic mindset, change becomes almost impossible, and policies and procedures become restrictive. Very few organizations are skilled at keeping these poles in balance, yet this is exactly what a flourishing organization much do. Quinn includes a 'Positive Organization Generator' at the back of his book that is worth the price of the book alone. It would be helpful for anyone wishing to become more balanced and healthier. Bi-lingual language. Balanced approaches. So helpful.

"In my estimation, another must-have resource to understand a dual operating system without losing your way is John Kotter's *Accelerate*. He also suggests that organizations must first have clearly aligned governing pathways. This creates a stable framework that protects from chaos or siloing. In the dual system, you must also have a strategy accelerator. A guiding coalition. The primary function of this group is agility and speed to what he calls, 'leap into the future.' Their secondary function is constant innovation and leadership development. This system allows for many more high-potential people to be given opportunities and grow.

"In a prior section, we have an example of an attempt to have a dual operating system[10] in the transition of a very significant and well-established church, but you could use this model, which is designed for the corporate world, in any setting."

Dr. Magnus shifted in his seat and then said, "Let's recap our model before taking a break. The leader in our model intentionally and irresistibly develops and mobilizes people. These people use engaging and transforming processes to move together toward a compelling and transforming purpose. It is this final part of the path that we will explore when we get together next."

---

10 *Accelerate*, 37.

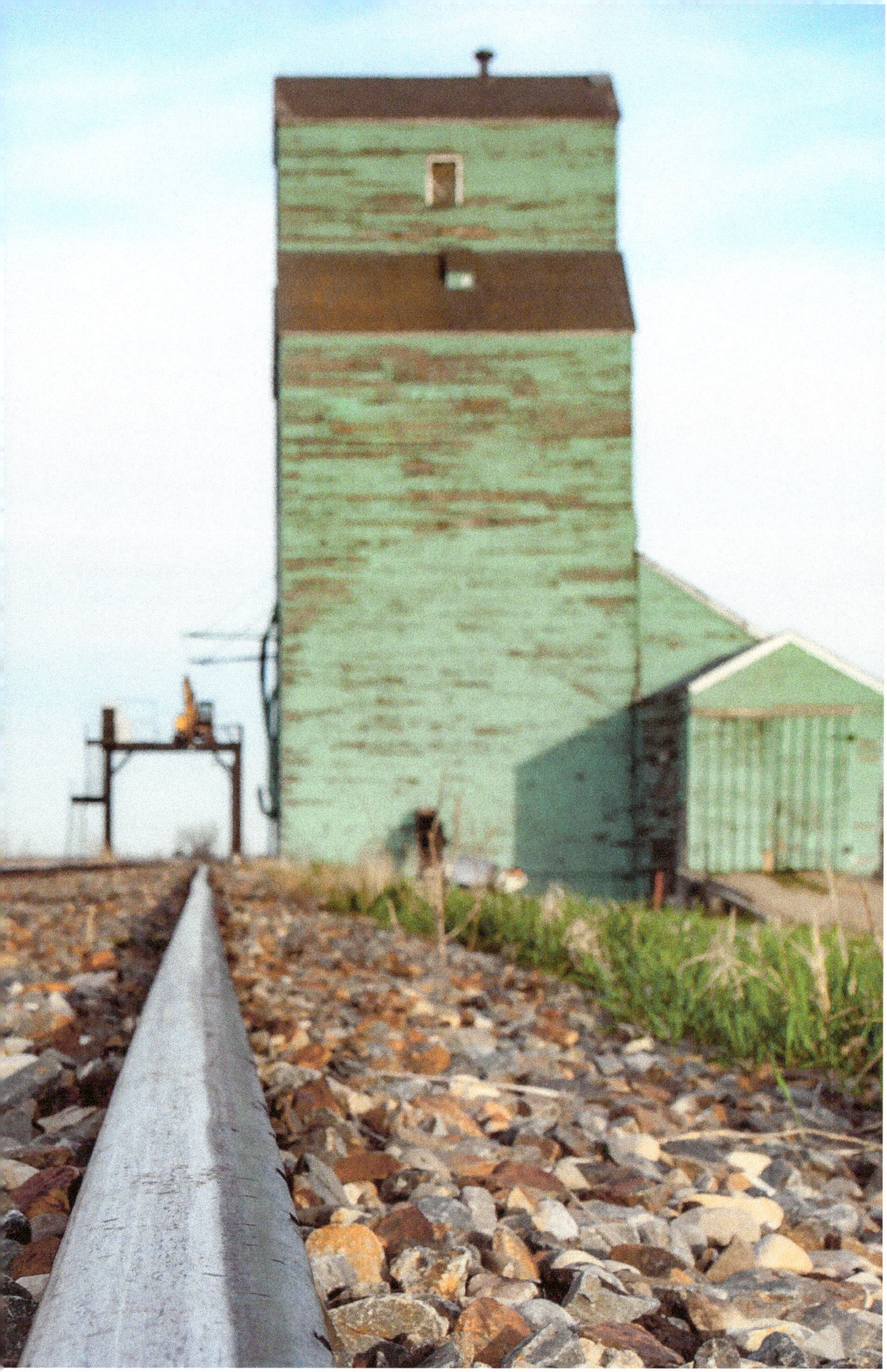

10. SUCCESSION

"It's time to talk about the last piece of the model. Hopefully, by now, we see how important it is to build high trust, high respect, high performing teams. And we've seen how the role of the leader is so crucial in crafting this kind of culture. If we want our teams and organizations to thrive after we leave, we cannot leave succession to chance. Effective leaders are intentional about developing others, so that the new leaders are ready to take their place.

"1 Kings 19:16-21 gives us a helpful picture of this. Elijah wants Elisha to be successful—see how close those two words are; they both start with success. I'd encourage you to look at this story later because it can be done well. Sometimes, leaders are focused on finishing well, and they plan carefully enough to prepare the organization and set the next leader up for success.

"There are four common approaches to transition or succession in organizations that I have observed.

"The first is what we could call a Pipeline Approach, where the leadership identifies high-potential people and intentionally helps them grow toward key roles. Normally the goal here is to pull the best up quickly by giving them lots of opportunities, training, and support.

"The second is what I like to call a Progressive Approach. We could draw it like this," he said, sketching the following model on the whiteboard.

"This approach involves a series of waves. In the first wave, a strong leader comes into their own and builds a strong organization around them. We see this with the upward swing of the first S curve. Even a very skilled leader will eventually reach their personal capacity and competency as the organization grows. If they insist on hanging on to or are expected by others to continue with the same style of leadership, they will burn out, leave or allow the organization to plateau and decline. However, if someone is wise enough to surround this leader with a team, the organization will be better positioned to move into its next season, which we show here as the next wave. As well as bringing diverse perspectives and skills, this team acts as additional arms to carry the burden of leadership. The people invited onto this leadership team represent the ability to work together well, despite diverse perspectives. Sometimes, someone must be brought in from outside if the needed skills are not available internally. For example, I find that many churches need to look outside for operational leaders as the congregation grows.

"Of course, the first step is ensuring that the people you move into these positions are ready for the additional responsibility. This requires a leadership culture in which stretch opportunities, coaching, and other supports have been offered. As people are elevated in the organization, part of their job description must be the intentional development of their team—whether paid or, as in the case of some non-profits and churches, volunteer. Creating this culture of leadership and development is very wise, and for Christian leaders, it enables us to develop a Kingdom view because many of the people we pour into will move on to other organizations, and you must learn to celebrate that.

"The third approach occurs in many organizations that have a long-term and much appreciated, strong leader. Many such organizations discover that it doesn't matter where they find a replacement for that leader because they are likely to be short-term. This happens because they will be expected to have the capacity and competencies of the person who has gone before, even though that person had numerous years to grow into that role and may have formed a culture that worked for *them*. In this case, organizations may bring in a transition leader. It is important to establish a previously agreed upon time span because this will enable the transitional leader to speak with more caring candour. It also helps them better leverage their opportunity and ensures they don't grow comfortable with the unhealthy parts of the culture. They need to make changes to set up the next leader for success."

"The fourth approach is to headhunt and find quality people who have gained experience and credibility elsewhere.

"Now, something that can often go wrong in succession is that we fail to celebrate the outgoing leader in an appropriate and attentive way. And a related issue is the leader's personal need to both process the transition and discover how to continue to contribute, normally in a new context. If this is not approached well by the leader, the Board, and others, there can be a significant loss to God's kingdom and a challenging time of grief for the outgoing leader.

"That brings us to another key point. People often ask me how much lead time they should give before retiring or moving on. Depending on the circumstances, I think one of the key criteria is how much time it will take for the Board to get their legs under them. Boards tend to choose good leaders and then let them lead. Which is good in many ways but bad if things start to go wrong and they do not have good accountability structures. If someone has been an exceptional and trusted leader, and if they have been in their position for decades, the Board may need three years to be ready for a significant change. They will need to take the time to ask some hard questions, do the hard work of discerning what kind of leader is needed for the future, shepherd the organization during the transition, orient the new leader, and celebrate the exiting one. It is possible to bring in a transitional leader, of course, but, in my opinion, this is more widely used than necessary if we planned better. Joshua, how did you decide how much lead time to give your Board?"

Joshua answered, "Our goal is for a seamless transition. This is critical so we can maintain the momentum of where God is taking us. We work in ninety countries and have four thousand people on our team. That's why I started five years before the end of my term to prepare myself and our organization for this transition. One of my top priorities is to work with my team to make sure they are ready for what will come next. Several years ago, we were not structured for growth or sustainability. The Ebola outbreak in 2013 revealed leadership gaps—cracks that needed fixing. As a result of what we learned during that season, we completely restructured our team, adding six new leaders to our global team and doubling the number of geographic leaders. When Covid hit, we were much better prepared to cope with that crisis. So, preparing well for my succession enabled us to more wisely and sustainably navigate even before I stepped down."

"That is so helpful. Thank you. You mentioned a seamless transition. And for any secure leader, that, of course, should be the goal. Insecure leaders secretly, or sometimes not so secretly, hope things fall apart after they leave. Perhaps they have the misguided belief that this will somehow demonstrate their good leadership. Yet even secure, mature leaders may find seamless transitions more challenging than we would like to think. No matter how gifted the new leader is. No matter what training and mentoring they have received. The fact is that they have not had the years of experience in this role that you have had. They lack the wisdom that comes from leading and learning in that role for all those years. Every transition is an act of faith as well as a disciplined process."

Joshua interjected, "This is something we have been reflecting on. However, I would also say that the opposite is also true. I am encouraging the Board not to look for someone like me, who has my life experience and gifting, but rather to look for the person needed for the next stage of the mission's history and journey with them as their strengths and priorities become evident."

"Well said." Dr. Magnus mused and then asked, "What has been more challenging than you expected, Joshua? Has your inner critic been getting in the way?"

"I would say it is my inner urgency rather than inner critic that is the most challenging. One of the hardest parts for me, now that the end of this chapter draws closer is to stay focused on where I am and not allow myself to feel a sense of urgency about what comes next."

Dr. Magnus nodded, "So honest, thank you. In my experience, Boards are often unprepared for leadership transition. One of the strategies I always suggest to them is that they establish two teams. One to carefully and prayerfully select and onboard a new senior leader; the other to support the existing leader carefully and prayerfully through the transition. Our goal for leaders who have served faithfully is that they leave feeling deeply cared for. And their spouse as well. I am working with numerous organizations on this right now. In one case, the spouse has felt completely left out. Their contribution to the organization has not been acknowledged, and their feelings about the transition have not even been considered. This is a missed opportunity to tend and care for our people—and model the way to emerging leaders."

Pointing at the board, he reminded us, "This model reminds us that every part must be infused with great *and* godly principles. We tend to forget that. We should look different in almost every way from what we see in other organizations that do not share our worldview."

Take a moment and reflect. Whatever your role is in your current organization. What are you doing to set things up well for whoever will come after you? If you were going to be the next person coming into your role, what would you want your successor to have left behind for you?

A few minutes later, Dr. Magnus said, "I have often been asked to help someone who has decided to resign because they are overwhelmed by the role. I always suggest that we set aside the idea of resigning until we understand better the root causes and whether alternatives might be possible. In almost every case, we discover that the demands on the leader were unrealistic and that, should they step down and someone else come in, within a short period of time, the new person would be in the same situation. Whenever you see patterns repeat themselves with new people, you know it is a systemic issue, not an individual one."

Wayne put up his hand and said, "I want to circle back to something we have talked about already because it is so important. We are watching what seems like a mass exodus of leaders in business and the church. It is concerning to observe, and I can't help but wonder what needs to happen so people aren't leaving prematurely?"

Dr. Magnus agreed. "The numbers are staggering. Of course, so much of what we have been talking about here is creating the kind of culture where people want to stay and are able to stay but let me make this personal. I once wrote a 21-page letter that a kind colleague did not hand in. Instead, they met with me and asked what was going on and what would need to change for me to feel I could stay. That conversation not only helped me clarify the root challenges but also form a plan for bringing these exact issues up in a more constructive way. Changes were made that I believe were better for everyone, and we carried on. Sometimes we need to leave, but often we need to find a way to identify and address the problems. Why? Rory Vaden's work is so important.[1] In a world where so many things are both important

---

[1] Rory Vaden, *Procrastinate on Purpose: 5 Permissions to Multiply Your Time, 2015,* TarcherPerigee.

and urgent, we need to discern what will have a lasting impact. He calls this 'Duration.' What will endure? What will have the best long-term impact on the organization? In my case, I knew that leaving would not actually fix anything. So, although in many ways it was harder to stay, I believed that was the great and godly thing to do in that situation. You need to discern this for yourself, of course, but for me, in that season, it was the right thing to do because it enabled us to restructure in a way that helped me thrive and has enabled several leaders since then to thrive as well."

Wayne thanked Dr. Magnus for sharing his story, then said, "That must have taken both humility and courage."

"We are all human. It is understandable that, at times, we want to leave prematurely because of the stress and strain. I guess God just gave me the insight, and I had surrounded myself with books and other resources that showed me there were options. Carefully considering your options through the lens of God's calling on your life and discerning what is best long-term helps give us the courage to try to apply what we are learning together here. There is a time to move on, I just hate to see people moving on prematurely. However, there does come a time to move on, and I have asked Marvin to share about the season of transition that he is in."

Marvin took a second to finish making his notes before standing to face the class. "One of the things I learned from you, Dr. Magnus, is that almost every pastor is an interim pastor, and every leader is an interim leader. In every case other than a startup or closeout, there will be someone before you and someone after you. As an interim leader, you honour your predecessor and pave the way for your successor. With that mindset, I did something that surprised many people. Long before the time when a church would normally start thinking about a successor for my role, I did two things. I took some training on transition and interim pastoring, and I initiated a conversation with our board that developed into a plan. There are really four options, and the first is a sudden transition due to death, illness, or moral failure. This can be the most challenging for a board and organization to navigate. The second option is someone who doesn't move on even though they are past their 'best before date.' Another approach is a short runway with a limited timeframe and little or no planning. Obviously, option four, a carefully thought through succession plan, is the best option but we planned for all four just in case.

"Each transition is of course unique and there is no template that works for all, but we wanted to glean principles that might be applicable in our setting and then adjust as needed. In speaking to other leaders who had transitioned well we discovered that some of the most successful outcomes came when the leader led the process. I spoke to our board, and they agreed. We also set a two-year time frame for this to unfold. Early in the process the board asked me to lead a Futures Team which was made up of board and staff members and an external coach who specialized in helping organizations with leadership transitions. This team took eleven months to gather information from our congregation, develop a communications plan, create a candidate profile, and discuss anything else that was deemed important for this team to consider or create in preparation for the board to appoint a pastoral search team the following year. In our context that will result in the board choosing one candidate to bring to the congregation for a vote.

"Dr. Magnus helped us here again when he suggested to the board that they also appoint a second team. I am not sure what to call it except a 'Help Marvin to transition well team.' We might not have considered this otherwise, and few leaders would feel comfortable asking for this even if they thought of it. His point was that the focus of transition is often on the incoming leader but that the way a church or organization handles the transition of the outgoing leader is equally important both for them and for the process and successor.

"There are some inherent challenges. First, for all parties to act with high integrity, grace, and transparency, recognizing the complicated range of emotions and expectations and longings that are part of the transition—both for the congregation or organization and for the outgoing leader. Secondly, for the outgoing leader to not be over- or under-involved in the process. I realized that I had a really important role to play in moving things forward without influencing things in inappropriate ways or being perceived as doing so in ways that could be problematic. Thirdly, there is the challenge of the board involving the church through data collection while also readying the church for the change, especially in a case like mine where I will have been their leader for close to 35 years by the time the transition is fully completed. And finally, there is the issue of timing. We announced two years out that we were beginning a transition process. The risk was that this was too early, and that would have a negative impact. The alternative was to try and keep it quiet, but we did not want something like that to leak out, so we decided to get out in front of it and be both transparent and intentional in our communication. Again, we sought others who had gone before, and, in the end, we borrowed a communication strategy that Beulah Alliance had used and graciously shared with us.

"So those are the challenges, but there are also incredible opportunities. Every transition has a plan—whether it is written down or not, whether it is thought out or not. A longer runway and intentional plan create the opportunity to engage more people and hopefully engender greater ownership when the decision is made about who is the next leader. It also gives people the opportunity to adjust to the upcoming change and shape the future.

"Our transition is unfolding in a way that I have not seen in any other church—and that is good because each situation is different. One thing we share in common with other Christian organizations is the opportunity to use times of change to invite people into prayer and listening to God and each other. In Acts 15, the Jerusalem Council came to a decision about something that was important and potentially divisive in the early church. And here is what it says in Acts chapter 15, 'it seemed good to the Holy Spirit and to us.' And that is my prayer for us as a church, that we can engage in a process that is well communicated, that is well structured, and that at the end of it, we can truthfully say, 'It seemed good to the Holy Spirit and to us.'"

Dr. Magnus shook Marvin's hand as they exchanged places, "There are so many valuable insights in what you shared, but I would like to focus on a few. First, I appreciated the intentionality that you and your board have put into considering how a change in senior leadership after so many years affects the people. In your case, the congregation. We know that people go through a whole range of emotions when change is thrust upon them, and providing opportunities to speak into and process what is happening is critical in building ownership but also in treating people as holistic human beings.

"Secondly, I really appreciated the Acts 15 model, which reminds us that we are 100% dependent on God to guide us, and we must also do our due diligence as leaders. In a world where transition is so often mishandled and people and organizations needless damaged, this is an example of transition handled well.

"Adam, as a Board Chair, you recently journeyed with a large organization through the succession of a senior leader. Can you tell us a bit about that?"

Adam took a deep breath and began, "As you suggest, we experienced a unique transition after twenty years of an established president. There were a few things that really stood out for me in the whole process:

1. As a Board Chair, I didn't know what I didn't know. Which was why it was so significant for us to embrace help. I'm not going to lie—it was costly. We spent sobering amounts of money to acquire counsel. Further, there's a saying from John Maxwell that kept proving true, 'However long you think it will take to do something, double it.' We kept making timelines and deadlines and discovering that four weeks turned into eight weeks, and two months turned into four months. And we had a significant choice to make as a board—do we do this fast, or do we do this well?

2. Which leads me to the second point. We kept asking, 'What is the wise thing to do?' Starting with the premise of asking for help and choosing not to simply reinforce our own bias led us to engage legal counsel and HR consulting, but it also ensured that we had conversations with the full board. Of all the things that I believe led to a successful and widely owned decision, this one was key. The whole board was involved in any major decisions around succession. There were no backroom handshakes or napkin deals. Did it slow things down? Considerably! Was it demanding and, at times, overwhelming? Absolutely. As Chair, I had to intentionally be aware of when I was engaging in a conversation or when we were approaching a decision, and I had to ensure that I didn't deliver something that wasn't mine to promise. This meant I had to govern myself. I kept thinking about what it would be like to be a board member receiving my report. If there was ever a point that I felt I would be uncomfortable not knowing or wondering why a decision was made without the board's involvement, I would step back and say, 'That will be something the board will need to discuss.'

3. I kept in mind the cost of things going poorly or off the rails. Sure, there would be severance and other financial costs, but the relational costs are what ultimately weaken the organization and halts momentum. It was an opportunity for me to test out what I've been coaching churches with for years . . .to imagine the worst-case scenario and ask, 'how much does that cost you?' Double or triple that amount, and I believe you'll be close to how much you should spend in the hiring (or in this case transition) process because the price we pay for things going wrong in HR impacts organizations deep and wide."

What did you most appreciate about this story? Have you had or observed a different experience? What were your key learnings?

Personalize it: What principles or practices have you built in—or do you need to begin to build in—to ensure healthy succession?

CONCLUSION

I didn't know whether I should be excited to go back and initiate the steps that I had laid out for myself and our team. I didn't feel ready, but does one ever feel truly ready for changes of this magnitude? In private conversation, Dr. Magnus had encouraged me to take it slowly, planning one step at a time and watching how the system reacted before moving on. He had connected me to someone else in my industry who was several steps further ahead in initiating a similar review of themselves, their team, their processes, and the alignment with their compelling purpose. Armed with the tools I had received and Dr. Magnus and this mentor on speed dial, I decided I was as prepared as I could be. I had already reached out to my prayer team, and they were praying for wisdom, favour, and resilience. In the quiet of that pre-class moment, I reminded myself of why this mattered, committed to do my best with the Lord's help and cried out for His help. Looking around, it looked like others might be doing the same.

Dr. Magnus seemed to sense our need. After giving us extra time to settle, he said, "As I reflected on how to end our time together, Ephesians 4 came to mind as a beautiful summary of so much of what we have discussed. I especially love the accessible way that Eugene Peterson has written it in *The Message*. Chapters one to three are filled with glorious theology.

"And now, as we reach chapter four, Paul switches to practice—as if he is saying, 'In light of all this truth, here is how to live.' He operationalizes it for them. I love this. I am handing out copies of verses one to sixteen."

Underline the phrases and words that relate to what we have been discussing. I count several but will highlight a few once you have read it.

> **4** ¹⁻³ In light of all this, here's what I want you to do. While I'm locked up here, a prisoner for the Master, I want you to get out there and walk—better yet, run!—on the road God called you to travel. I don't want any of you sitting around on your hands. I don't want anyone strolling off, down some path that goes nowhere. And

mark that you do this with humility and discipline—not in fits and starts, but steadily, pouring yourselves out for each other in acts of love, alert at noticing differences and quick at mending fences.

⁴⁻⁶ You were all called to travel on the same road and in the same direction, so stay together, both outwardly and inwardly. You have one Master, one faith, one baptism, one God and Father of all, who rules over all, works through all, and is present in all. Everything you are and think and do is permeated with Oneness.

⁷⁻¹³ But that doesn't mean you should all look and speak and act the same. Out of the generosity of Christ, each of us is given his own gift. The text for this is,

He climbed the high mountain,
He captured the enemy and seized the plunder,
He handed it all out in gifts to the people.

Is it not true that the One who climbed up also climbed down, down to the valley of earth? And the One who climbed down is the One who climbed back up, up to highest heaven. He handed out gifts above and below, filled heaven with his gifts, filled earth with his gifts. He handed out gifts of apostle, prophet, evangelist, and pastor-teacher to train Christ's followers in skilled servant work, working within Christ's body, the church, until we're all moving rhythmically and easily with each other, efficient and graceful in response to God's Son, fully mature adults, fully developed within and without, fully alive like Christ.

¹⁴⁻¹⁶ No prolonged infancies among us, please. We'll not tolerate babes in the woods, small children who are easy prey for predators. God wants us to grow up, to know the whole truth and tell it in love—like Christ in everything. We take our lead from Christ, who is the source of everything we do. He keeps us in step with each other. His very breath and blood flow through us, nourishing us so that we will grow up healthy in God, robust in love.[1]

---

1 Ephesians 4:1-16, *The Message*

"Look at how he starts—don't walk, run! Run where? On the road God called *you* to travel. Not someone else's road. Your road. Don't sit on your hands, wander off or go in fits and starts—be focused, intentional, and consistent. Live with humility and discipline. Pour yourself out in acts of love for one another. Notice the differences but don't let them create fences between you. Stay together. I love this. Stay together—inwardly and outwardly. We have One Lord. Everything is permeated with Oneness, yet we are all unique. We have all been given a unique gift. Leadership gifts are intended to train Christ's followers in skilled servant work until we are all moving rhythmically and easily with each other and becoming mature adults—alignment, engagement, gift-based service, development, personal accountability, telling the truth in love, tending to one another, higher purpose, God dependence, robustness—it's all here!"

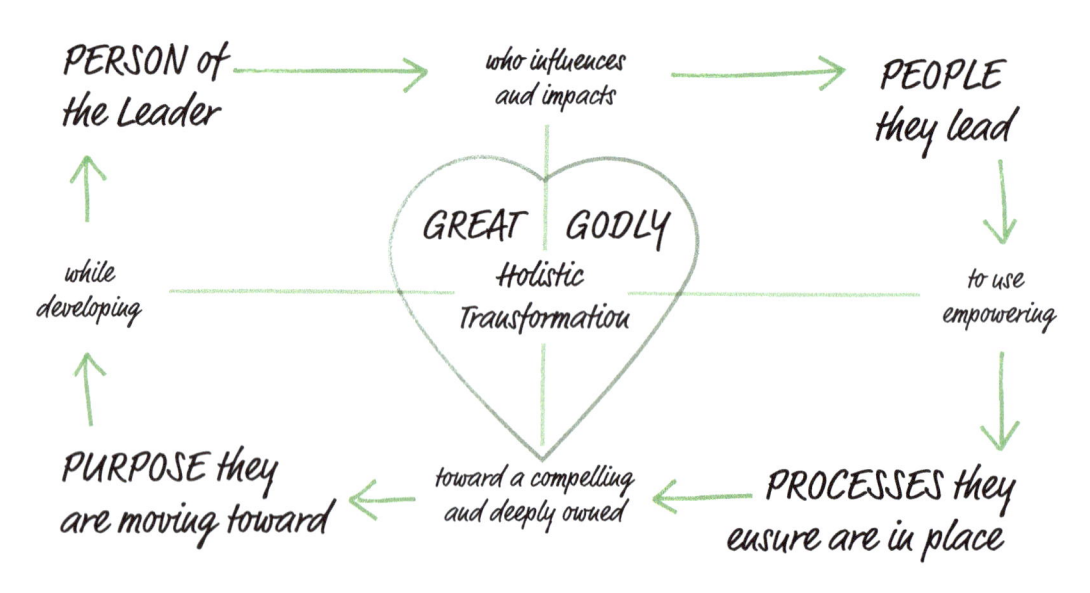

PERSON of the Leader → who influences and impacts → PEOPLE they lead

GREAT GODLY Holistic Transformation

while developing ↑ … ↓ to use empowering

PURPOSE they are moving toward ← toward a compelling and deeply owned ← PROCESSES they ensure are in place

Copyright 2023, Paul E. Magnus

Personalize it before we close: Is there one of the lenses that requires more attention at this point in your personal leadership? What is needed?

How can you think about your organization more holistically using this model?

How could it inform you and your team's approach to planning, execution, and measurement?

Given this high purpose and calling so beautifully expressed by Paul as guided by the Holy Spirit, what is your sense of your own leadership and your heightened purpose?

I recently read Ryan Leak's book *Leveling Up* and was inspired by his 12 questions to offer these adapted ones to you:

1. What is your definition of success as a leader?
2. What do you perceive it is like to be on the other side of you?
3. How can you get better and who might best help you with clarity on that?
4. What credit can you give away, to whom and why?
5. What risk do you need to take?
6. Who knows who you really are, and how well do they know you?
7. Whose dream do you need to support?

Dr. Magnus chuckled and said, "Of course, we could do this whole class again, walking backwards this time around the model. How does your compelling vision—your purpose—inform and empower your processes? How do your processes bring life and freedom, and both direction and agency to the people? How are the people a reflection of both who you are as a leader and a sufficient representation of all that you are not? What does their growth and engagement show about your leadership and the leadership they are receiving from their managers? And how is your team shaping you—challenging your thinking, enabling you to envision and do more than you could do on your own, keeping you humble and on your knees?

"And how is all this informed by and responsive to the growing heart at the centre of it all? But that will have to be a class for another day because, for now, all I want to say is, 'go in peace to love and to serve the Lord.' I believe in you. Christ died for you. The Holy Spirit is present to you. Go and holistically lead with diligence and heart."

And under my breath, I whispered, "With your help, Lord, Amen."

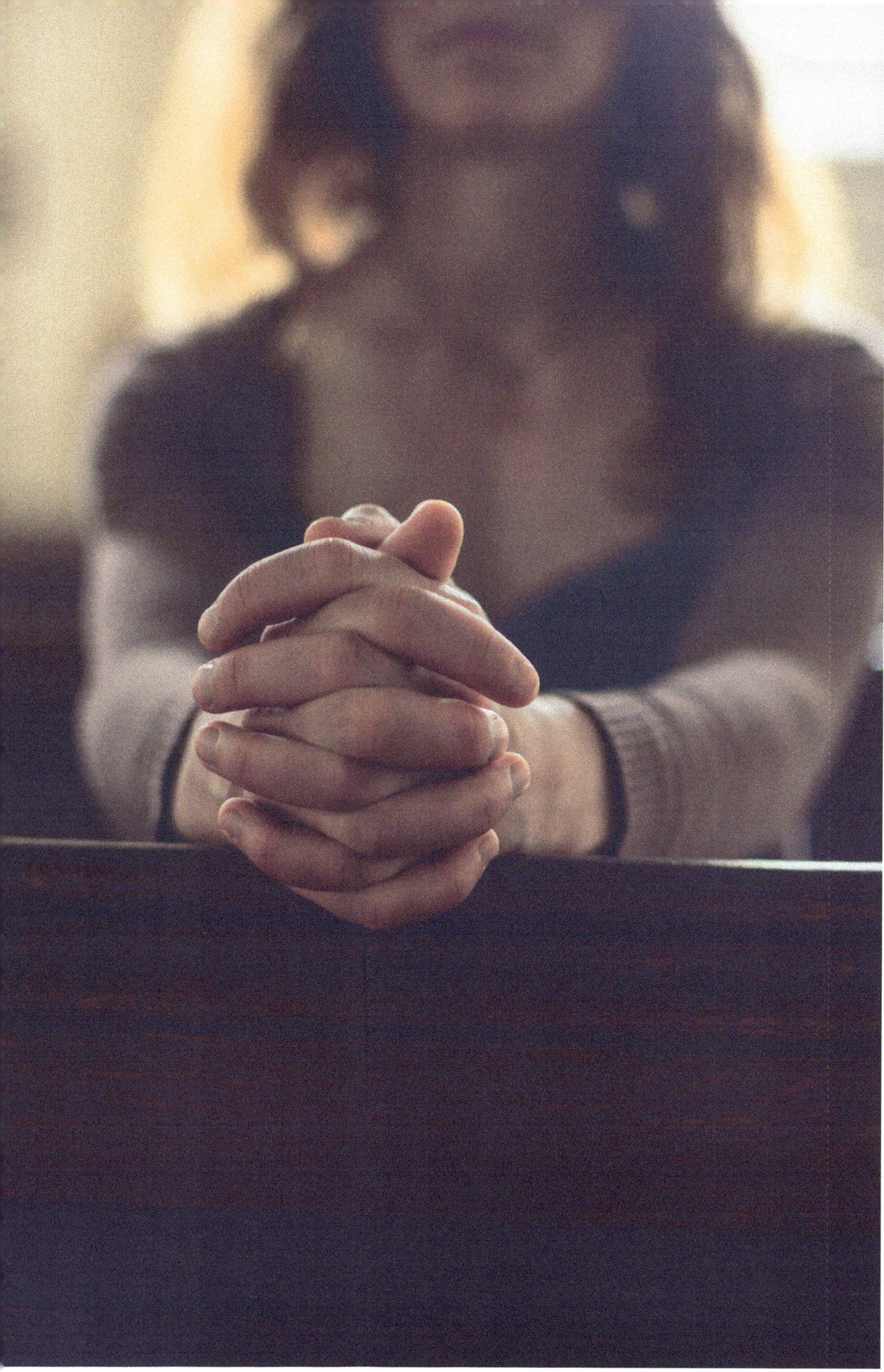

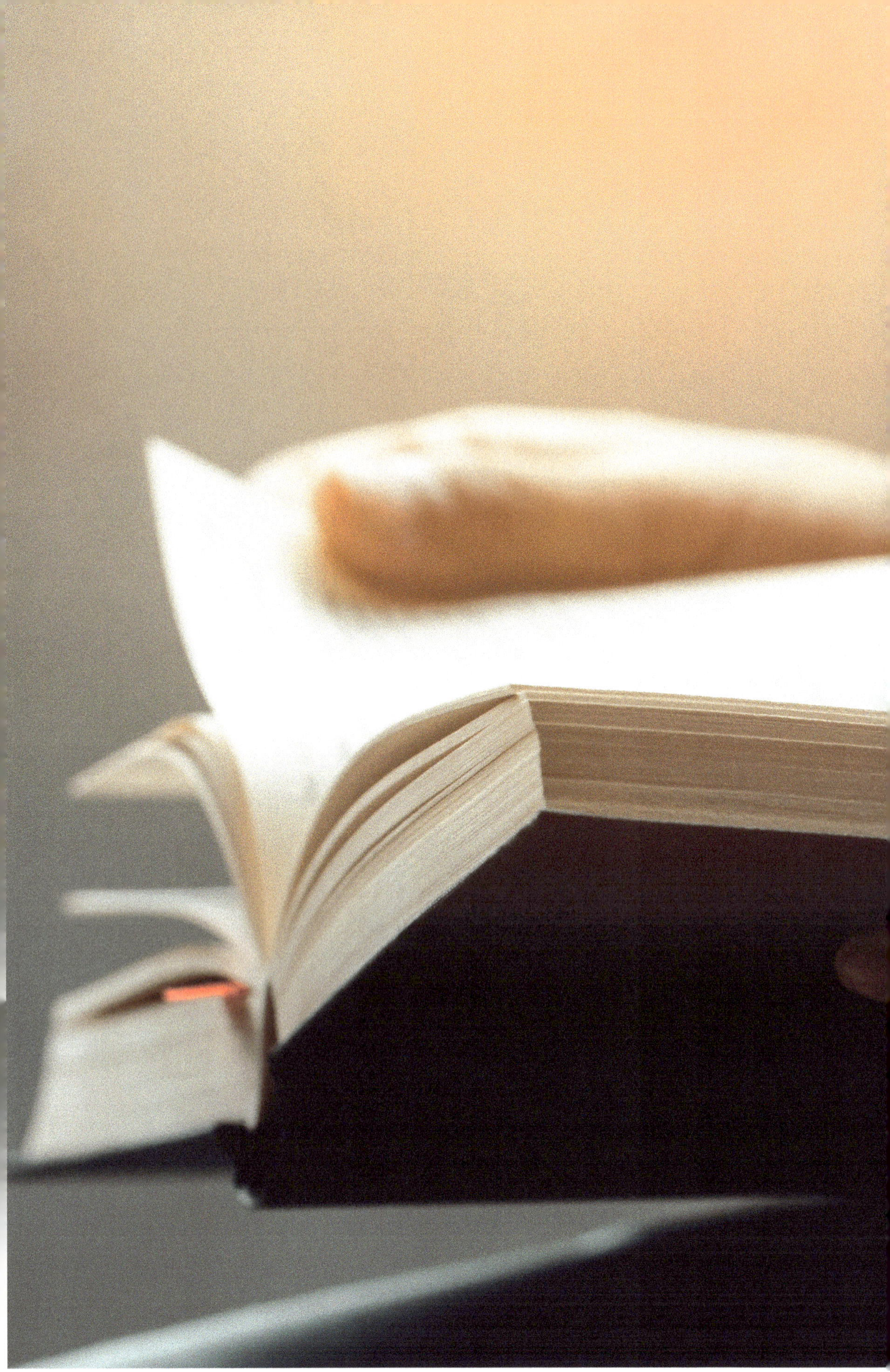

APPENDIX
DR. MAGNUS' BOOKSHELF

"Some of you have been asking for a curated list of the resources that have shed so much light on leadership for me over the years. As I look over my bookshelf, I see that some are so thumbed and marked up as to be barely readable. Some have been loaned out to so many leaders that the fingerprints on them would tell their own story. Others are quite new, and I am still processing their meaning and how they overlap with the other resources here.

"These books, along with the diverse and rich career opportunities God has provided, have shaped my over 50 years of teaching and practice. I hope you find them helpful. And I sincerely hope you pass on to others what you are learning. If you don't, you may just get a phone call from me.

"I have done my best to arrange them by topic for ease, but of course, several could fit in many categories.

Great and Godly Leadership
Mike Bonem did some great work on this in his book by the same title, *In Pursuit of Great and Godly Leadership: Tapping the Wisdom of the World for the Kingdom of God*.[1]

Great Leadership
Jim Collins changed the thinking of leadership in all domains—business, non-profit and the church—in his book *Good to Great*.[2] He talks about the risk of settling for good and offers practical yet well researched insights into how to move from good towards organizational greatness.

---

1 Mike Bonem, *In Pursuit of Great and Godly Leadership: Tapping the Wisdom of the World for the Kingdom of God*, Jossey-Bass, 2012.

2 Jim Collins, *Good to Great: Why Some Companies Make the Leap... And Others Don't*, Harper Collins, 2001.

Willie Piettersen's *Strategic Learning: How to Be Smarter than Your Competition and Turn Key Insights into Competitive Advantage*.[3] Don't let the title turn you off. Or the fact that it is a bit older. There are great nuggets in this book to help you and your team think about how to maximize your God-given potential.

And who can forget Steven Covey's *Primary Greatness: The 12 Levers of Success*[4] and *The Eighth Habit: From Effectiveness to Greatness*.[5]

Godly Leadership
Robert Lewis and Rob Wilkins' classic *The Church of Irresistible Influence: Bridge Building Stories to Help Reach Your Community*[6] came out in 2001 and had a big impact on me at the time. The irresistibility of Jesus. The call on the church to be equally countercultural and irresistible.

One of the things I love about the life of Jesus is the way He *did* things is. The Gospel of John is especially helpful here. What Jesus taught is crucial, but so is the way he lived and led. For over almost eight decades I have been learning about this remarkable God who became man. And he fascinates me more and more the more I read about him! Have you seen John Ortberg's book *Who is This Man: the Unpredictable Impact of the Inescapable Jesus*[7]? So helpful!

Holistic Leadership
I like Kouzes and Posner, authors of the seminal book *The Leadership Challenge*,[8] they don't try to define leadership. They describe the practices

---

[3] Willie Piettersen, *Strategic Learning: How to Be Smarter than Your Competition and Turnkey Insights into Competitive Advantage*, Wiley, 2010.

[4] Steven Covey. *Primary Greatness: The 12 Levers of Success*, 2015.

[5] Steven Covey's *The Eighth Habit: From Effectiveness to Greatness*.

[6] Robert Lewis & Rob Wilkins, *The Church of Irresistible Influence: Bridge Building Stories to Help Reach Your Community*, 2001.

[7] John Ortberg, *Who is This Man: the Unpredictable Impact of the Inescapable Jesus*, Zondervan, 2014.

[8] James Kouzes and Barry Posner, *The Leadership Challenge*, Jossey-Bass, 6th Ed., 2017.

and commitments of effective leaders that begins with modelling the way, and is followed by inspiring a shared vision, challenging the process, and enabling others to act. This is similar to the construct I have created. Although I began it before their books came out, I have been both influenced by, and confirmed in my instincts by their research.

THE HEART OF LEADERSHIP

Spiritual Quotient
I mentioned John Ortberg's *Soul Keeping*[9] because he approaches the question of tending our soul holistically. I also love Dallas Willard's *Renovation of the Heart.*[10]

Ken Shigematsu, *God in My Everything*[11] had a significant impact on my thinking about how God both weaves through and supports every part of our lives and leadership.

Ruth Haley Barton's book *Strengthening the Soul of Your Leadership* [12]is another good resource here although I don't find her work as holistic as some others.

Andy Stanleys' *Enemies of the Heart: Breaking Free for the Four Emotions that Control You*. It addresses the health of our core—both as a leader and we could apply this to our organization. Proverbs 4:23 tells us to "above all else guard [our] heart, for everything you do flows from it" (NIV) Stanley identifies the roots of our simmering volcanoes as unprocessed guilt, anger, greed, and jealousy. These bear fruit in attitudes and actions. A valuable book to have on your shelf if you want to dig below the surface.

---

9 John Ortberg, *Soul Keeping: Caring for the Most Important Part of You*, Zonderan, 2014.

10 Dallas Willard. *Renovation of the Heart: Putting on The Character of Christ*, 20th Anniversary Ed., Tyndale House Publishers, 2021.

11 Ken Shigematsu, *God in My Everything: How an Ancient Rhythm Helps Busy People Enjoy God,* Zondervan, 2013.

12 Ruth Haley Barton, *Strengthening the Soul of Your Leadership: Seeking God in the Crucible of Ministry*, FORMATIO, 2018.

Another book I mentioned above is Parker Palmer's *Let Your Life Speak*.[13] Such a great resource for considering our soul and our vocation.

Emotional Quotient and Character

When it come to our emotional intelligence Daniel Goleman's work is seminal. In *Primal Leadership*[14] he applies it specifically to leadership.

I also like Goleman's book, *Focus*.[15] In it he addresses what Nobel prize winning economist, Herbert Simon, predicted more than two decades ago—that our age of information overload would create attention poverty. We see that all around us, don't we? One important take away for me from this book was how self-awareness strengthens our awareness of our surroundings.

Peter Scazzero's *Emotionally Healthy Spirituality*[16] is an important book for everyone but perhaps especially for church leaders.

Travis Bradberry and Jean Graves take a slightly different approach in their book *Team EQ 2.0*.[17] As the name suggests their embedded instruments and insights enable us to think more broadly than our own emotional intelligence.

Brené Brown's work on vulnerability and empathy is so important and I really like her book, A*tlas of the Heart*.[18]

---

13 Parker Palmer, *Let Your Life Speak: Listening for the Voice of Vocation*, Jossey Bass, 1999.

14 Daniel Goleman, Richard Boyatzis & Annie McKee. *Primal Leadership: Unleashing the Power of Emotional Intelligence*, Harvard Business Review Press, 2013.

15 Daniel Goleman, *Focus: The Hidden Driver of Excellence*, Harper, 2015.

16 Peter Scazzero, *Emotionally Healthy Spirituality: It's Impossible to be Spiritually Mature While Remaining Emotionally Immature*, Zondervan, 2017.

17 Travis Bradberry and Jean Graves, Team EQ 2.0, 2022

18 Brené Brown, *Atlas of the Heart: Mapping Meaningful Connection and the Language of Human Experience*, Random House, 2021.

The Bain Institute[19] has done some great research around centered, inspirational leadership. Their model outlines thirty-three characteristics clustered in four areas. So comprehensive.

Mindset Quotient

Adam Grant's *Think Again: The Power of Knowing What You Don't Know*,[20] provides amazing insights into how to examine assumptions and biases. One of my favorite insights is that it is as important to unlearn as it is to learn because it is highly likely that we are wrong in several of our important opinions. Imagine becoming the kind of person who gets excited by being proven wrong! I am not talking about the core tenets of our faith, I am talking about things like strategy, cultural awareness, and perspective. He points to underlying causes like pride and confirmation biases because our mindsets are grounded in our worldview and our character. Grant shows how pride leads to an overconfidence cycle but humility to a rethinking cycle that can lead to deeper, broader, and more helpful insights.

When it comes to helping us think long term in a short-term world, I really like Dorie Clark's *The Long Game*[21] and Simon Sinek's 2019 book T*he Infinite Game*.[22] Sinek stresses the importance of having a just cause that is compelling enough that people will sacrifice for it and it can have infinite time horizons. Sounds a lot like the calling Jesus left His disciples doesn't it!

We don't focus nearly enough on the character of the leader. That is one of the reasons I so appreciated Sarah Summers book *Leadership Above the Line*.[23] She gives language to this important topic and offers powerful strategies to enable us to recognize and address mindsets and behaviours that are 'below the line.'

---

19 Bain Institute, https://www.bain.com/insights/how-leaders-inspire-cracking-the-code/

20 Adam Grant, *Think Again: The Power of Knowing What You Don't Know*, Viking, 2021.

21 Dorie Clark, *The Long Game: How to be a Long Term Thinker in a Short Term World,* Harvard Business Review Press, 2021.

22 Simon Sinek, *The Infinite Game*, Portfolio, 2019

23 Sarah Summer, *Leadership Above the Line: A Character Based Leadership Tool that leads to Success for You and Your Team*, Tyndale House Publishers, 2006.

Another great book is Marie Forelo's *Everything is Figureoutable.*[24] Just think what a difference that would make to our organizations if we believed that!

We talked about the things on repeat in our head when we discussed John Acuff's excellent book *Soundtracks: The Surprising Solution to Overthinking.*[25]

One resource I have found helpful regarding understanding our influence is Vanessa Bohn's *You Already Have More Influence Than You Think.*[26] Her research shows that people are more likely to listen to and appreciate your opinion than you would imagine. Your voice matters and we can't let our inner critic or limiting assumptions stop us from speaking up.

I really like Rory Vaden's P*rocrastinate on Purpose: 5 Permissions to Multiply Your Time.*[27] There is a time and place to procrastinate, and he walks us through when those are and how to maximize those opportunities.

Another important self-awareness resource is Daniel Pink's *The Power of Regret, How Looking Backwards Moves us Forward.*[28] He outlines four universal regrets and how they can affect our self-awareness, motivation and planning.

And when it comes to staying in a learner mindset Marilee Adams *Change Your Questions, Change Your Life*[29] is exceptional.

Physical Quotient and Energy
Looking back over the literature we see how the thinking has changed about time management. For many years it was considered an important part of leadership. Then Jim Loehr and Tony Schwartz, wrote, *The Power of Full*

---

24 Marie Forleo, *Everything is Figureoutable,* Portfolio, 2020.

25 John Acuff, *Soundtracks: The Surprising Solution to Overthinking.* Baker Books, 2021.

26 Vanessa Bohns, *You Already Have More Influence Than You Think: How We Underestimate Our Power of Persuasion and Why It Matters*, 2021.

27 Rory Vaden, P*rocrastinate on Purpose: 5 Permissions to Multiply Your Time, 2015,* Tarcher-Perigee.

28 Daniel Pink. *The Power of Regret, How Looking Backwards Moves Us Forward*, 2022.

29 Marilee Adams, *Change Your Questions, Change Your Life: 12 Powerful Tools for Leadership, Coaching and Results,* 4th Ed. Berrett- Koehler Publishers, 2022.

Engagement: Managing Energy NOT Time is the Key to High Performance[30] and many people began to think about how to best do that, sometimes at the expense of managing their time well. Whenever a pendulum swings far in one direction it will often swing back in the other before settling out somewhere in the middle. That is what happened when people like Carey Nieuwhof wrote *At Your Best: How to Get Time, Energy and Priorities Working in Your Favor.*[31] The point of course is to manage your time *and* your energy.

Author and speaker Tasha Eurich argues that, when it comes to things like self-awareness and decision making, 'what' may be a more important question than 'why.' She says, 'What can I do about this situation?' is often a stronger question than 'why did this happen?' 'Why me?' may be less helpful than 'What's most important to me and how can I ensure that stays a priority during this difficult time?'

In her book *Insight*[32] Eurich says that 'why' points us backward. 'What' points us forward, giving us a sense of agency and giving us space to think about how we want to respond. Thinking back over my career, if I had focused on why I didn't get some opportunities I would have grown resentful or left. Instead, I asked, 'what can I do to ensure that doesn't happen again?'"

Social and Connection Quotient
I mentioned Amy Edmondson's book earlier, *The Fearless Organization*[33] as this is such an important and timely topic. I cannot stress enough how crucial and interrelated psychological safety, courage and respect are for effective leadership.

---

30 Tony Schwartz, *The Power of Full Engagement: Managing Energy NOT Time is the Key to High Performance.* Free Press, 2005.

31 Carey Nieuwhof, *At Your Best: How to Get Time, Energy and Priorities Working in Your Favor,* Waterbrook, 2021.

32 Tasha Eurich, *Insight: Why We are Not as Self Aware as We Think, and How Seeing Ourselves Clearly Helps Us Succeed at Work and Life,* Currency, 2017.

33 Amy Edmondson, *The Fearless Organization; Creating Psychological Safety in the Workplace for Learning, Innovation and Growth,* Wiley, 2018.

In 2018 Vanessa Van Edwards published *Captivate: The Science of People*[34] to help leaders understand people. Then in 2022 *Cues: Master the Secret Language of Charismatic Communication*[35] came out, teaching everyone how to be more impactful at connecting and communicating using both verbal and nonverbal cues. I think one of the most important things that I have learned from Vanessa is how to connect with people faster and more effectively by being aware of our competency and warmth cues.

Another great resource for this is Buckingham's 2022 book *Love+Work*.[36] He acknowledges that the adage 'do what you love' may be harder than it looks and gives some great ideas on how to decode what our strengths are. One of my favorite parts of Buckingham's research is how important the specifics of your job are. For example, some people become a doctor to help people, but they don't love many of the day-to-day tasks of their job. The more we can drill down to what we love to do the more clarity we will have on what God has wired us for. The great thing is that this does not necessarily mean a career move. More often it means using the latitude our jobs provide to do things a bit differently.

Gordon MacDonald talks about the value of running in the company of the happy few. I love that. He talks about perseverance in adversity. His book, *A Resilient Life*[37] and Tom Rath's book *Vital Friends: The People you Cannot Afford to Live Without*[38] paint a picture of the link between relationships and both workplace effectiveness and wellbeing.

---

[34] Vanessa Van Edwards, *Captivate: The Science of People*, Portfolio, 2018.

[35] Vanessa Edwards, *Cues: Master the Secret Language of Charismatic Communication*, Portfolio, 2022.

[36] Marcus Buckingham, *Love+Work: How to find what you love, love what you do and do it for the rest of your life*, Harvard Business Review Press, 2022

[37] Gordon MacDonald, *A Resilient Life: You Can Move Ahead No Matter What,* W. Publishing Group, 2006.

[38] Tom Rath, *Vital Friends: The People you Cannot Afford to Live Without*, Gallup Press, 2006

A book that powerfully links relational intelligence to purpose is Dharius Daniels, *Relational Intelligence: The People Skills You Need for the Life of Purpose You Want*.[39]

THE PERSON OF THE LEADER

We mentioned the seminal work that Robert Clinton did about lessons and stages of leadership in *The Making of a Leader*.[40] While not meant to be prescriptive this resource is so helpful in enabling us to identify what God may be doing at various seasons of our lives and how we can partner with Him to grow in character, confidence and competence.

One of the books that I personally think should still be available is Neil Cole *Journeys of Significance*. Cole seeks to apply Clinton's framework to the apostle Paul's life. So helpful. The life and leadership of Paul have been an inspiration to me most of my life—and not just because we share the same first name. He wasn't perfect but look at the impact of his life! We have records of him ministering in Damascus, Jerusalem, Antioch, Cyprus, Perga, Iconium, Lystra, Derbe, Syria, Cilicia, Phrygia, Galatia, Troas, Philippi, Thessalonica, Athens, Corinth, Ephesus, Macedonia, Greece, Tyre, and Rome. And look at how teachable he was. He did a 180 degree turn when God revealed Himself to him. He changed his worldview in countless ways to align with the Gospel. He dedicated his life to caring candor—teaching the truth laced with love and pastoral care. And he was focused. Remember Philippians 3:8? 'That I might know Christ...'

When it comes to considering the rationale behind our leadership, I like Lencioni's *The Motive*.[41] The title says it all.

---

[39] Dharius Daniels, *Relational Intelligence: The People Skills You Need for the Life of Purpose You Want*, Zondervan, 2020.

[40] Robert Clinton, *The Making of a Leader: Recognizing the Lessons and Stages of Leadership Development,* The Navigators, 2012.

[41] Patrick Lencioni, *The Motive: Why So Many Leaders Abdicate Their Most Important Responsibility*, Jossey Bass, 2020.

Another book I have found helpful is Henry Thompson, *Stress Effect: Why Smart Leaders Make Dumb Decisions and What to Do About It*.[42] His focus on building resilience is worth the price of the book and I like the way he links resilience with purpose and rituals that build wellbeing.

I mustn't forget *Canoeing the Mountains*[43] by Bollsinger. From his vantage point as a long-term pastor and then VP of Fuller Seminary, he stresses the importance of adaptive leadership. He says that when the context changes, we are tempted to use our old approach with additional vigor when what is needed is a new approach. How do we lead the church in this season? How do we lead ourselves? I appreciate Bollsinger's comments about how the problems we face today are often a result of the solutions we implemented yesterday. This doesn't necessarily mean that they were wrong then, it just means that they need fresh eyes today. So helpful.

When it comes to thinking about leadership temptations and possible derailers three important resources are Nouwen's *In the Name of Jesus*, Lencioni's *5 Temptations of a CEO* [44] and Dotlich and Cairo's *Why CEO's Fail*.[45] Christian leaders should probably read these books every year, or more frequently as needed!

Related to leadership temptations is the important work the Arbinger Institute does around self-deception. I especially like their book *Leadership and Self Deception*.[46] We so easily deceive ourselves and the cost to this is more significant than we realize resulting as you may recall in our self-betrayal and the dehumanization of others.

---

42 Henry Thompson, *Stress Effect: Why Smart Leaders Make Dumb Decisions and What to Do About It,* Jossey-Bass, 2010.

43 Todd Bolsinger, *Canoeing the Mountains: Christian Leadership in Uncharted Territory,* PRAXIS, 2018.

44 Henri Nouwen, *In the Name of Jesus: Reflections on Leadership,* Crossroad, 1992.
 Patrick Lencioni, *The Five Temptations of a CEO: A Leadership Fable,* Jossey-Bass, 2008.

45 David L. Dotlichi & Peter C. Cairo, *Why CEO's Fail: The 11 Behaviors that Can Derail Your Climb to the Top and How to Manage Them,* Jossey-Bass, 2003.

46 The Arbinger Institute, *Leadership and Self Deception: Getting Out of the Box,* Berrett-Koehler Publishers, 2018.

I also want to point out Gene Getz's book *Elder and Leaders*[47] and James Robertson's *Overlooked*[48] here as a possible resource for church contexts.

THE PEOPLE

As I already mentioned two books that should be on every leader's shelf or desk are Steven R. Covey's *The Speed of Trust: The One Thing that Changes Everything*[49] and Patrick Lencioni's *The Five Dysfunctions of a Team.*[50] Trust is the foundation of a team and essential to leadership.

Go Together: How the Concept of Ubuntu will Change How You Live, Work and Lead[51] by Shola Richards is such a powerful book. Richards uses the South African term Ubuntu to refer to 'the power of our shared humanity, a deep level of kindness, consistent generosity, and our innate duty to support each other on our journey we call life.' This is a great resource on civility in the workplace and creating actionable team norms. The stats in his book are staggering. Well worth reading. As is his earlier book *Making Work Work.*[52]

In Liz Wiseman *Multipliers: How the Best Leaders Make Everyone Smarter*[53] she describes how Multipliers, unlike their opposites—who Wiseman calls Diminishers—are not intimidated by talented people. They attract them and find ways to stretch them, invest in them, and help them make their best

---

[47] Gene Getz, *Elders and Leaders: God's Plan for Leading the Church- A Biblical, Historical and Cultural Perspective.* Moody Publishers, 2003.

[48] James T. Robertson, *Overlooked: The Forgotten Stories of Canadian Christianity,* New Leaf Network Press, 2022.

[49] Steven R. Covey, *The Speed of Trust: The One Thing that Changes Everything,* Free Press, 2008.

[50] Patrick Lencioni, *The Five Dysfunctions of a Team,* Jossey-Bass, 2002.

[51] Shola Richards, *Go Together: How the Concept of Ubuntu will Change How You Live, Work and Lead* Stirling Publishing, 2018.

[52] Shola Richards *Making Work Work: The Positivity Solution for Any Work Environment,* Stirling Publishing, 2016.

[53] Liz Wiseman *Multipliers: How the Best Leaders Make Everyone Smarter,* Harper Business, Revised, 2017.

contribution. Multipliers are not afraid of differences of opinion. In fact, they welcome them and use them to create rigorous debate. I love her work.

Liz Wiseman's 2021 book *Impact Players: How to Take the Lead, Play Bigger and Multiply Your Impact*[54] also sheds a lot of light. She demonstrates that what differentiates 'Impact Players' from good players comes down to both mindset and quality. And here is why her work is so important. It is in the most challenging situations that 'Impact Players' are most likely to show up differently. When problems are complex, roles are unclear, there are unforeseen obstacles and moving targets, and when the demands are unrelenting. If it isn't on your bookshelf, it should be.

I mentioned how grateful I was at the time to John Maxwell for his *5 Levels of Leadership*[55] as it helped me to move beyond 'doing it all' to empowering people. If you cannot make this leap, you will not be able to grow your leadership capacity.

Adam mentioned *The Service Profit Chain*,[56] and while an older resource I believe it is still relevant today because it shows the link between tending our team and the health of the organization. This may be even more important now than ever.

If there is one source that impacted my thinking more than almost any other nonbiblical book it is probably Hersey and Blanchard and team's *Management of Organizational Behavior: Leading Human Resources*.[57] Notice the byline—leading human resources. To be a leader means to take people seriously. Why? Because every person has been made in God's image.

---

[54] Liz Wiseman, *Impact Players: How to Take the Lead, Play Bigger and Multiply Your Impact*, Harper Business, *2021*.

[55] John Maxwell, *5 Levels of Leadership: Proven Steps to Maximize Your Potential*, Center Street, 2013.

[56] James, L. Heskett, W. Earl Sasser, Jr. & Leonard A. Schlesinger, *The Service Profit Chain: How Leading Companies Link Profit and Growth to Loyalty, Satisfaction and Value*. Free Press, 1997.

[57] Paul Hersey, Kenneth Blanchard & Dewey E. Johnson, *Management of Organizational Behavior: Leading Human Resources*, 9th Ed. Pearson College, 2008.

In my opinion, one of the reasons that we are experiencing many of the problems that we are is because we have swung away from the importance of management. In the historical swing back and forth between management and leadership we have lost sight of how interconnected and critical they both are. Marcus Buckingham's book *The One Thing You Need to Know... About Great Managing, Great Leading, and Sustained Individual Success*[58] offers such important light here. He draws a Venn diagram with 3 circles labeled competence, confidence and focused. The one thing the leader must do is build confidence by rallying people toward a better future. The one thing organizations must do it build competence by matching the right people to the right role. The one thing a great manager must do is help the individuals on their team discover their strengths and focus on maximizing that. We have neglected management. We delegate our people's development to people who don't see them in the trenches the way we do—or should. Who don't understand what our department needs to achieve and what the individual's strengths are.

Buckingham also talks about the power of a sustaining culture to support these three crucial and overlapping areas. This is the one thing that everyone in the organization must take responsibility for.

Ellen Duffield's *Theology of Thriving*[59] reminds us of just how important it is to focus on people, purpose, and product or service. Rooted in Genesis 1, this is the most comprehensive and insightful book on the topic I have read.

And I can't leave this section without mentioning Tim Rath's book *Vital Friends*.[60] As a leader one of our most crucial roles in building a place of community and belonging for people. A place where people can develop genuine and life-giving friendships.

---

[58] Marcus Buckingham, *The One Thing You Need to Know... About Great Managing, Great Leading, and Sustained Individual Success,* Free Press, 2005.

[59] Ellen Duffield, *A Theology of Thriving: Belonging, Being, Contributing,* Shadow River Ink, 2023.

[60] Tom Rath, *Vital Friends: The People You Can't Afford to Live Without,* Gallup Press, 2006.

Encouragement

The 5 Languages of Appreciation in Workplace[61] by Gary Chapman and Paul White is a great resource for knowing how to meaningfully demonstrate that you value the members of your team.

You may recall we talked about the different things that motivate us. I really like Daniel Pink's book *Drive: The Surprising Truth About What Motivates Us,*[62] here.

Making Work Work: Positivity Solution for Any Work Environment[63] by Shola Richards tells a powerful story. Richards had become desperate. He couldn't tolerate his work anymore when he realized that he could dedicate his life to making workplaces a space that people wanted to work at. He identified components that make the acrostic REAL. Relentless respect—for ourselves and others. That is where I get this language. Endless Energy. Addressing workplace negativity. Lasting leadership.

Empowering

I told you how important Blanchard and team's *3 Keys to Empowerment*[64] was to my leadership when it first came out. While it is an older resource it is still very helpful.

Embodiment

When it comes to thinking about the important of modelling and mentoring, I so appreciate John Maxwell and Jim Dornan's book *Becoming a Person of Influence.*[65]

---

61 Gary Chapman & Paul White, *The Five Languages of Appreciation in the Workplace: Empowering Organizations by Encouraging People,* Northfield Publishing, 2019.

62 Daniel Pink, *Drive: The Surprising Truth About What Motivates Us,* Riverhead Books, 2011.

63 Shola Richards *Making Work Work: The Positivity Solution for Any Work Environment,* Stirling Publishing, 2016.

64 Ken Blanchard, John Carlos & Alan Randolph, *The 3 Keys to Empowerment: Release the Power Within People for Astonishing Results.* Berrett-Koehler Publishers, 1999.

65 John Maxwell and Jim Dornan, *Becoming a Person of Influence: How to Positively Impact the Lives of Others,* 1997.

THE PROCESSES

Communication

We talked about Kim Scott's excellent book *Radical Candor*.[66] Using different language she is really talking about the polarity between truth and grace that Jesus modeled for us and that we must learn as leaders. She has multiple charts and insights to help us do just this.

The next resource I would like to recommend is *Crucial Conversations*.[67] Another great Grenny, Patterson, McMillan, Switlzer, and Gregory book. I have to say, the more crucial the conversation the important it is that there is safety. And when something is crucial that is when it is hardest to make it feel safe. The authors describe a crucial conversation as one where the stakes are high, the opinions differ, and emotions are elevated. I especially like their concept that the more words it takes for us to describe something the higher the likelihood that we were not prepared enough for the crucial conversation.

In Judith Glasser and Ross Tartell's *Conversational Intelligence*[68] I especially like the way the neuroscience of conversation is explained. It provides a helpful dashboard that correlates levels of trust to the quality of our conversations—from transactional to transformational—and gives insights into the internal dialogues that are stifling our ability to co-create.

Co-creation

Patrick Lencioni to the rescue again with his incredibly helpful book, *The Advantage: Why Organizational Health Trumps Everything Else in Business*.[69] Do you have a copy of this on your bookshelf? Every leader should. His six questions alone are worth their weight in organizational health gold—why

---

[66] Kim Scott, R*adical Candor: How to Get What You Want by Saying What you Mean,* St. Martin's Press, 2019.

[67] Joseph Grenny, Kerry Patterson, Ron McMillan, Al Switlzer and Emily Gregory, *Crucial Conversations: Tools for Talking When the Stakes are High,* McGraw Hill, 3rd Ed. 2021.

[68] Judith Glasser & Ross Tartell. *Conversational Intelligence: How Great Leaders Build Trust and Get Extraordinary Results,* Routledge, 2016.

[69] Patrick Lencioni, *The Advantage: Why Organizational Health Trumps Everything Else in Business.* John Wiley and Sons, 2012.

we exist, how we behave, what we do, what are our strategic anchors, what matters most, and who must do what. They enable us to build clarity and alignment. Without this kind of clarity and alignment we have at best silos—Lencioni has a book about that too—and at worst chaos. Therefore, I like to talk about interlinking teams. This requires hungry, humble, Smart leaders. I'd recommend his assessment, available at https://www.tablegroup.com.

Then there is *Team of Teams: New Rules of Engagement for a Complex World* by Stanley McChrystal.[70] This book has really been shaping my thinking recently. He claims that one result of the complexity of our world is that even though we are data rich we are still uncertain. But the part I love best is how to actualize a fast moving start up mentality, even within large or long existing organizations.

Co-delivering

I love McChesney and team's *The 4 Disciplines of Execution*[71] because it offers such practical light on how to operationalize and execute. And the other book I mentioned that focuses on this topic is simply called *Execution*[72] by Bossidy and Charan. Again, I am giving you some newer resources and some classics, and this is a classic.

Robert Quinn's 2019 book, *The Economics of Higher Purpose*[73] and his earlier, *The Positive Organization*[74] are both excellent. The latter shows us how to create dual mind maps and offers sample step by step working processes.

---

70 Stanley McChrystal, *Team of Teams: New Rules of Engagement for a Complex World*, Portfolio, 2015

71 Chris McChesney, Sean Covey, Jim Huling, Scott Thele & Beverly Walker, *The 4 Disciplines of Execution: Achieving Your Wildly Important Goals,* Revised and Updated, Simon and Schuster, 2021.

72 Larry Bossidy and Ram Charan, *Execution: The Discipline of Getting Things Done*, Currency, 2002.

73 Robert Quinn, *The Economics of Higher Purpose,* Berrett-Koehler, 2019.

74 Robert Quinn, *The Positive Organization: Breaking free from Conventional Cultures, Constraints, & Beliefs,* Berrett-Koehler, 2015.

Mark Gerzon offers some great insights in his book, *Leading Through Conflict: How Successful Leaders Transform Differences into Opportunities*.[75] He suggests that leaders in today's polarized world of seemingly intractable problems, must become skilled at mediation—at helping individuals and groups find a third way. William Ury's *Getting to Yes: Negotiating Conflict* book, DVD, or YouTube are also great resources.

Drake gave us some practical application of a dual operating system. To learn more about this I suggest reading John Kotter's *XLR8*.[76]

Vern Harnish's *Scaling Up: How a Few Companies Make it and the Rest Don't*.[77] There are so many great tools in here, most importantly perhaps the one--page strategic plan. *Mastering the Rockefeller Habits 2.0* looks at how few companies make it, and why the rest don't.

I like Greg Satell's *Mapping Innovation*[78] as he describes how innovation in a startup and innovation in an established organization require two different processes. He also brings a fresh perspective as much of his work has been done in Eastern Europe.

When it comes to thinking about co-creation and culture another important book is Robert Quinn's *Rational Management*.[79]

Patrick Lencioni has another hit with *The 6 Types of Working Genius*.[80] Knowing how each member of your team best contributes to the whole is invaluable.

---

75 Mark Gerzon, *Leading Through Conflict: How Successful Leaders Transform Differences into Opportunities,* Harvard Business Review Press, 2006.

76 John Kotter, *XLR8, Accelerate*, Harvard Business Review Press, 2014.

77 Vern Harnish, *Scaling Up: How a Few Companies Make it and the Rest Don't,* ForbesBooks, Revised, 2014.

78 Greg Satell, *Mapping Innovation: A Playbook for Navigating a Disruptive Age*, McGraw Hill, 2017.

79 Robert Quinn, *Beyond Rational Management: Mastering the Paradoxes and Competing Demands of High Performance,* Jossey Bass, 1992.

80 Patrick Lencioni, *The 6 Types of Working Genius,* Matt Holt, 2022.

And of course, we can't forget Jim Collins *Good to Great* and Joiner and Josephs *Leadership Agility*.[81]

Polarities

Two easy to read, Canadian, and very helpful books on polarities are Tim Arnold's *Lead with And*,[82] and *The Power of Healthy Tension*.[83] His models alone are well worth the price of the books.

Systems Thinking

Kotter's *Our Iceberg is Melting*[84] provides an apt metaphor for the sinking feeling we can experience when it feels like we are doing everything right, but everything is going wrong. Easy to read yet such a powerful and memorable way to think about systems.

A much more comprehensive resource is Peter Senge's *The Fifth Discipline: the art and practice of a learning organization*.[85] His explanation of effective dialogue is alone worth reading this book but he also covers so many other important topics.

Co-owning

Coming from a military context *Extreme Ownership*[86] gives different but still very helpful insights into how to build teams of people who both 'get it' and are committing to 'doing it' for each other's sakes as well as the good of the mission.

---

[81] Jim Collins, *Good to Great: Why Some Companies Make the Leap and Others Don't*, Harper Business, 2001.
Bill Joiner and Stephen Josephs, *Leadership Agility: 5 Levels of Mastery for Anticipating and Initiating Change*, Jossey-Bass, 2006.

[82] Tim Arnold, *Lead with And: The Secret to Resilience and Results in a Polarized World*. Tim Arnold, 2022.

[83] Tim Arnold. *The Power of Healthy Tension: Unite Your Team. Spark Change. Get Unstuck.* HRD Press, 2017.

[84] John Kotter, *Our Iceberg is Melting: Changing and Succeeding Under Any Circumstances*, Portfolio, 2016.

[85] Peter Senge, *The Fifth Discipline: The art and practice of the learning organization*, Currency, 2006.

[86] Joko Willink & Leif Babin, *Extreme Ownership: How US Navy Seals Lead+ Win*, St Martin's Press, 2017.

Co-changing

Grenny, Patterson, Maxfield, McMillan, and Switlzer's *Influencer: The New Science of Leading Change*[87] is one of the most helpful books on this topic in my opinion.

Coaching

Coaching is an important skill that every leader and manager should develop. I find Michael Simpson's *Powerful Leadership Through Coaching*[88] a helpful resource here. He gives a 3D model to teach the actual 'how' of coaching as well as practical examples of how to practice an abundance mindset when developing others.

Great leaders, like David, also knew how to both preach to and coach themselves. Helen Tupper & Sarah Ellis', *You Coach You*[89] is a great resource for this.

Co-measuring

It can be tempting to assume that the important but intangible outcomes we seek are impossible to measure but this is a myth. If you are wondering how to think about this differently, I suggest Douglas Hubbard's *How To Measure Anything: Finding the Value of Intangibles in Business.*[90]

Co-governance

The books I referred to when we talked about board governance were Max De Pree's *Called to Serve*,[91] Fredric L. Laughlin and Robert C. Andringa's *Good*

---

[87] Joseph Grenny, Kerry Patterson, David Maxfield, Ron McMillan, & Al Switlzer, *Influencer: The New Science of Leading Change,* McGraw Hill, 2nd Ed. 2013.

[88] Michael Simpson, *Powerful Leadership Through Coaching: Principles, practices and Tools for Leaders and Managers at Every Level,* 2020.

[89] Helen Tupper & Sarah Ellis, *You Coach You,* Penguin Business, 2022.

[90] Douglas Hubbard, *How To Measure Anything: Finding the Value of Intangibles in Business.* Wiley; 3rd edition, 2014.

[91] Max De Pree, *Called to Serve: Creating and Nurturing the Effective Volunteer Board,* Eerdmans, 2001.

Governance for Non-Profits[92] Jim Brown's *The Imperfect Board Member*[93] and John Carver's *Boards That Make a Difference.*[94] Together they give us a good overview of the important work of board governance.

THE PURPOSE

We talked about Simon Sinek's excellent book *Find Your Why.*[95] I really like his work and found this book particularly helpful.

I also really appreciate Robert Quinn's *Economics of Higher Purpose*[96] as he outlined both a business case for focusing here and counterintuitive steps to enable us to do this well.

Any of the books Tom Rath writes or contributes to are good, and when it comes to thinking about purpose and contribution, I like his *Life's Great Question: Discover How you Contribute to The World.*[97]

Erwin McManus describes himself as a storyteller, activist and creative. His book *Chasing Daylight*[98] challenges us to seize the moment and make our lives count. So good.

---

92 Fredric L. Laughlin and Robert C. Andringa, *Good Governance for Non-Profits: Developing Principles and Policies for an Effective Board,* AMACOM, 2007.

93 Jim Brown, *The Imperfect Board Member: Discovering the Seven Disciplines of Governance Excellence,* Jossey-Bass, 2006.

94 John Carver, *Boards That Make a Difference: A New Design for Leadership in Nonprofit and Public Organizations,* Jossey- Bass; 3rd ed. 2006.

95 Simon Sinek, *Find Your Why: A Practical Guide for Discovering Purpose for You and Your Team,* Portfolio, 2017.

96 Robert Quinn, *The Economics of Higher Purpose: Eight Counterintuitive Steps for Creating a Purpose Driven Organization,* Berrett-Koehler, 2019.

97 Tom Rath, *Life's Great Question: Discover How you Contribute to The World,* Silicon Guild Books, 2020.

98 Erwin Raphael McManus *Chasing Daylight: Seize the Power of Every Moment,* Nelson Books, 2005.

I like Max Lucado's Venn diagram of God's glory, my strengths, everyday opportunities as outlined in his book *The Cure for the Common Life*.[99]

Christine Caine's *Unashamed: Drop the Baggage, Pickup your Freedom, Fulfill Your Destiny*[100] tells her powerful story. And I also really like Paula Faris' *Called Out: Why I Traded Two Dream Jobs for a Life Calling*. [101]

A few videos I also really appreciate are: Max Lucado's "The Cure for the Common Life," Marcus Buckingham's "Call to Clarity" and Daniel Pink's "Why We Do What We Do."

In closing: *In the spirit of lifelong learning, I would deeply appreciate any feedback you might offer on how to get better as a leader and how to produce more benefit on the subject of Christian leadership for those coming after me. Please email me at pmagnus@briercrest.ca*

---

[99] *Max Lucado, The Cure for the Common Life: Living in Your Sweet Spot,* Thomas Nelson Publishers-Lucado Books, 2005.

[100] Christine Caine, *Unashamed: Drop the Baggage, Pickup your Freedom, Fulfill Your Destiny,* Thomas Nelson, 2018.

[101] Paula Faris, *Called Out: Why I Traded Two Dream Jobs for a Life Calling,* Bethany House Publishers, 2020.

BIBLICAL REFERENCES

Genesis 1, 19, 94, 168, 227
Genesis 3, 14
1 Kings 19, 84, 198
1 Samuel 30, 55
Nehemiah, 54-7, 125
Psalm 8, 19
Psalm 19, 19
Jeremiah 17, 94
Ezekiel 34, 93

Matthew 4:4-8, 82
Matthew 9:21, 55
Matthew 25, 72
Mark 10:42, 1, 43, 56, 93
John 1, 19
John 1:14, 131, 133
John 1:3, 133
John 5, 19, 59
John 14:6, 133
John 14-17, 89, 91, 110, 116, 192
John 15:18, 89
John 16:25, 89
John 17, 34
John 21, 19
Acts 6, 56
Acts 15, 11, 215

Romans 8:28, 66
Romans 12, Intro and 43, 138
1 Cor., 43
1 Cor. 8:6, 133
2 Cor. 10:4-6, 28
Galatians 3:28, 90
Gal. 5:22-23, 43
Eph. 4:1-6, 208-209
Phil. 1, 25, 26
Phil 3:8, 223
Phil. 4:8, 28
Hebrews 1, 133
James 1, 67
James 4, 30, 67

Biblical Leaders
    David, 17, 55, 82
    Jesus, 1, 4, 10, 18, 19, 25, 29, 34, 43, 46, 53, 55, 56, 58, 59, 67, 68, 82, 86, 89, 90, 91, 93, 97, 108, 112, 116, 132, 133, 134, 140, 150, 166, 167, 172, 216, 219, 229
    Nehemiah, 54-7, 125
    Paul, 25, 223

INDEX OF TOPICS

APEST, 85

Appreciative Inquiry, 55, 68, 70, 124-33, 171

Board Governance, 179-196, 234

Burnout, 21, 84, 85, 110

Co-envisioning, 124ff, 120-121

Communication, 1, 86, 114, 115, 121, 132f

Co-learning, 121, 141ff

Co-creation, 48, 119, 120, 121, 146, 166, 170, 172, 186, 229

Co-owning, 12, 121, 147, 172, 232

Co-delivering, 120, 121, 149ff, 230

Co-measuring, 121, 157ff, 233

Co-changing, 121, 156, 186, 233

Co-governing, 161, 178ff, 195

Courage, 31, 38, 54ff, 61, 69
    Teachability, 61, 62
    Moral, 61, 62
    Physical, 61, 63
    Intellectual, 61, 62
    Emotional, 61
    Disciplined, 61, 62
    Perseverance, 61
    Empathetic, 61, 63
    Social, 61,
    Crisis, 67

Double Loop learning, 142-3

Dual Operating Systems 154, 160, 161, 195, 196, 231

Enneagram Assessment, 85

Great and godly leadership,
    Thanks, 2, 3, 4, 6, 7, 12, 13, 14, 15, 19, 20, 86, 119, 150, 165, 172, 202, 203, 215

Leaders
    Heroic, 48
    Post heroic, 48
    Catalyst, 48
    Synergist or Holistic, 48

Leadership
    Heart of, 17ff
    Temptations, 81ff
    Derailers, 83ff
    Self-deception in, 93, 224
    Centered, 14, 20, 29-31, 43, 82, 84, 116, 133, 136, 219

Leadership Definitions, 5, 10
    History of, 6

Holistic Leadership
    Lenses, components, 6, 7

Reading
    A book a week, 8

Relational congruence, 70, 71

First follower, 10

Motivators, 95

Network, 11, 107, 182

Polarities, 4, 12, 70, 73, 88, 89, 91, 100, 108, 109, 122, 124, 132, 159, 172, 232

Positive Deviants, 74

Strategic learning, 34, 53, 73, 75, 76, 119, 122, 142, 143, 216

Strategic thinking, 48, 76, 124ff, 160
Synergy, 120, 121, 122
Systems thinking 124, 129ff, 150, 232
Teams, 10, 12, 32, 33, 48, 70, 72, 97, 100, 105-107, 109, 110, 111, 113-114, 119, 120, 122, 127, 132, 139, 148, 149, 151, 154, 157, 160, 180, 186, 195, 199, 201, 230, 232
   Adaptive, 107

Trust, 3, 14, 32ff, 62, 85, 106ff
Wall of Wonder, 55, 126

INDEX OF AUTHORS

Adams, Marilee, 22, 220
Andringa, Robert, 186, 233
Acuff, John, 25, 26, 220
Arbinger Institute, 93, 224
Bass and Burns, 57, 101
Benni, Warren, 12
Blanchard, Ken, 101, 108, 226, 228
Bolsinger, Todd, 70
Bossidy, Larry and Ram Charan, 149, 230
Brown, Brené, 54, 137, 218
Brown, Jim, 183
Bohn, Vanessa, 92, 220
Buckingham, Marcus, 5, 37, 38, 173, 174, 222, 227, 235
Carver, John, 187, 234
Clarke, Dorie, 73, 76, 124, 219
Cole, Neil, 46, 223
Collins, Jim, 3, 46, 47, 101, 166, 173, 215
Covey, Sean, 149

Covey, Steven, 32, 106
Clinton, Robert, 44, 45, 46, 101, 223
De Pree, Max, 183, 233
Detert, James, 105
Dotlich, David and Peter Cairo, 83, 224
Duffield, Ellen, 168, 169, 227
Edmondson, Amy, 35, 36, 221
Eurich, Tasha, 50, 221
Fiorina, Carlie, 140
Forleo, Marie, 71
Gates, Bill, 12
Getz, Gene, 151, 226
Hubbard, Douglas, 189, 233
Hiemstra, Rick and Kindsay Callaway, 40, 115
Hesselbein, Frances, 47-48, 95, 101, 166, 232
Johnson, Dewey E., 226
Joiner, Bill and Stephen Josephs, 47
Kilman, O'Hara and Strauss, 67

Kotter, John, 154, 196
Lawler, Edward, 114
Lencioni, Patrick, 82, 96, 97, 106, 115, 152, 189, 192, 223, 224
Maxwell, John, 100, 112, 206, 226, 228
    And Jim Dornan, 117, 228
McChesney, Chris, 149, 156, 230
McGrath, Rita, 125
Newbigin, Lesslie, 128
Northouse, Peter, 2
Nouwen, Henri, 58, 82, 224
Palmer, Parker, 12, 218
Patterson, Kerry, 159, 229, 233
Pialat, Gyzel, 48
Pink, Daniel, 95, 165, 166, 169, 220, 228, 235
Ortberg, John, 18, 216, 217
Quinn, Robert, 154, 155, 165, 175, 195, 196, 230, 231, 234
    And Kim Cameron, 154
Rath, Tom, 166, 167, 168, 222, 227, 234
Richards, Shola, 138, 225, 228
Robertson, Jamie, 158, 225
Satell, Greg, 146, 231
Scott, Kim, 132, 229
Sinek, Simon, 88, 143, 170, 171, 219, 234
Shigematsu, Ken, 18, 217
Schaeffer, Francis, 19
Stanley, Andy, 175, 217
Summer, Sarah, 26, 219
Thompson, Henry, 23, 224
Trobisch, Ingrid, 38
Vaden, Rory, 192, 202, 220
Welch, Jack, 47

Wilberforce, William, 57
Willink, Joko and Leif Babin 148, 232